This Book Belongs To:

_____

Date Range:

_____ *To* _____

Dedicated to all those that feel lost without a plan, empty without creativity, and in a funk without expressing themselves. I feel your pain. I've been there. This type of journaling helped me. I hope it helps you too! ~Tina

| 16 | *Tuesday* | *April* | ☀ |

The fun part of fauxbonichi is that you can plan, journal, and scrapbook all in one book. Keep track of big events, write down the small happenings in your life, and even throw your to-do's onto your book.

- Add washi tape to add some color
- Print out pictures and glue them in
- Use your planner stickers!
- Draw, doodle, paint, get creative and have fun.

Remember - there are no rules! Art journal, write your thoughts, plan your day....it is whatever you want to make it!

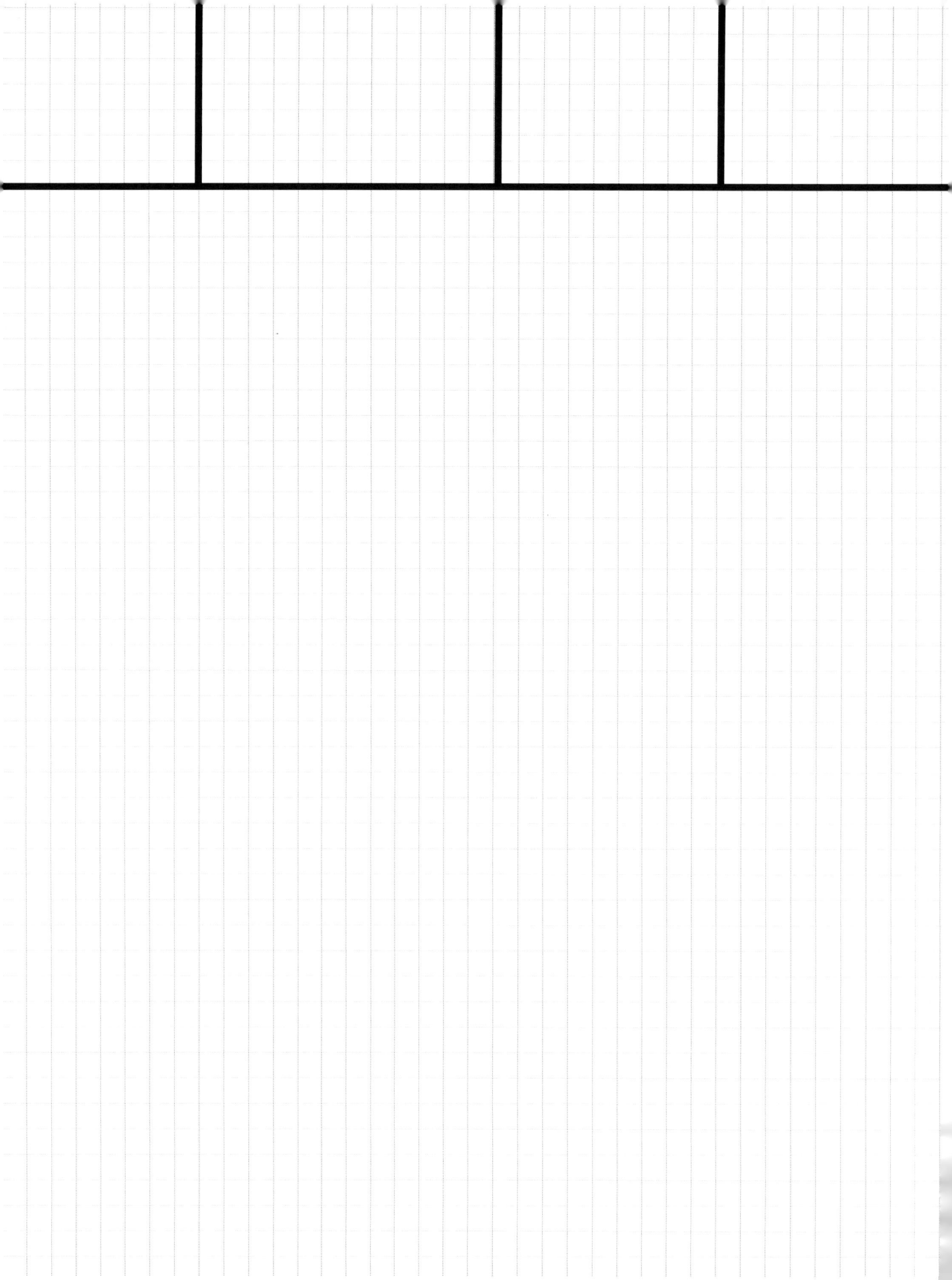

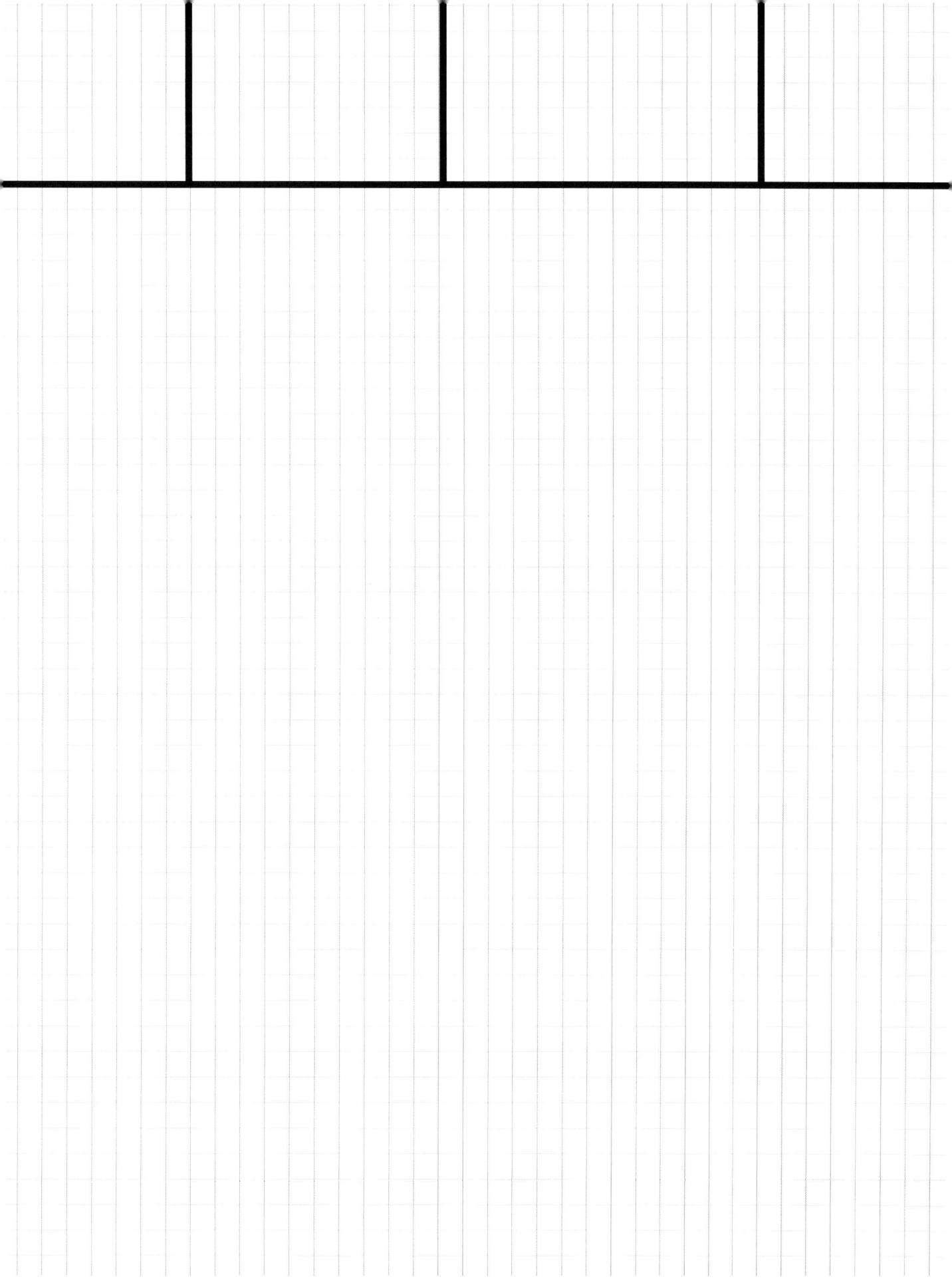

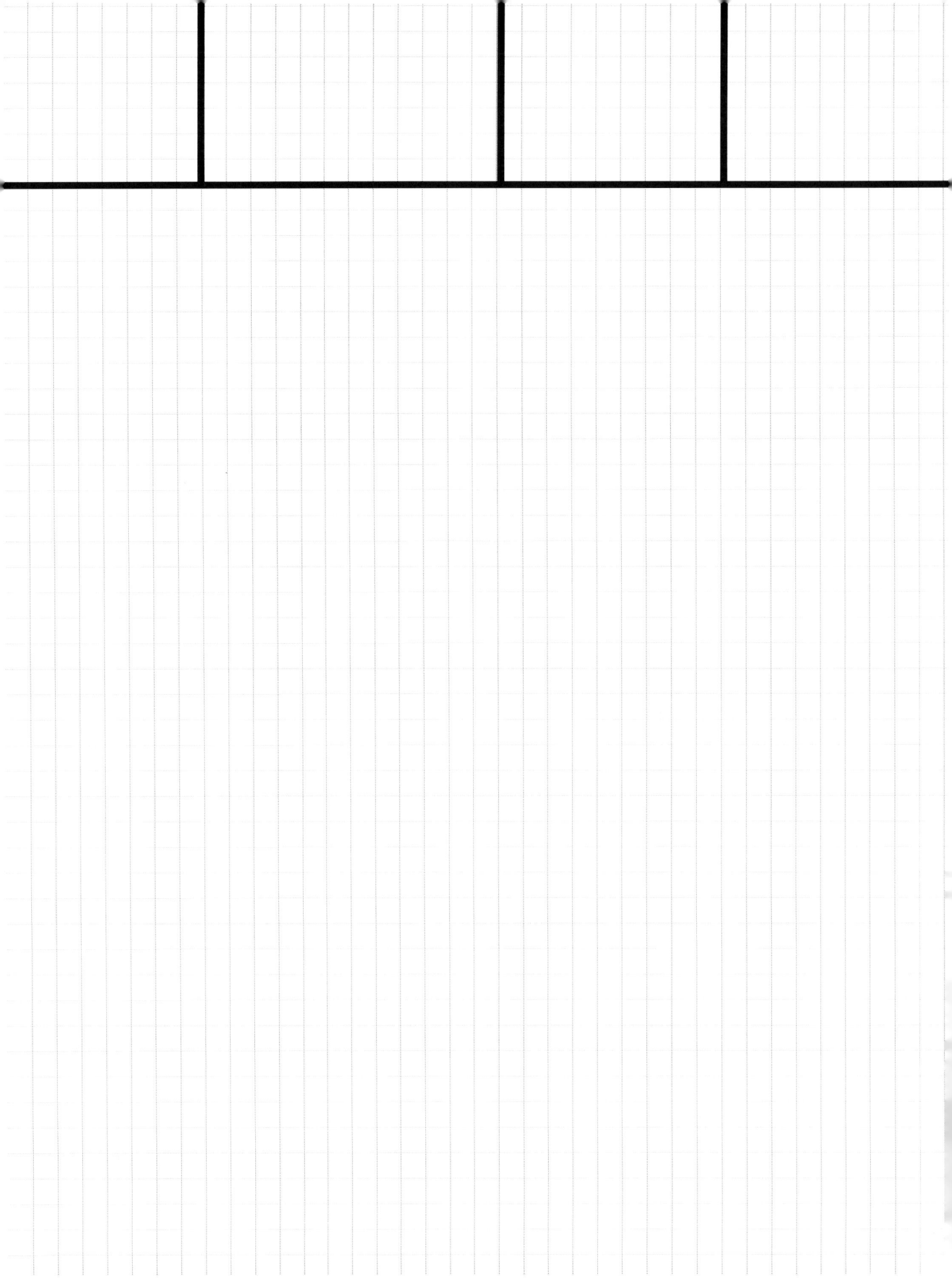

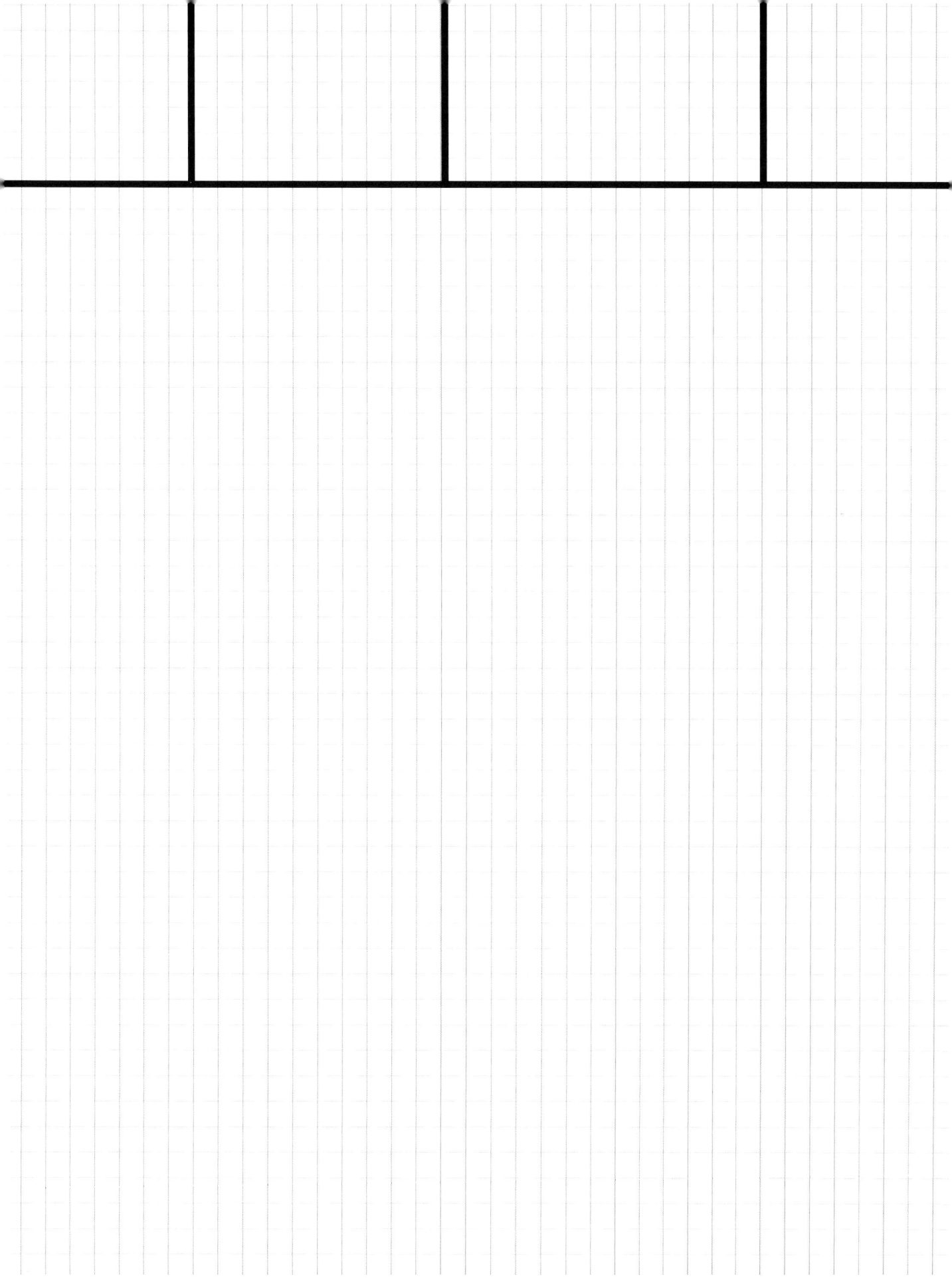

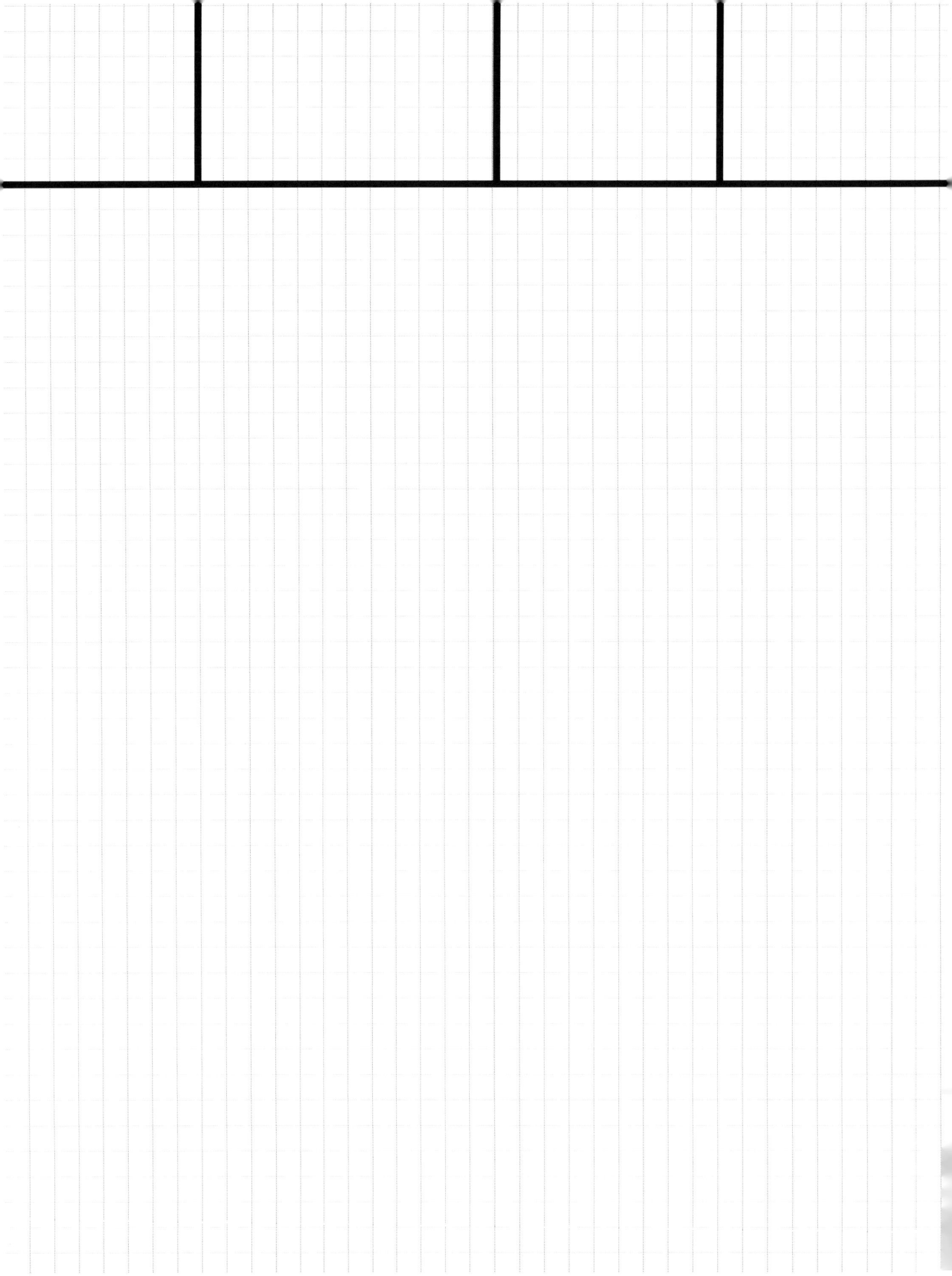

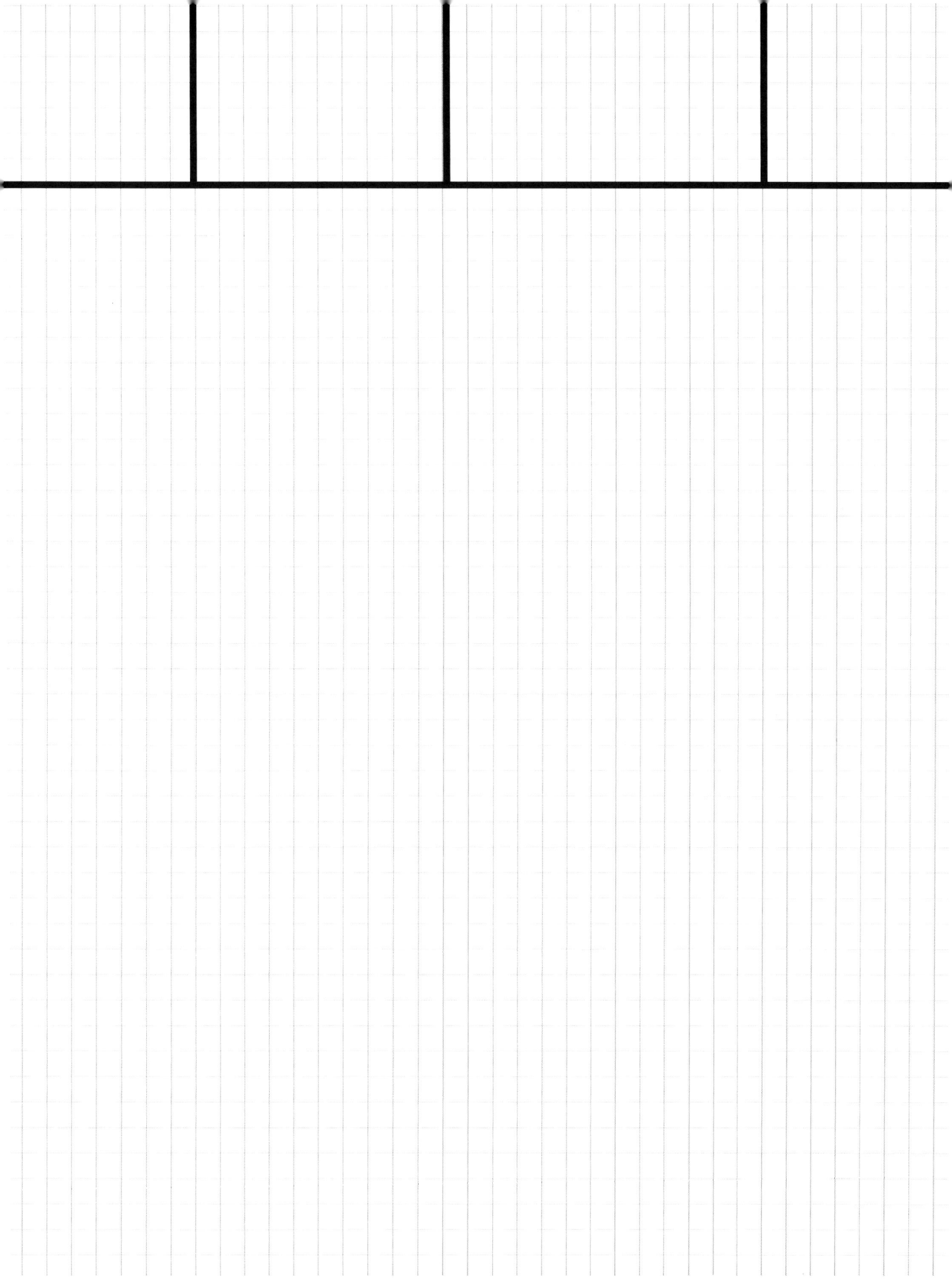

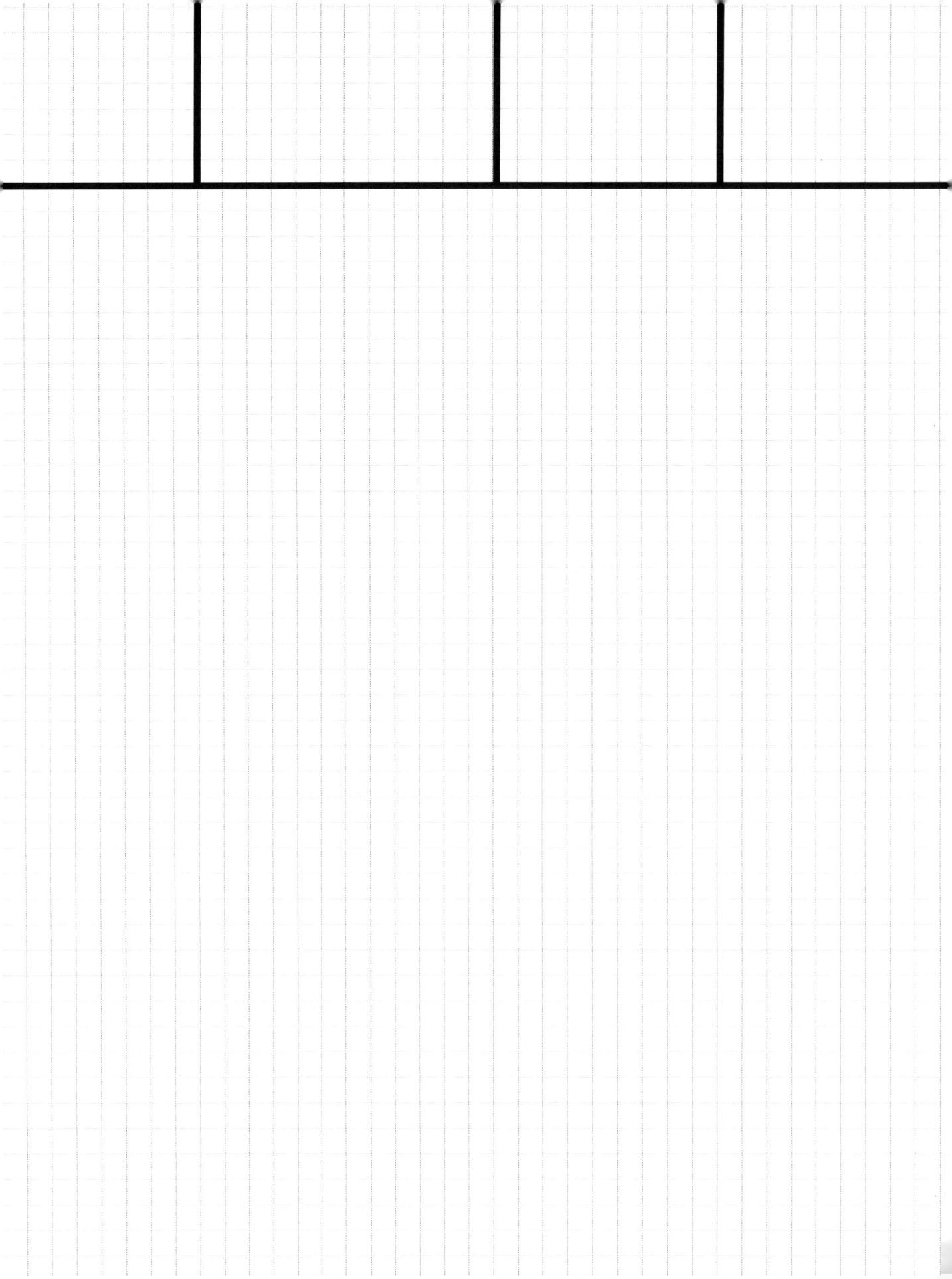

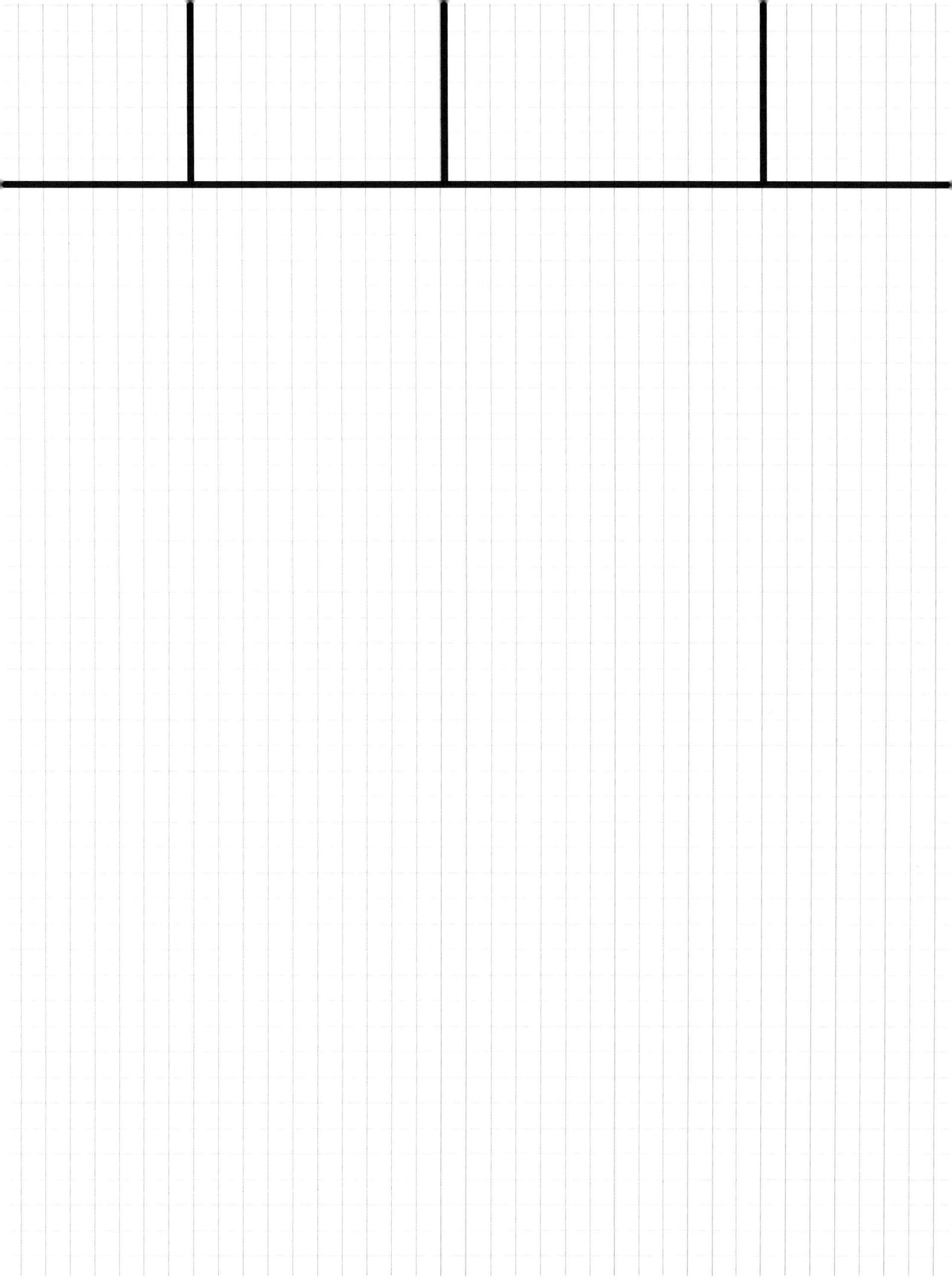

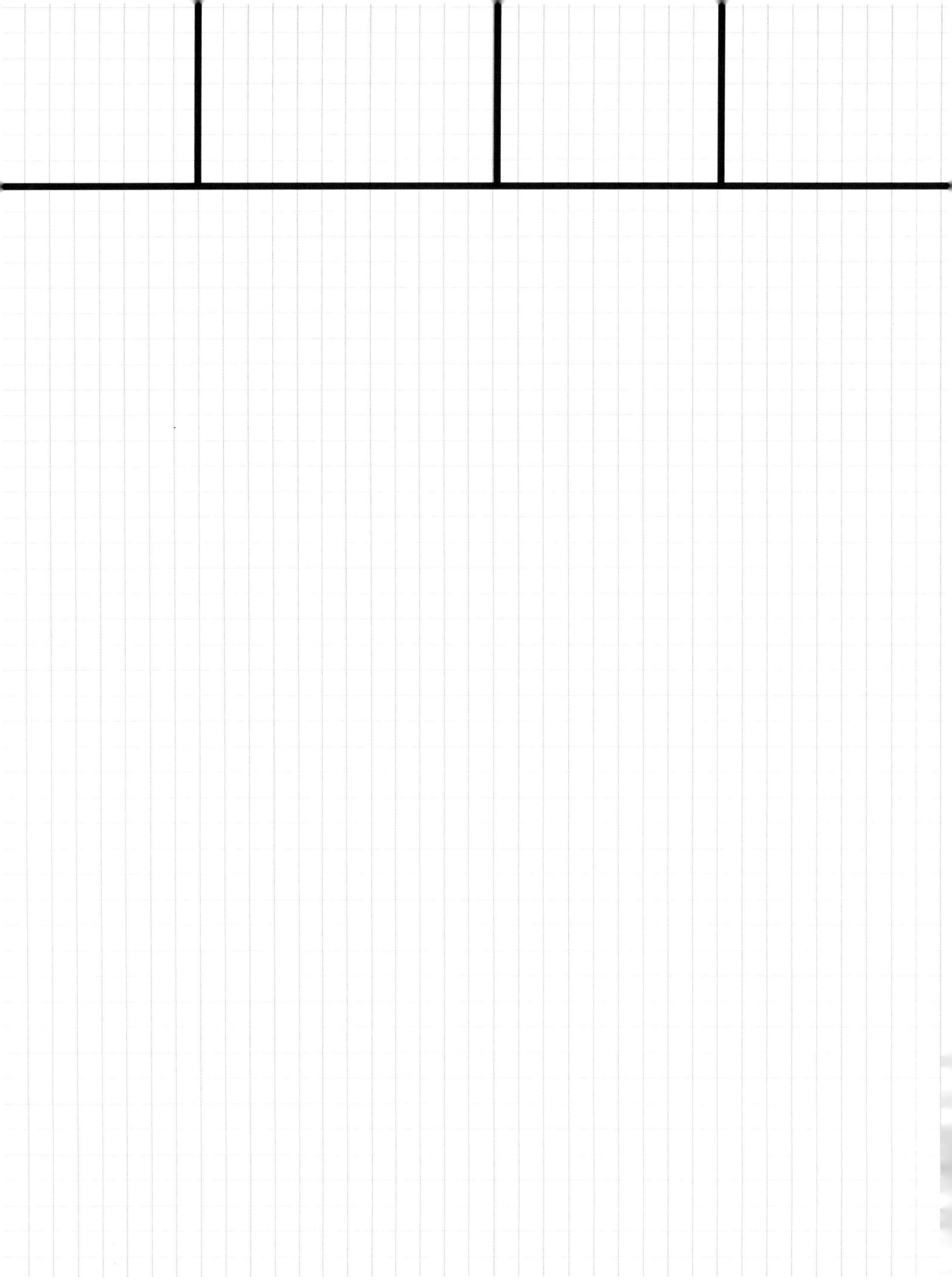

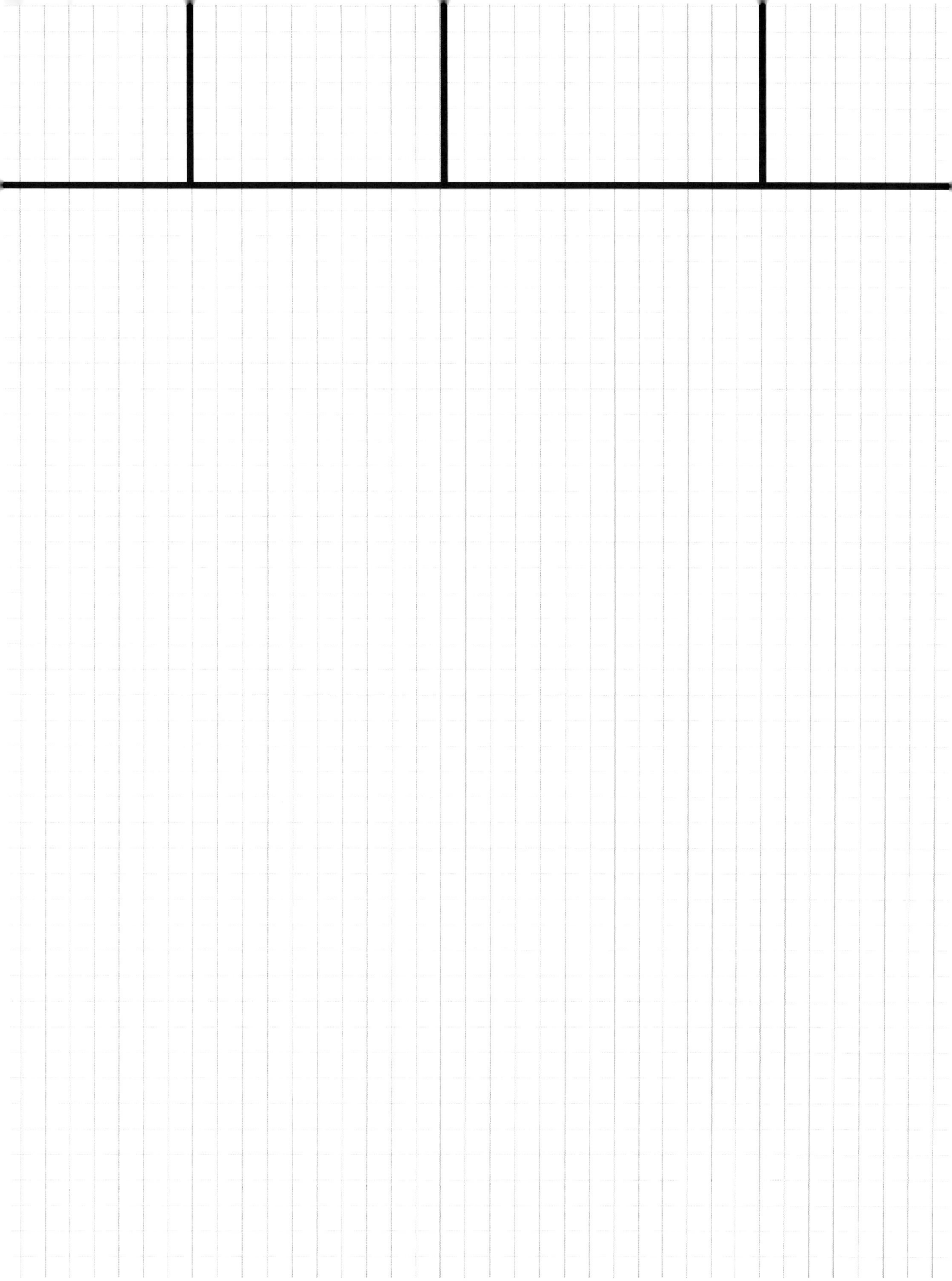

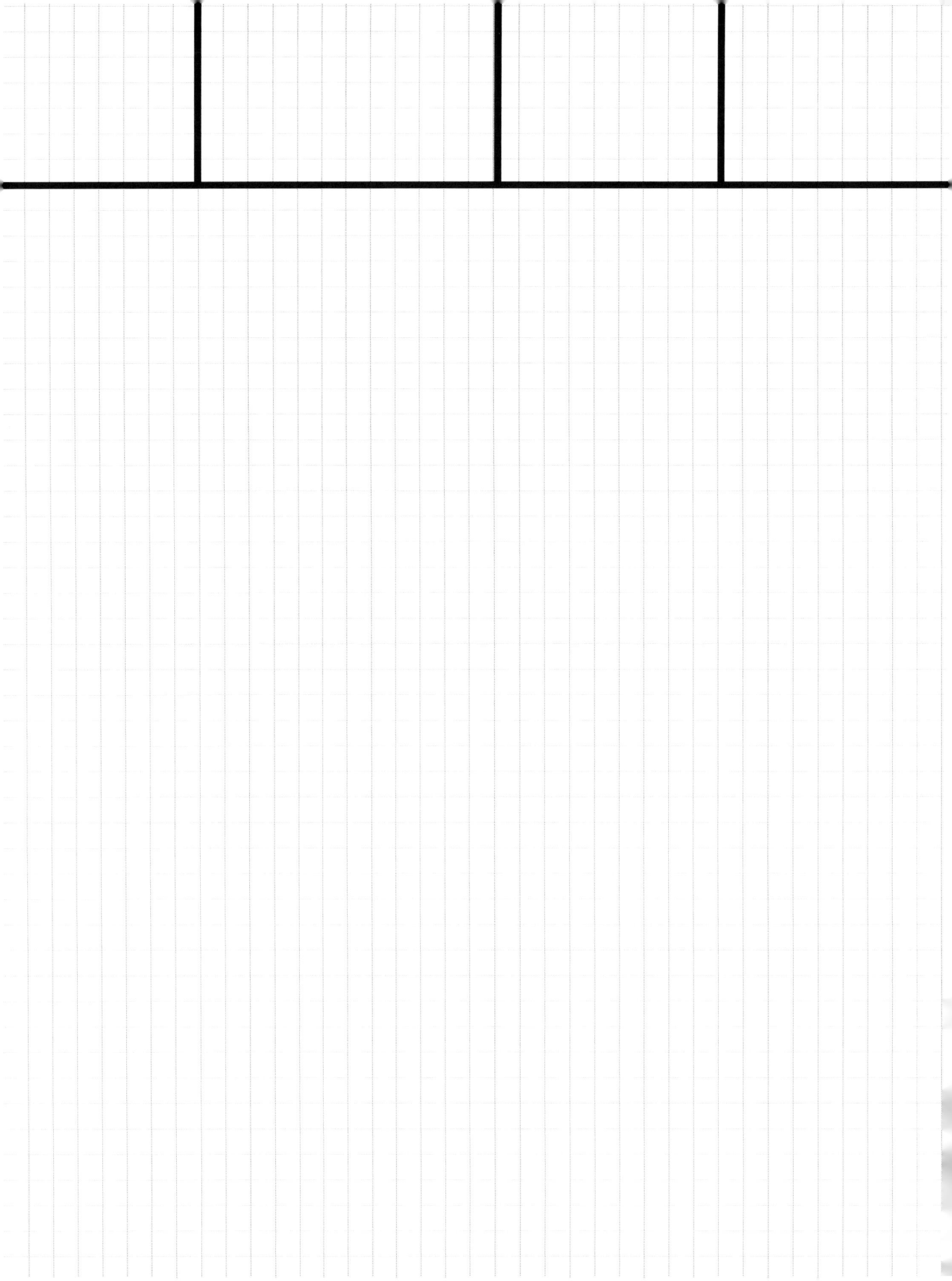

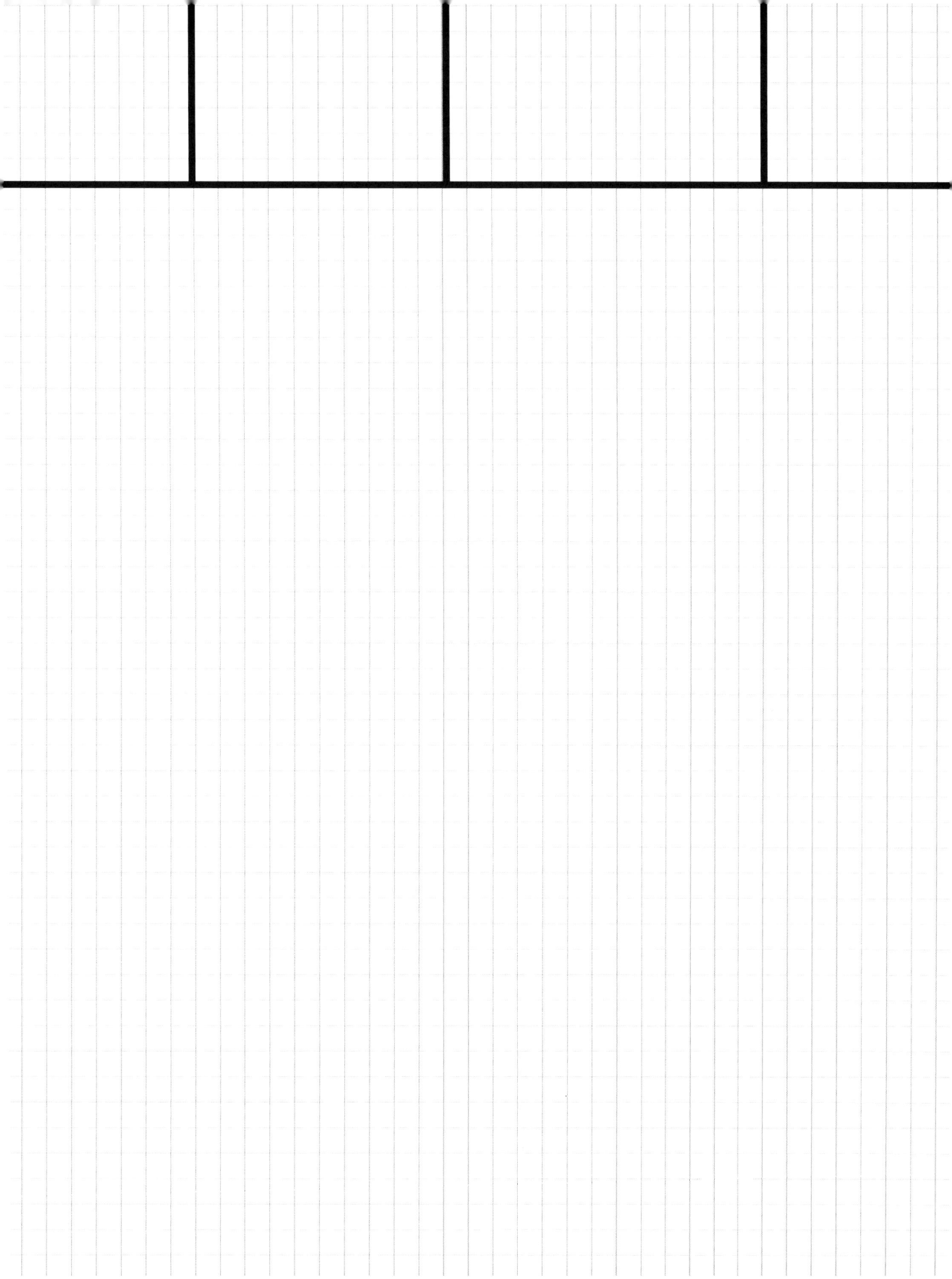

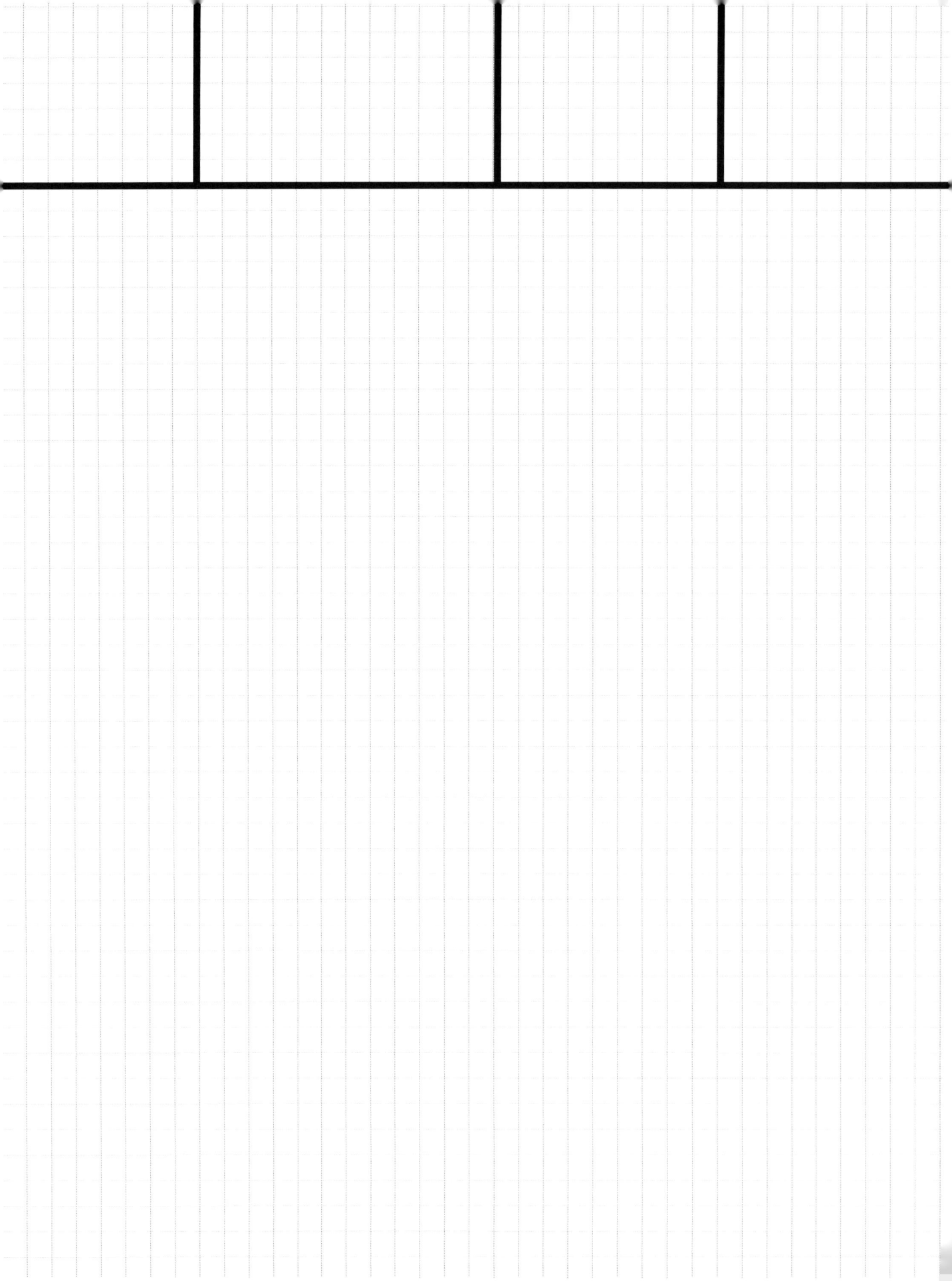

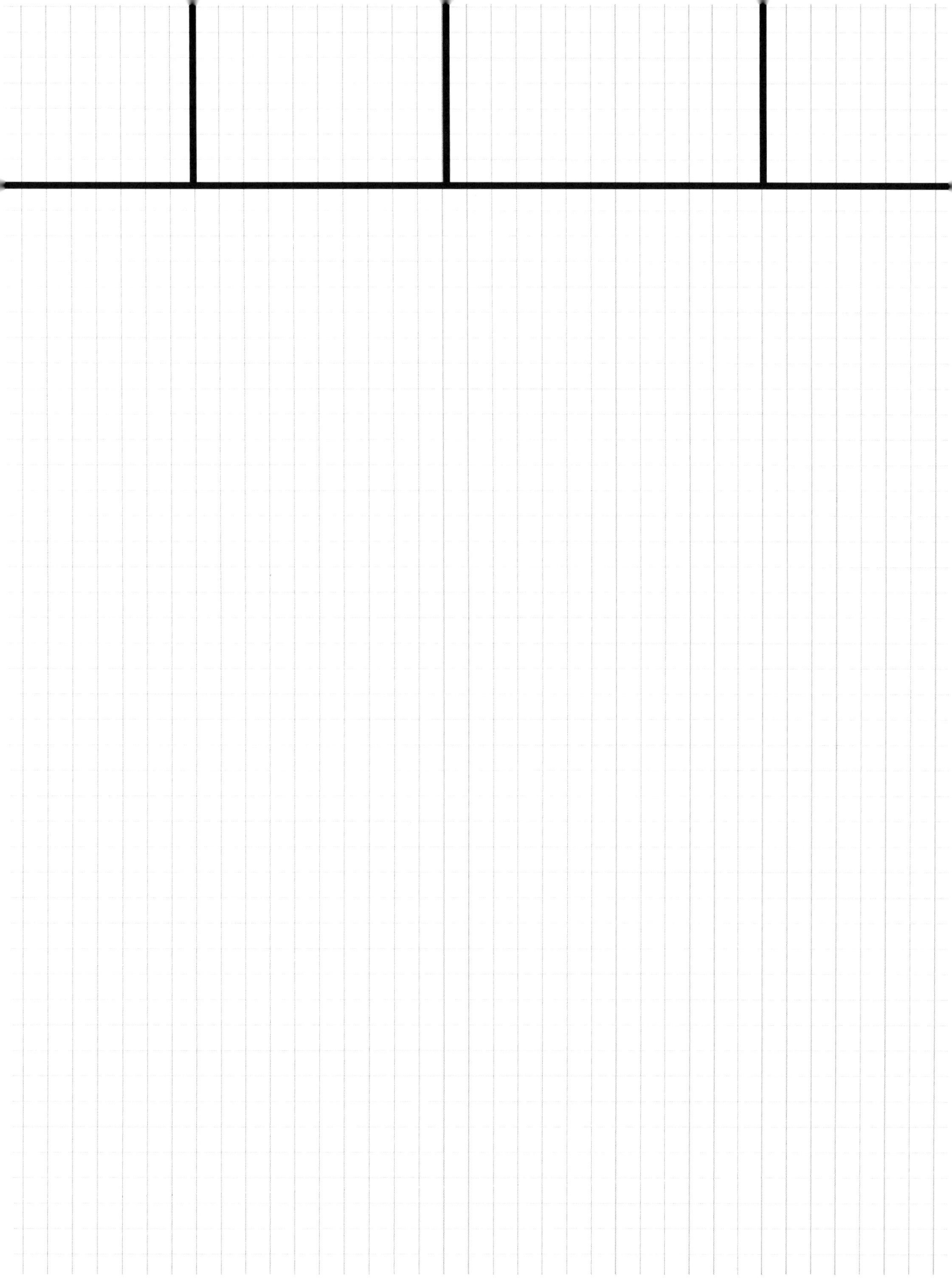

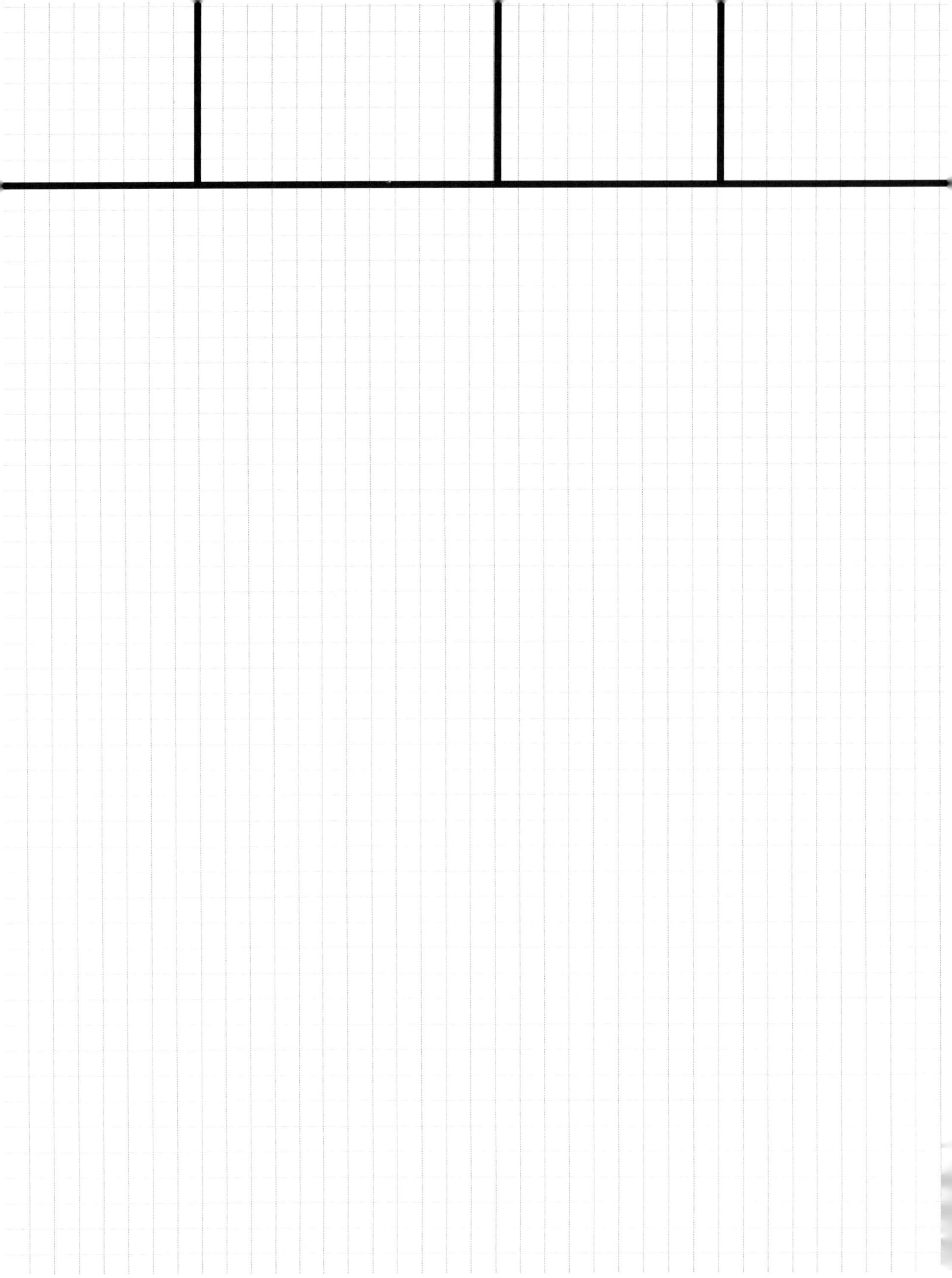

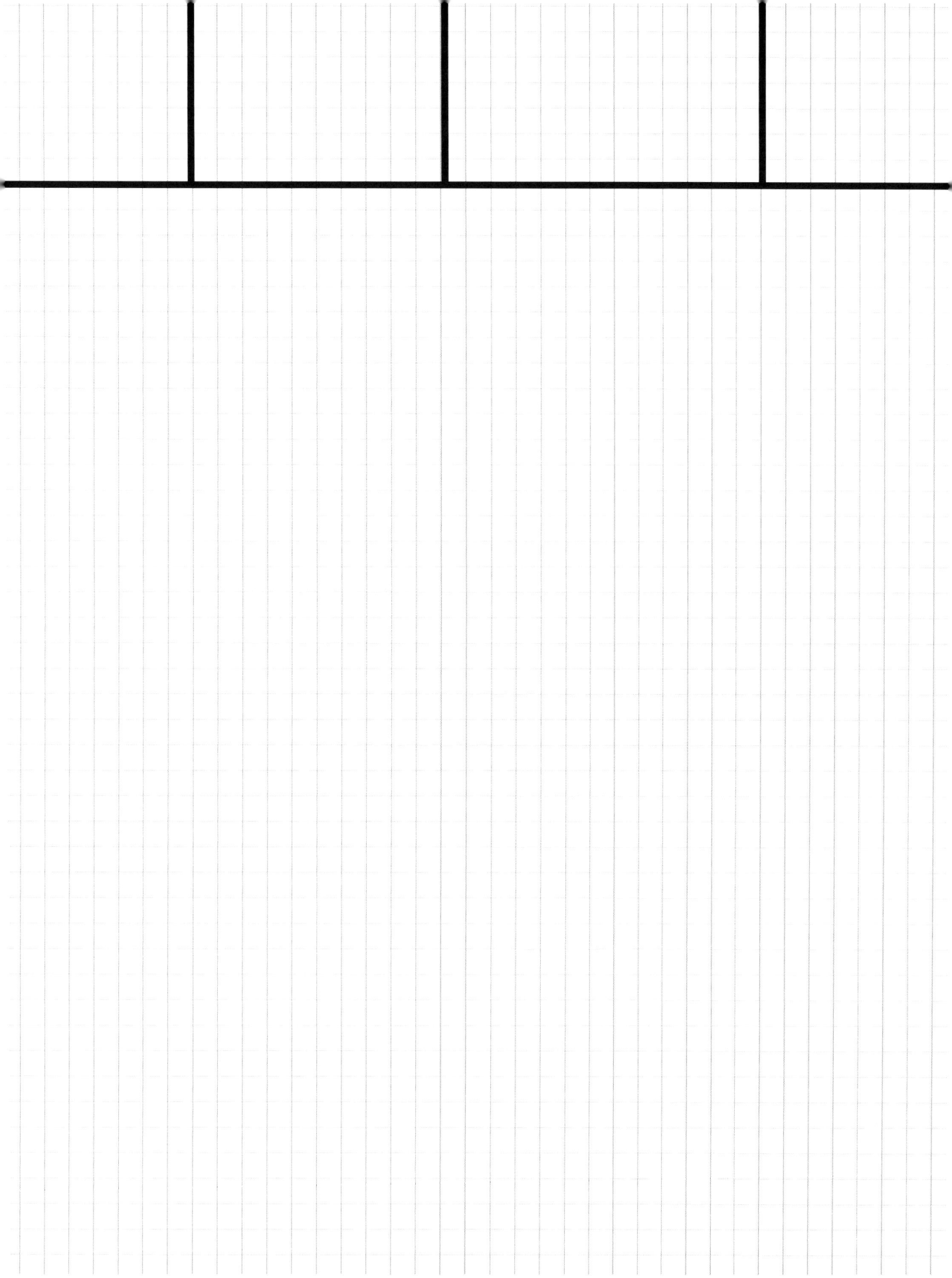

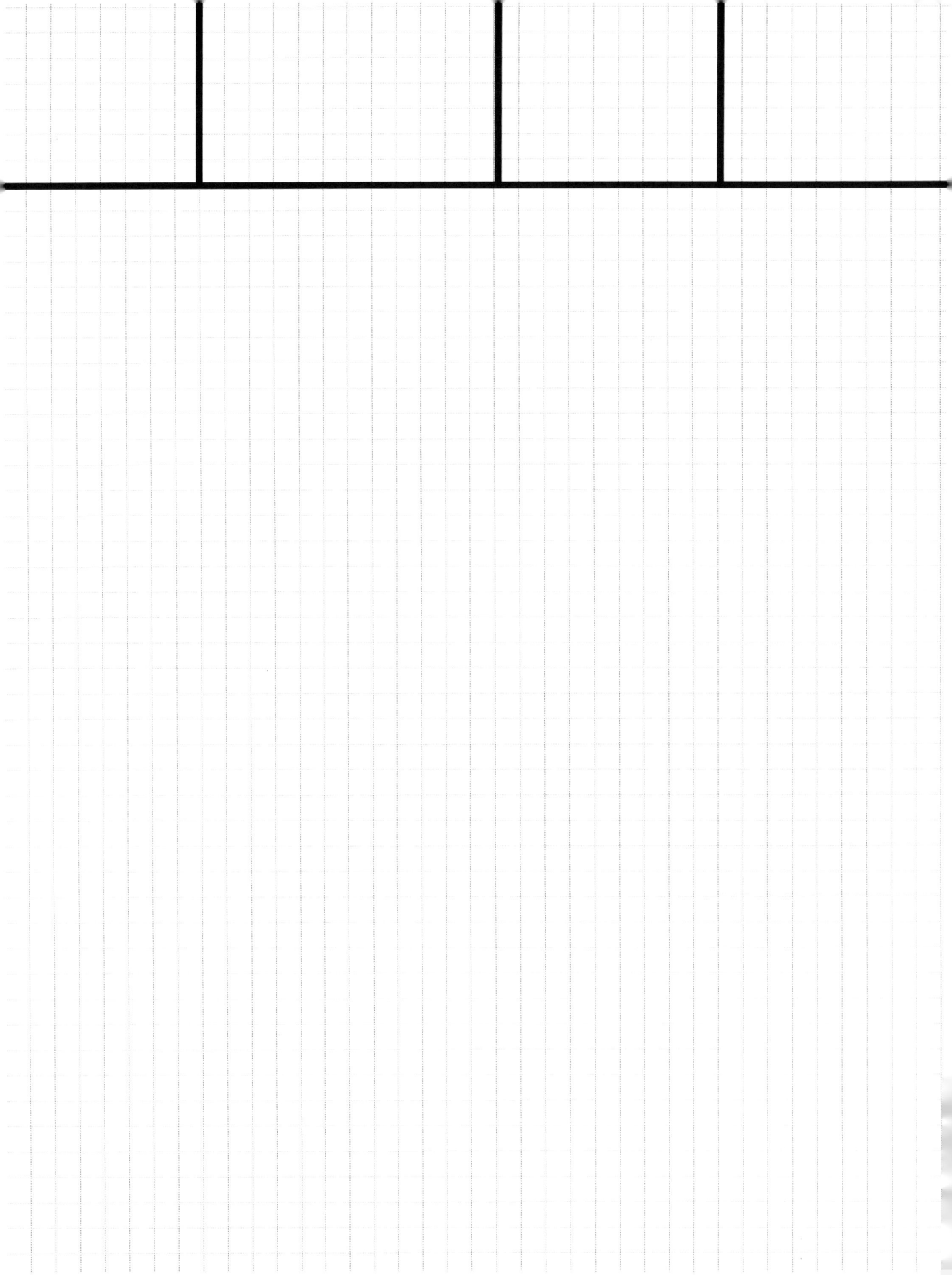

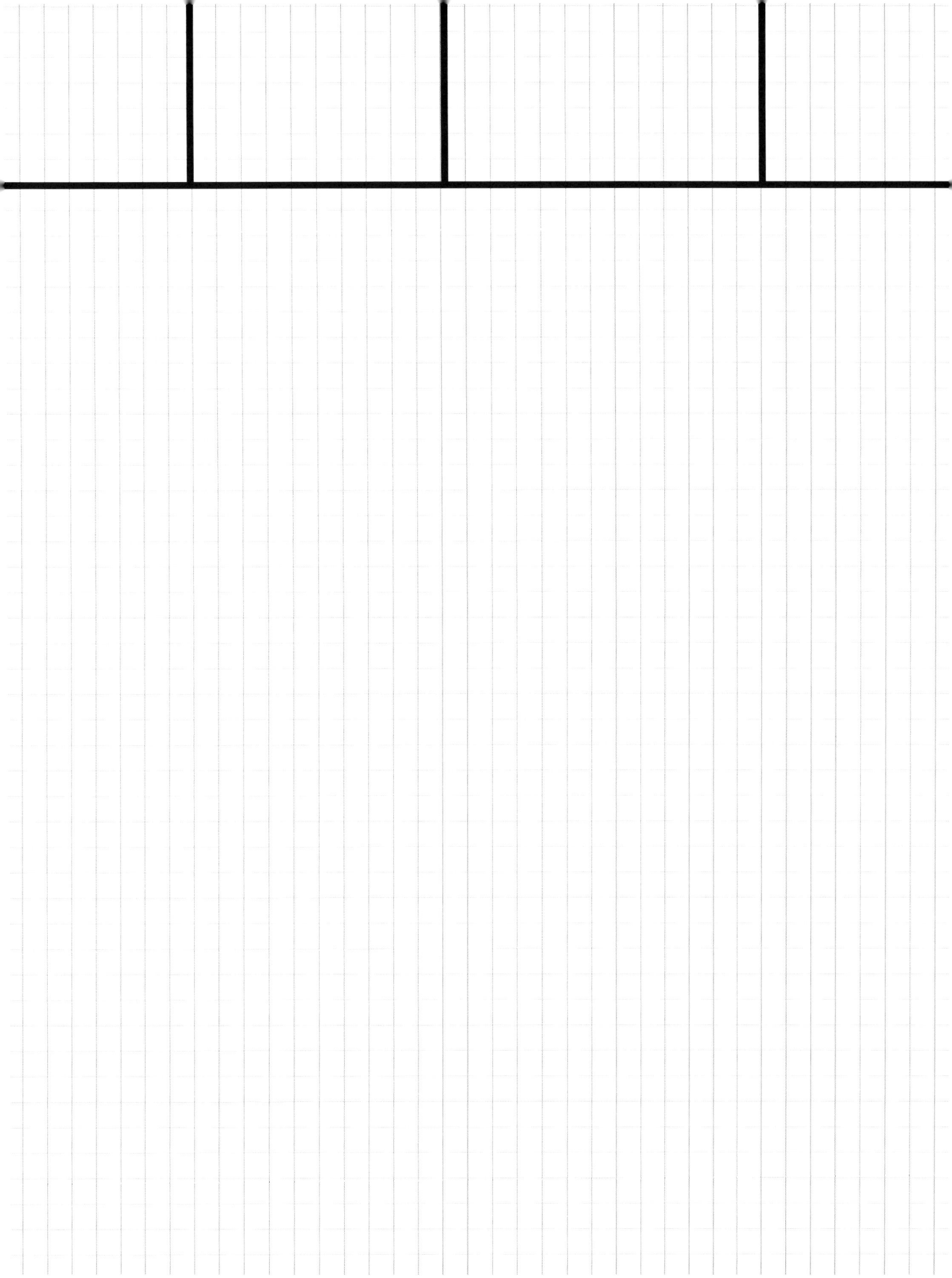

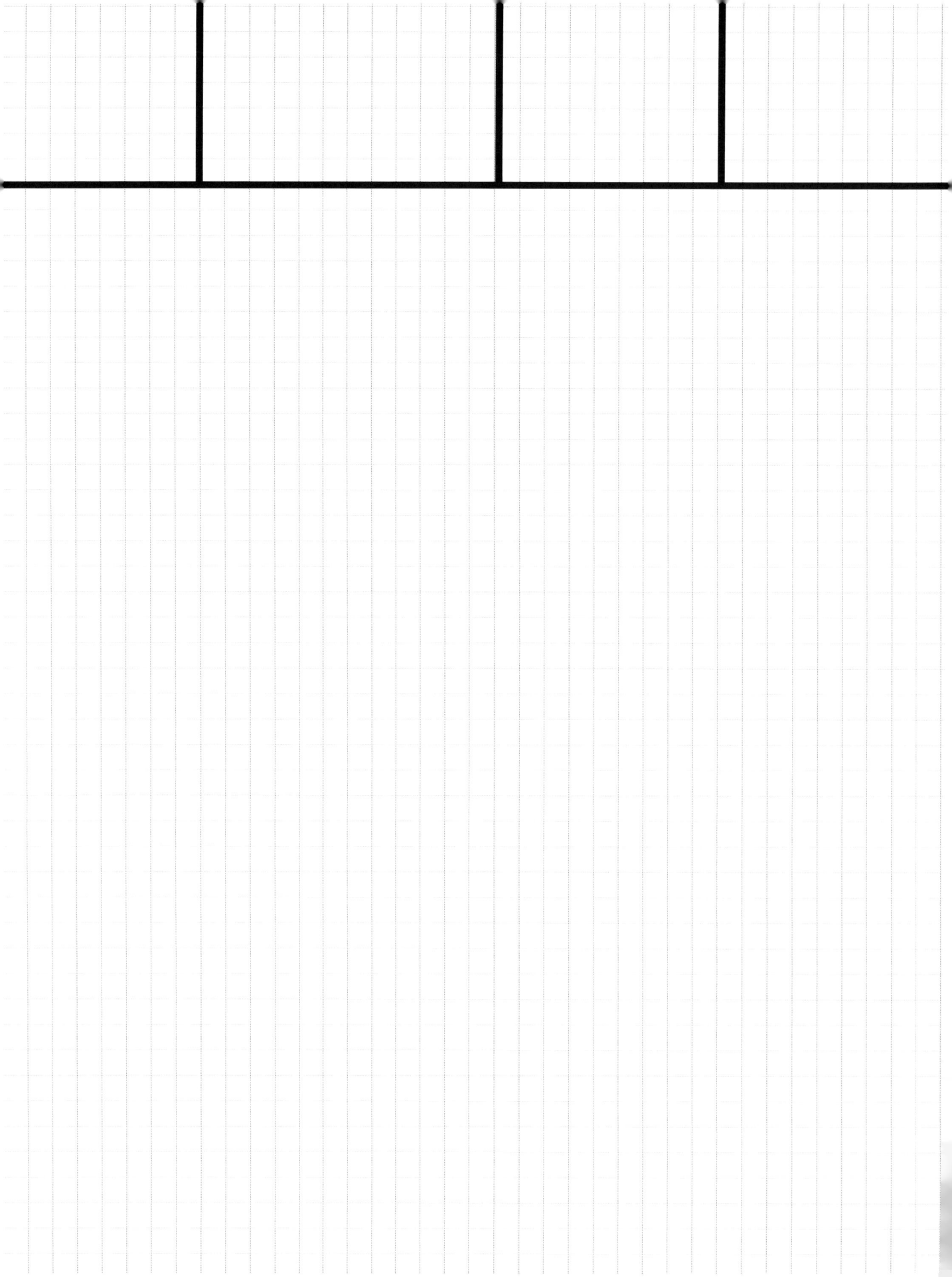

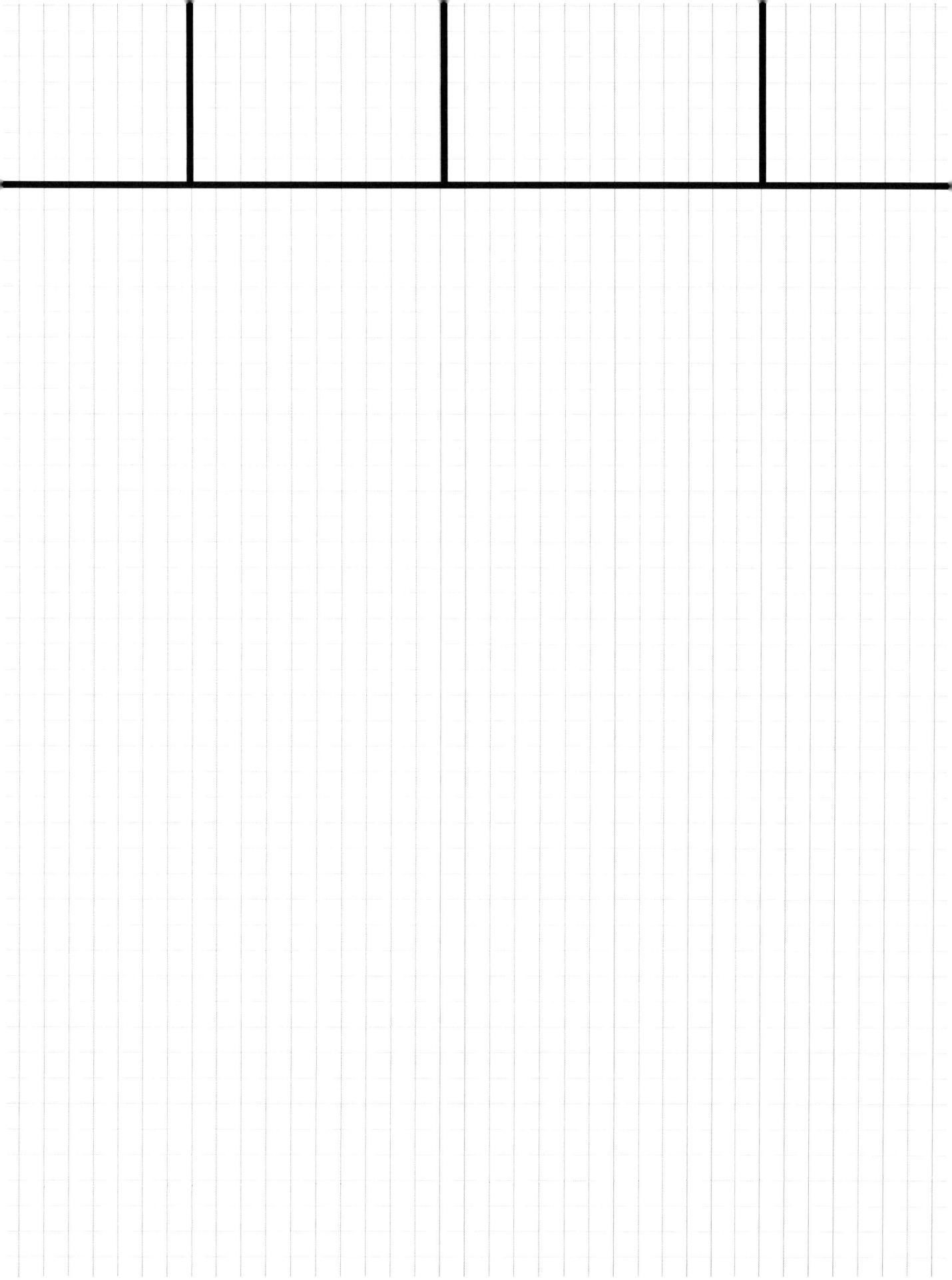

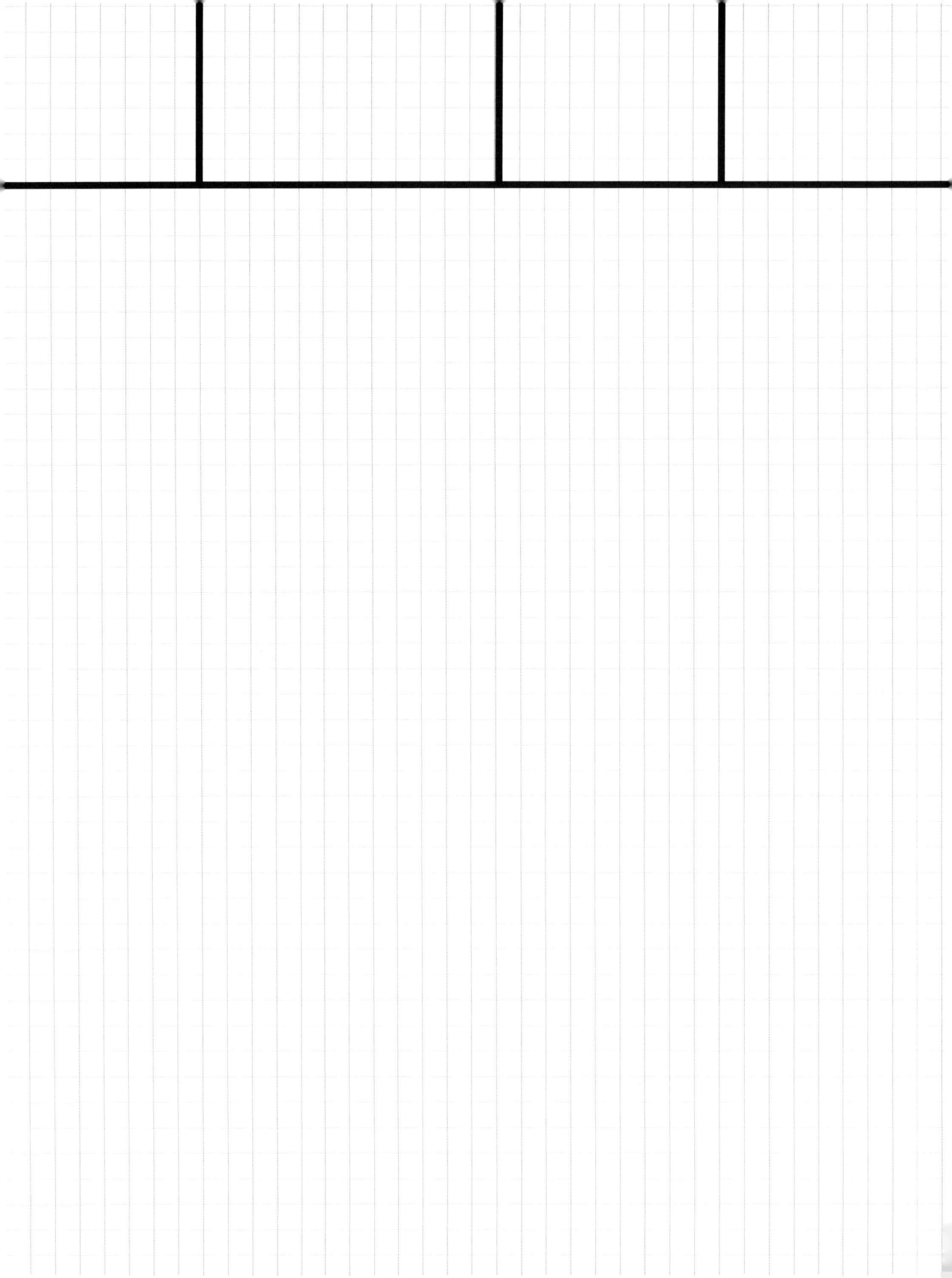

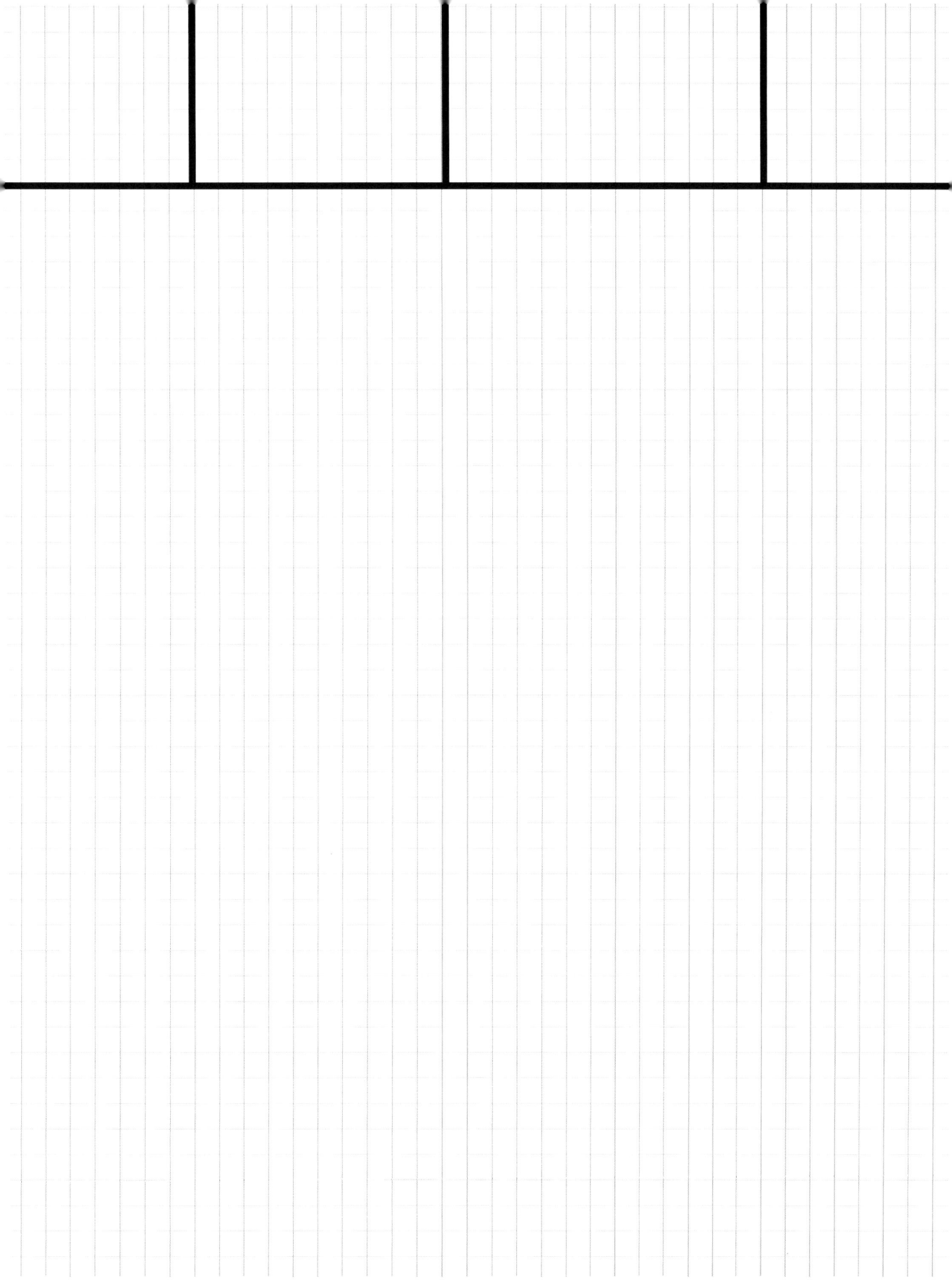

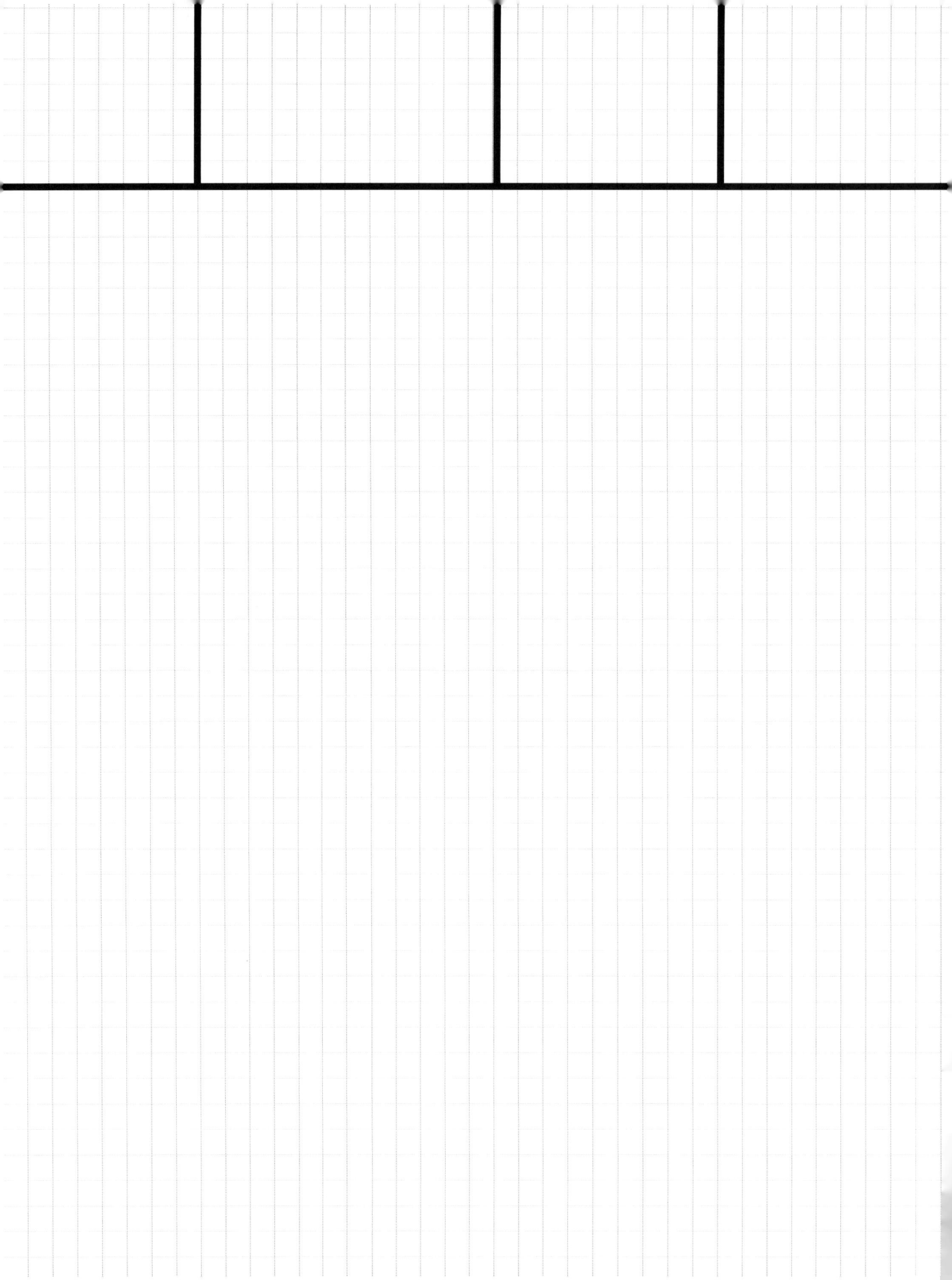

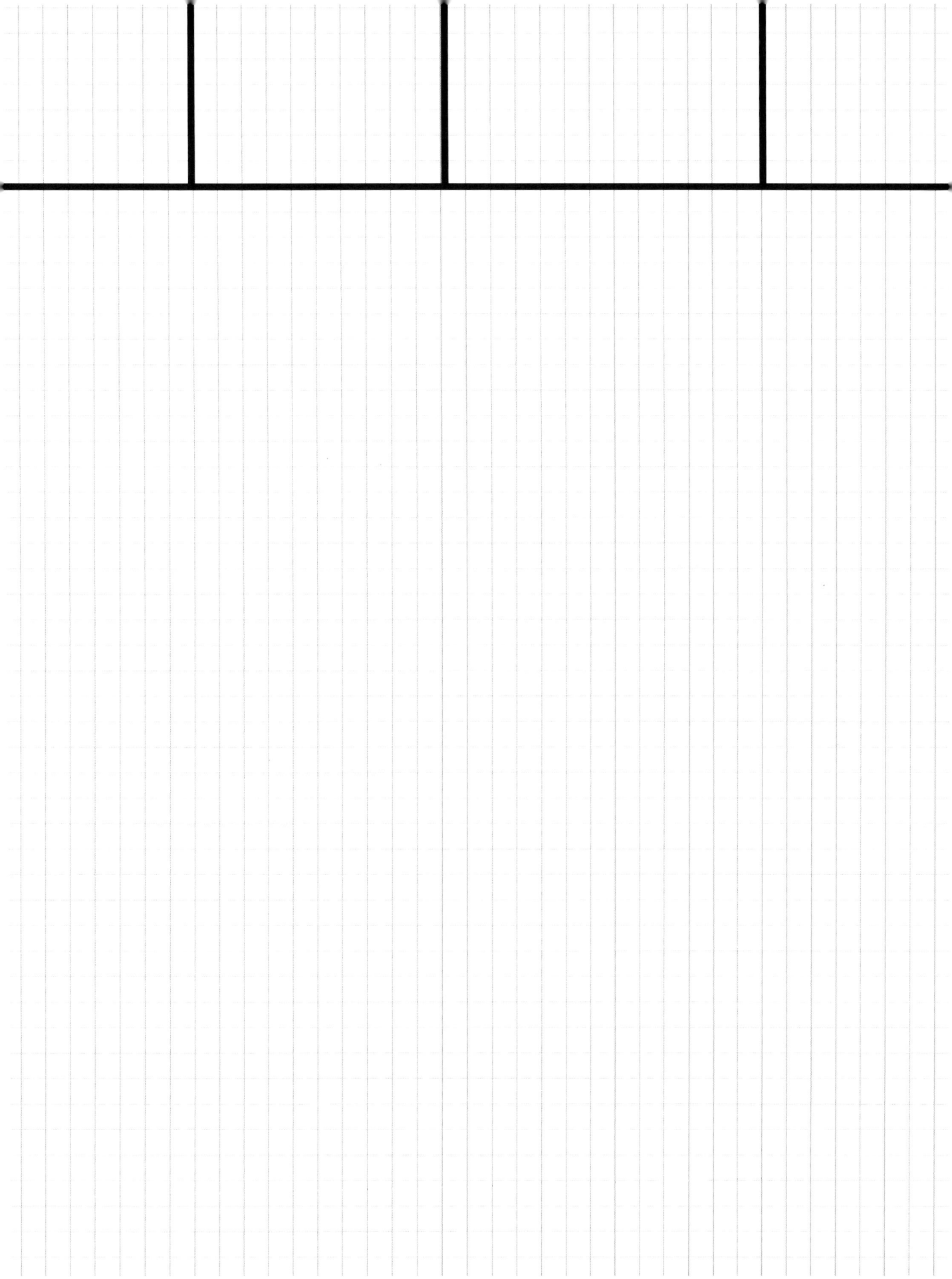

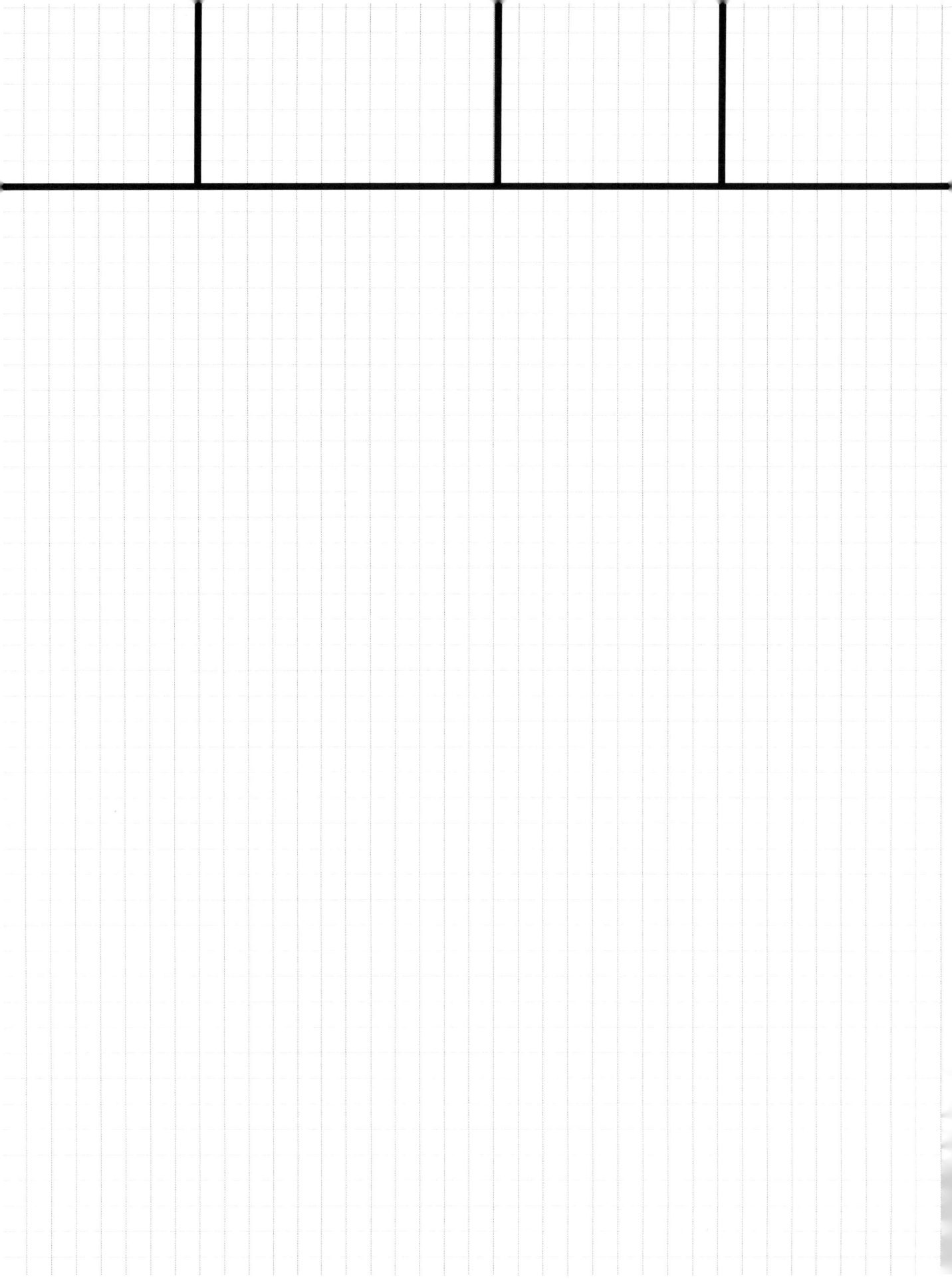

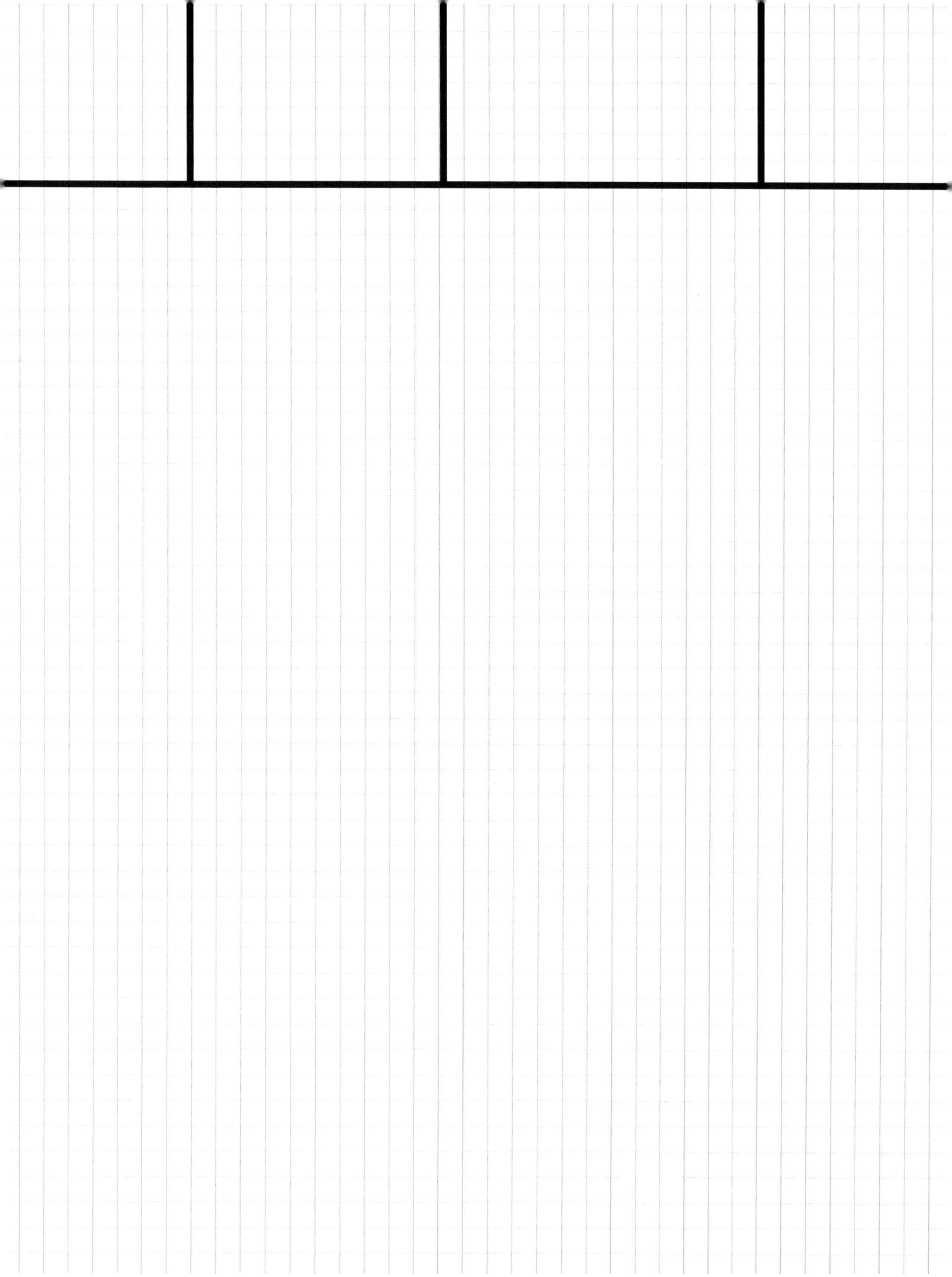

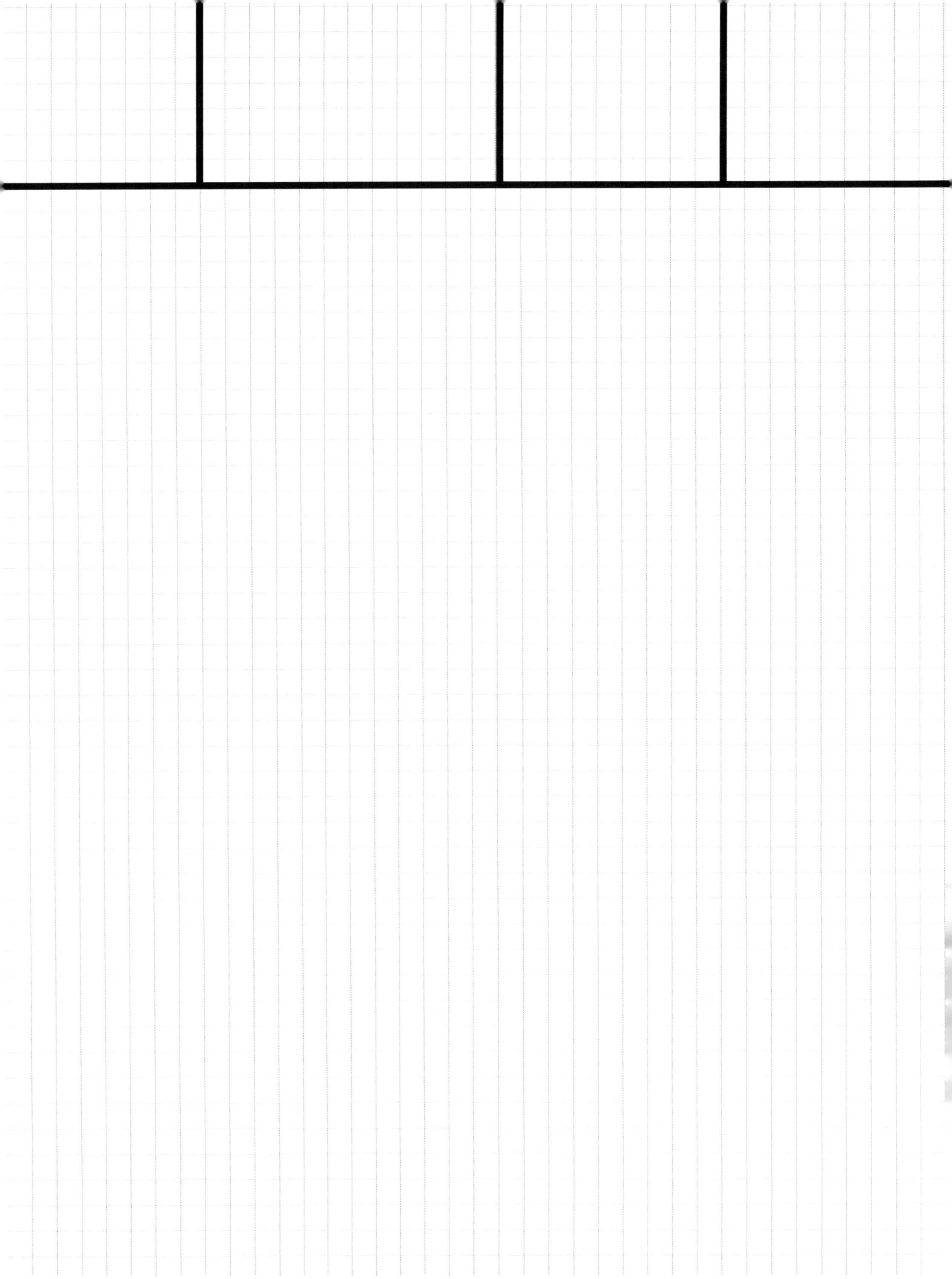

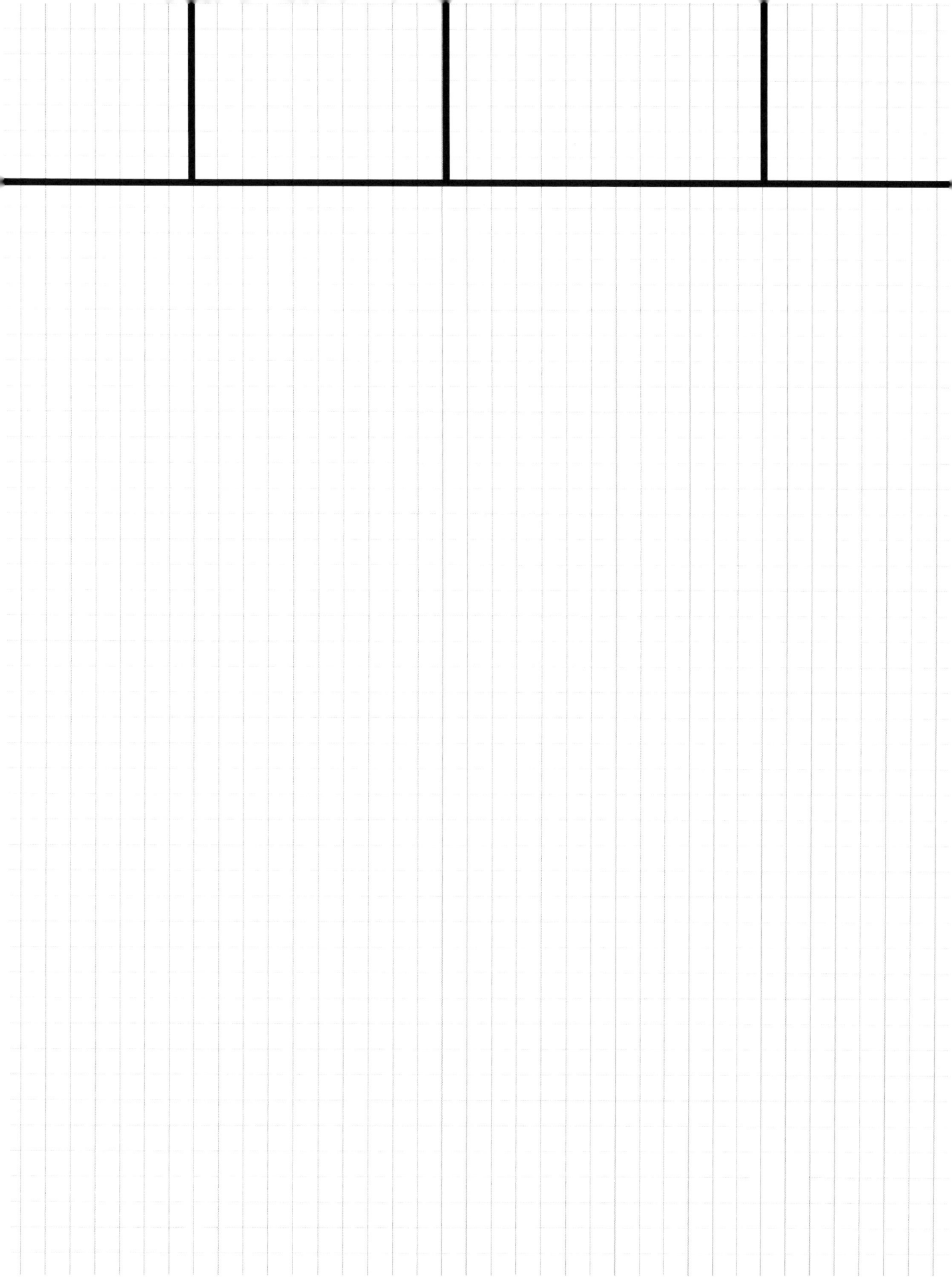

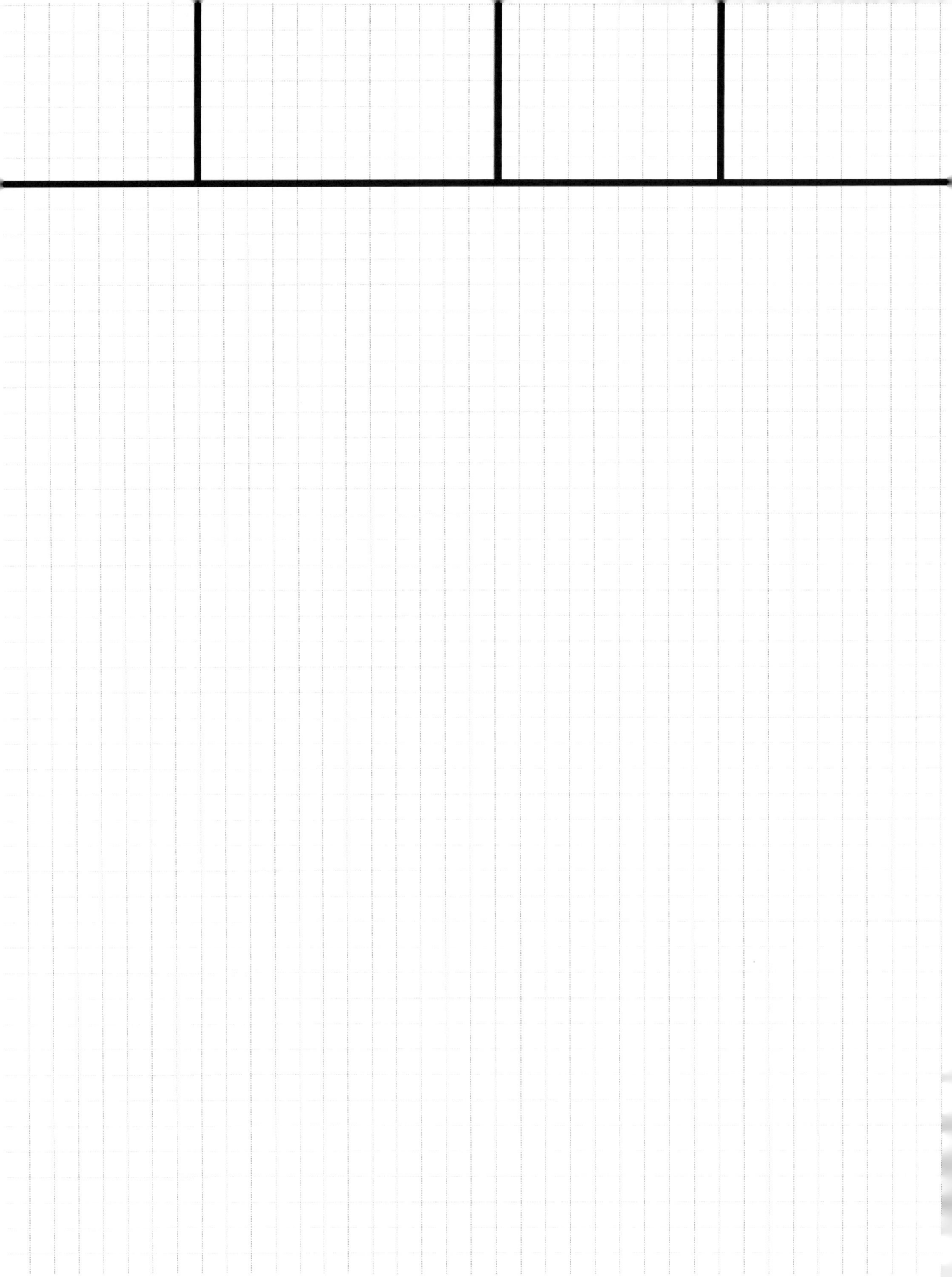

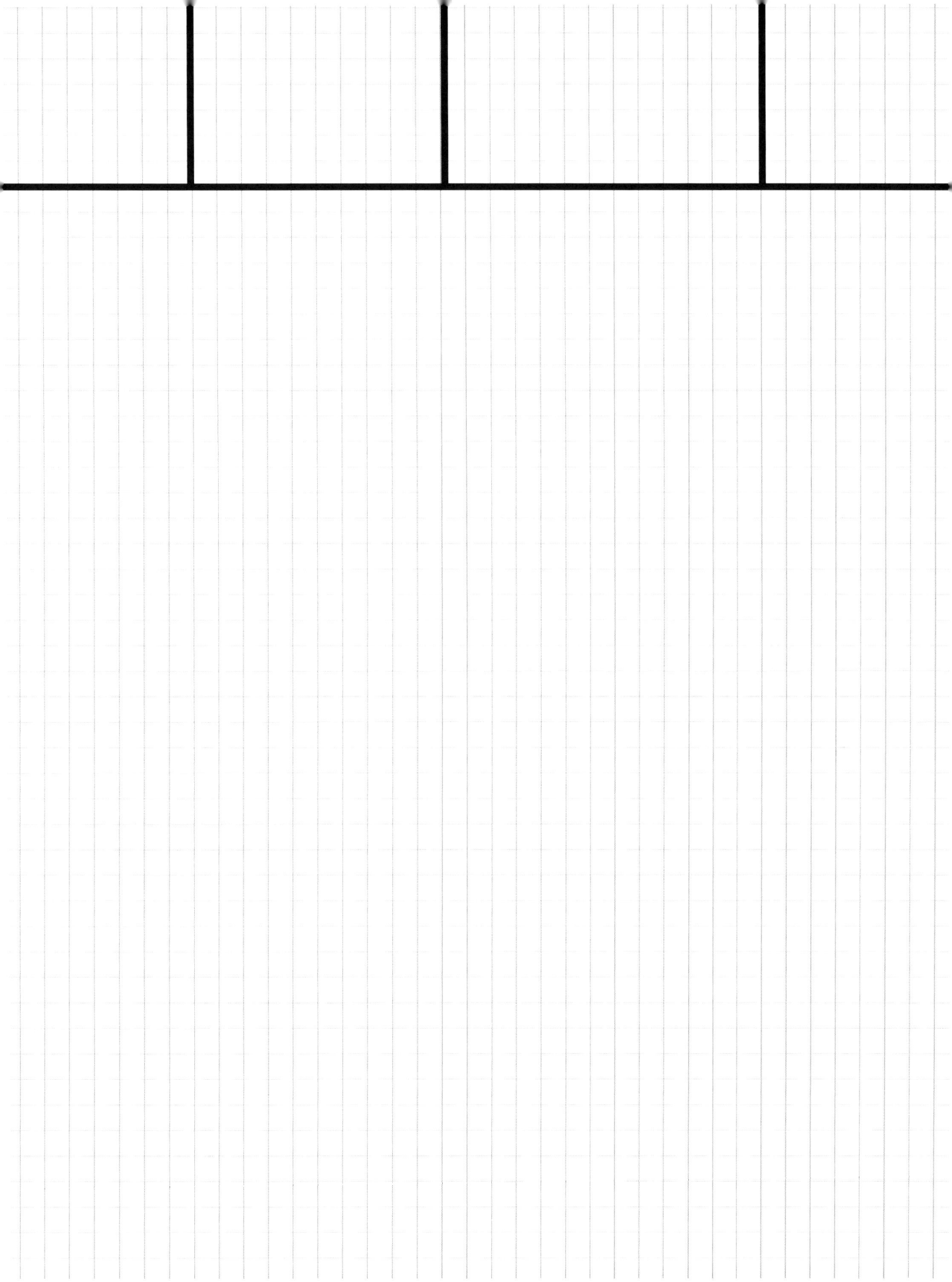

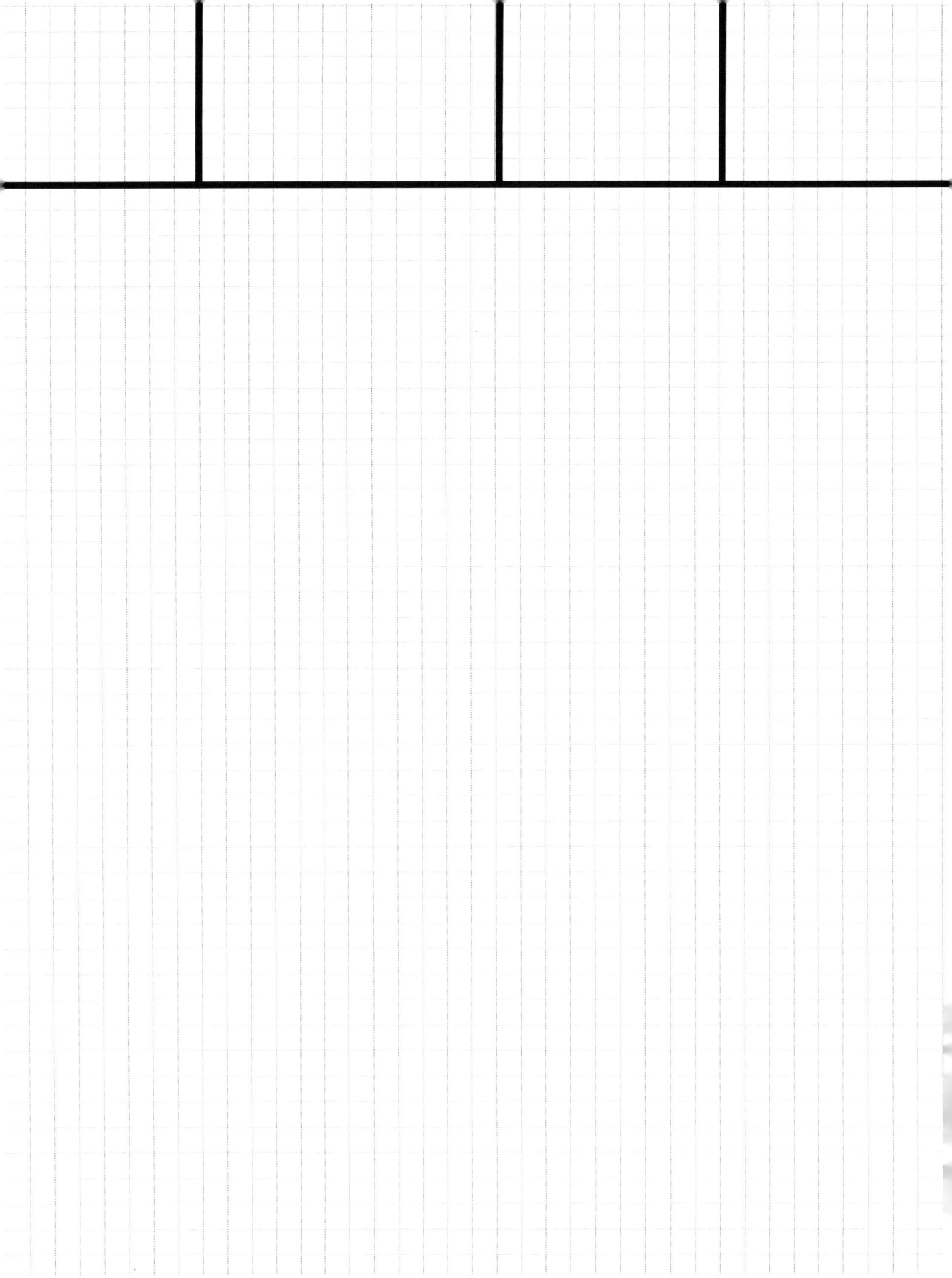

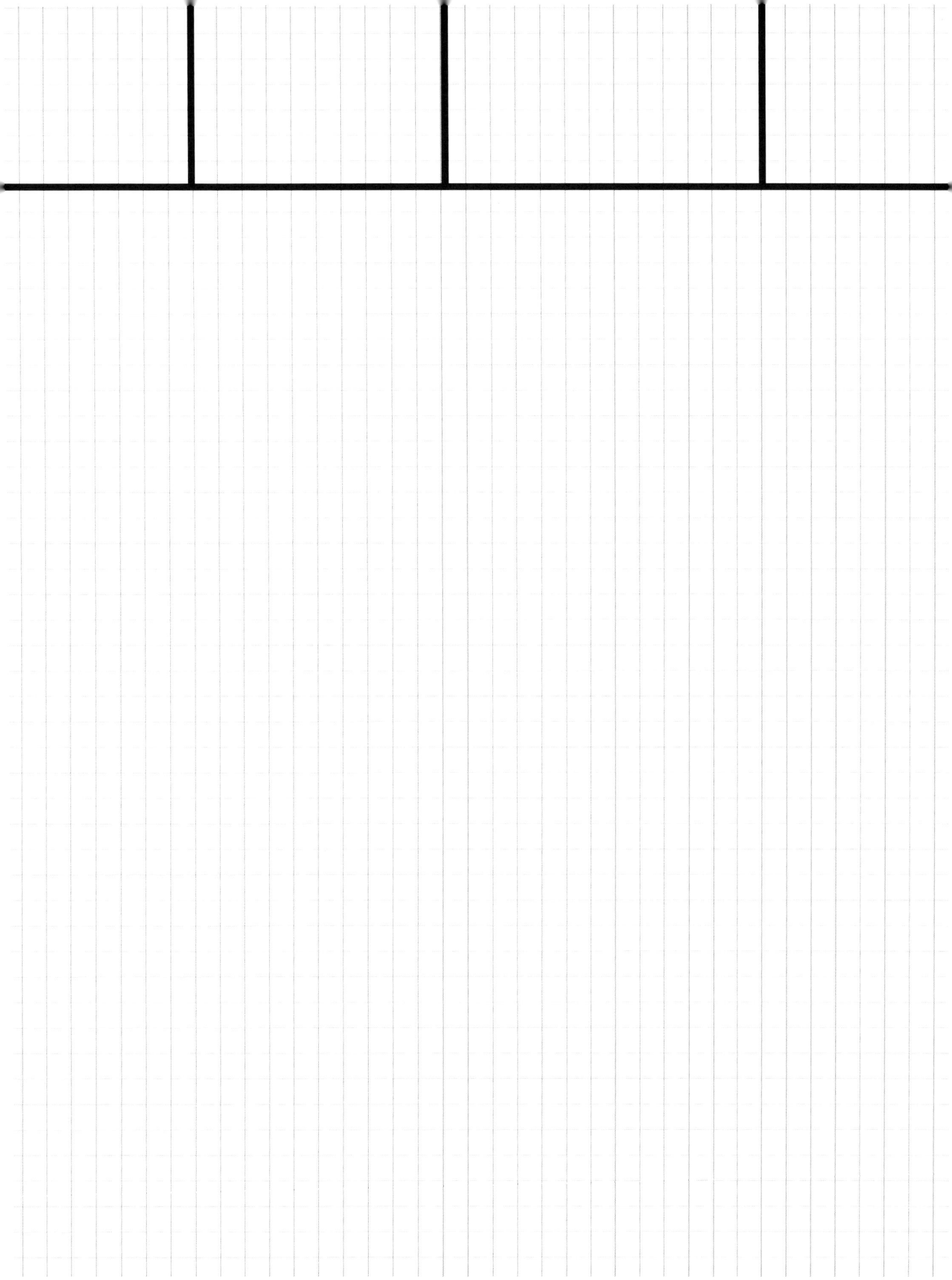

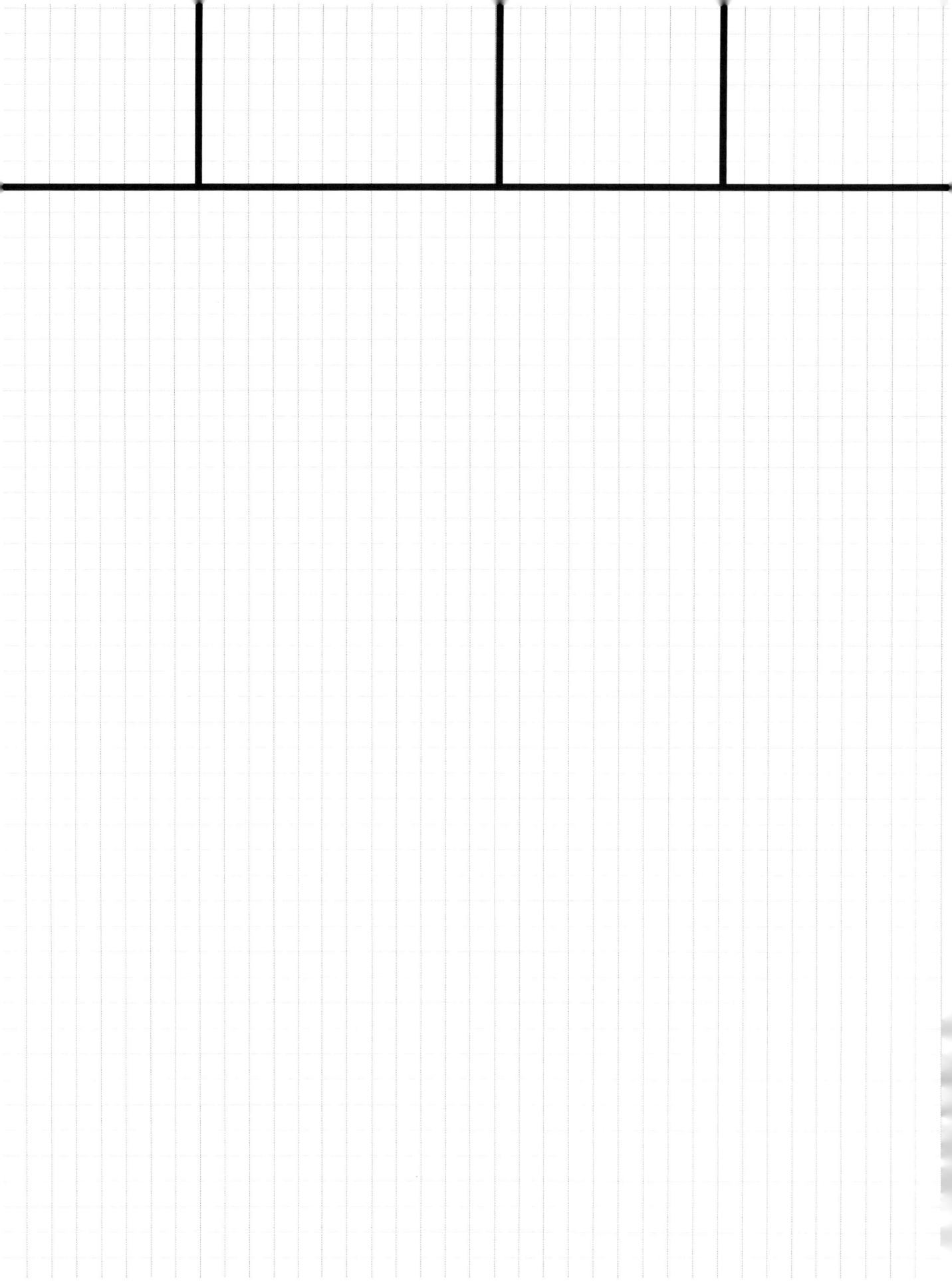

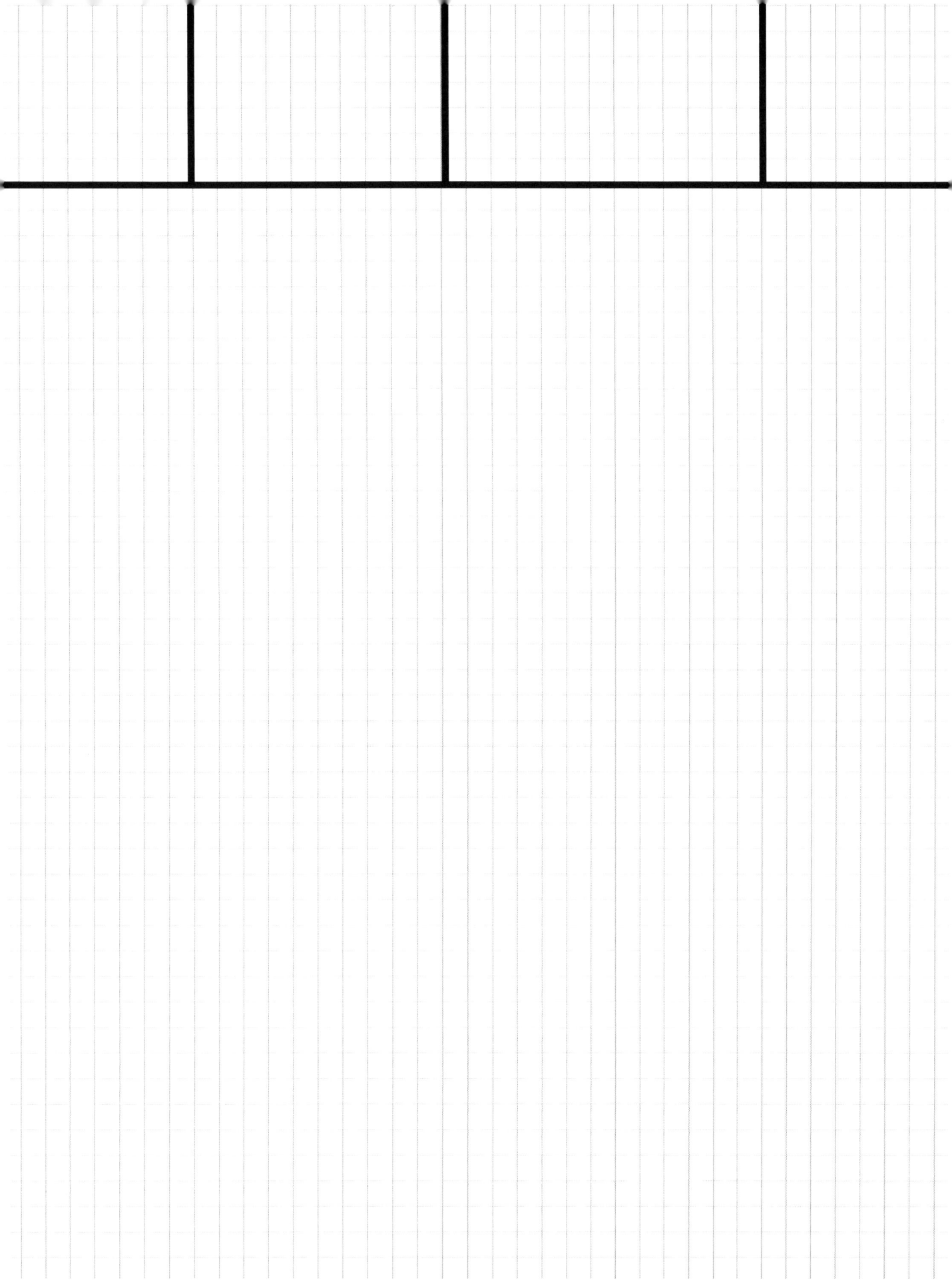

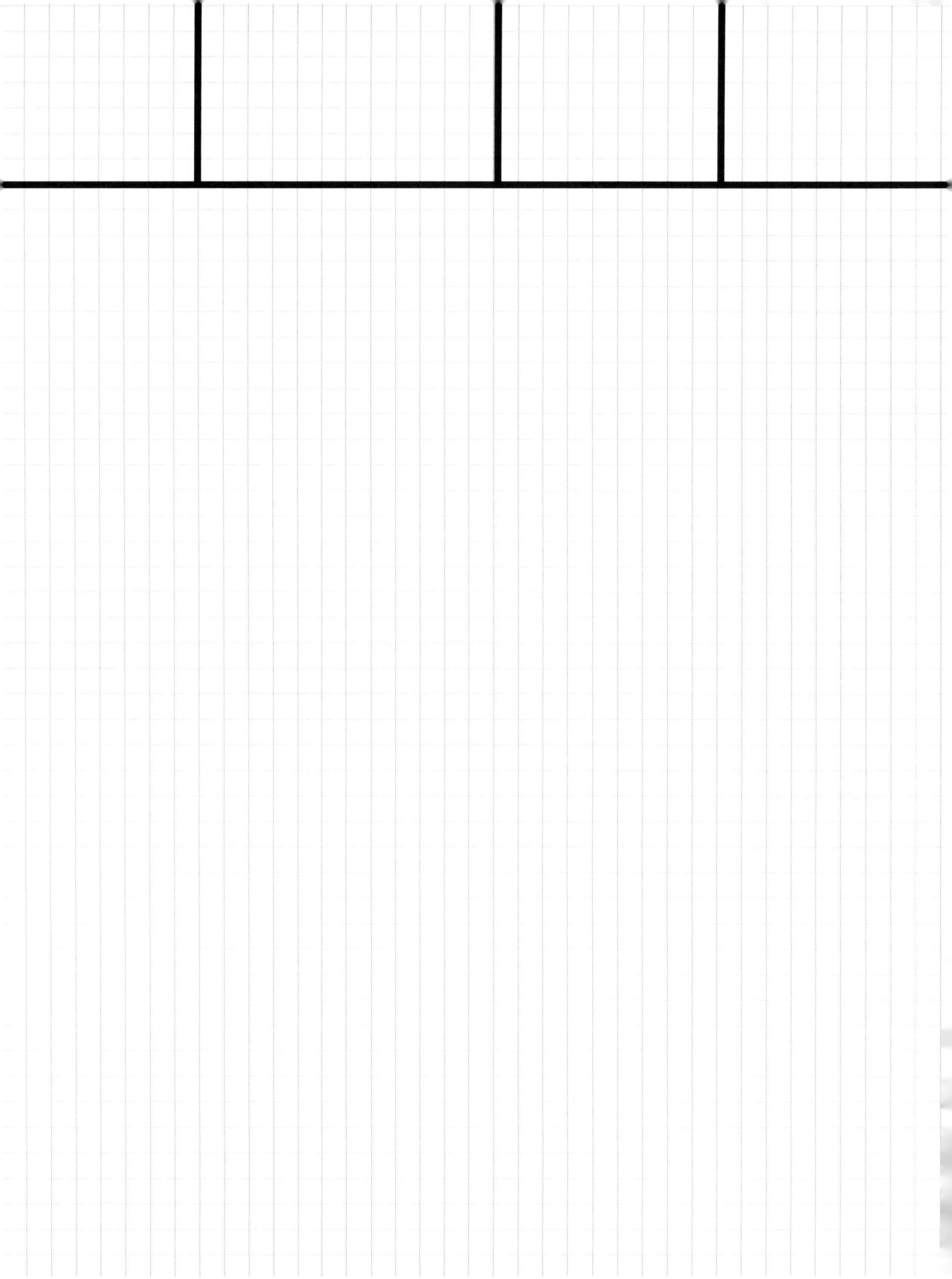

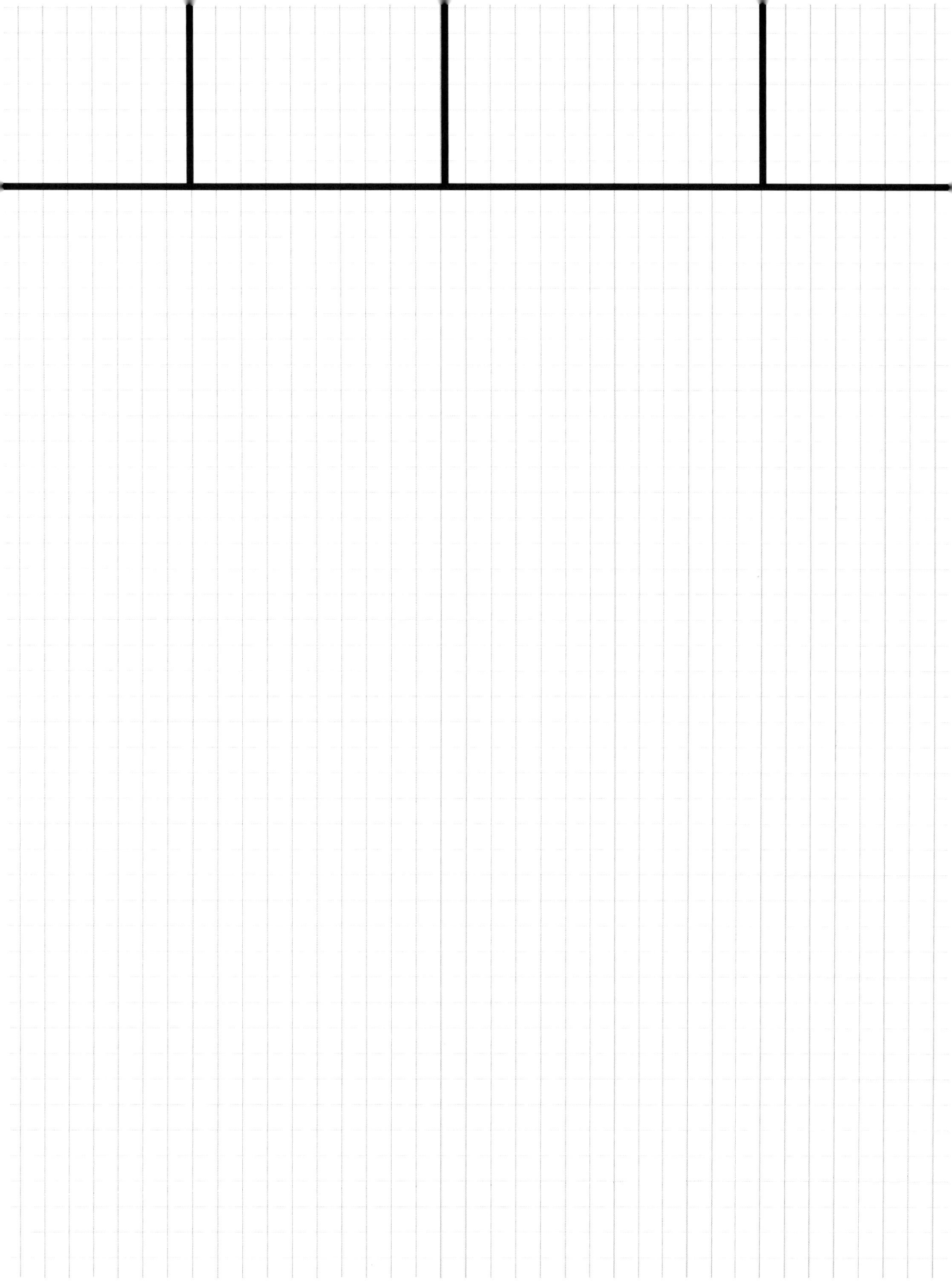

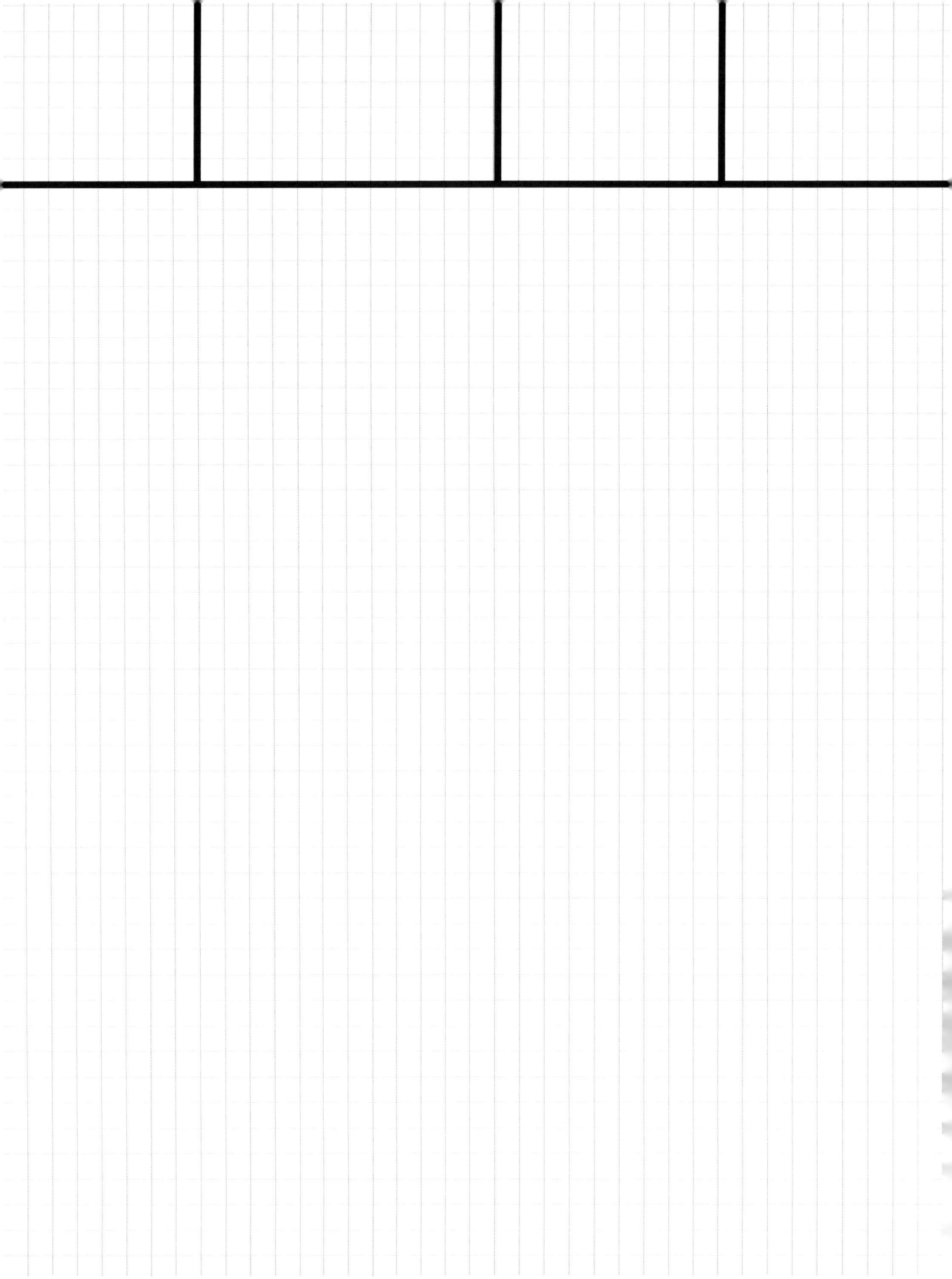

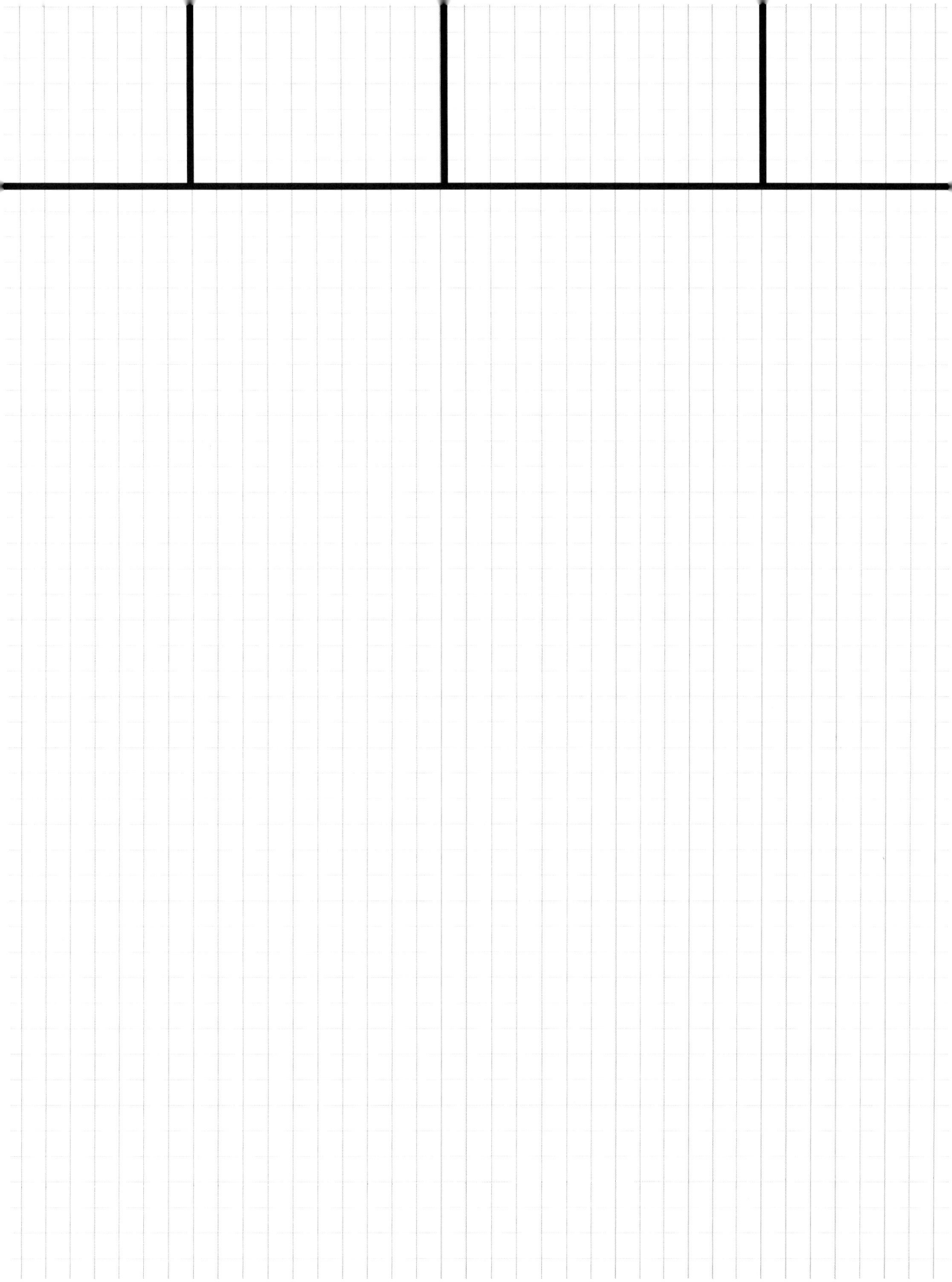

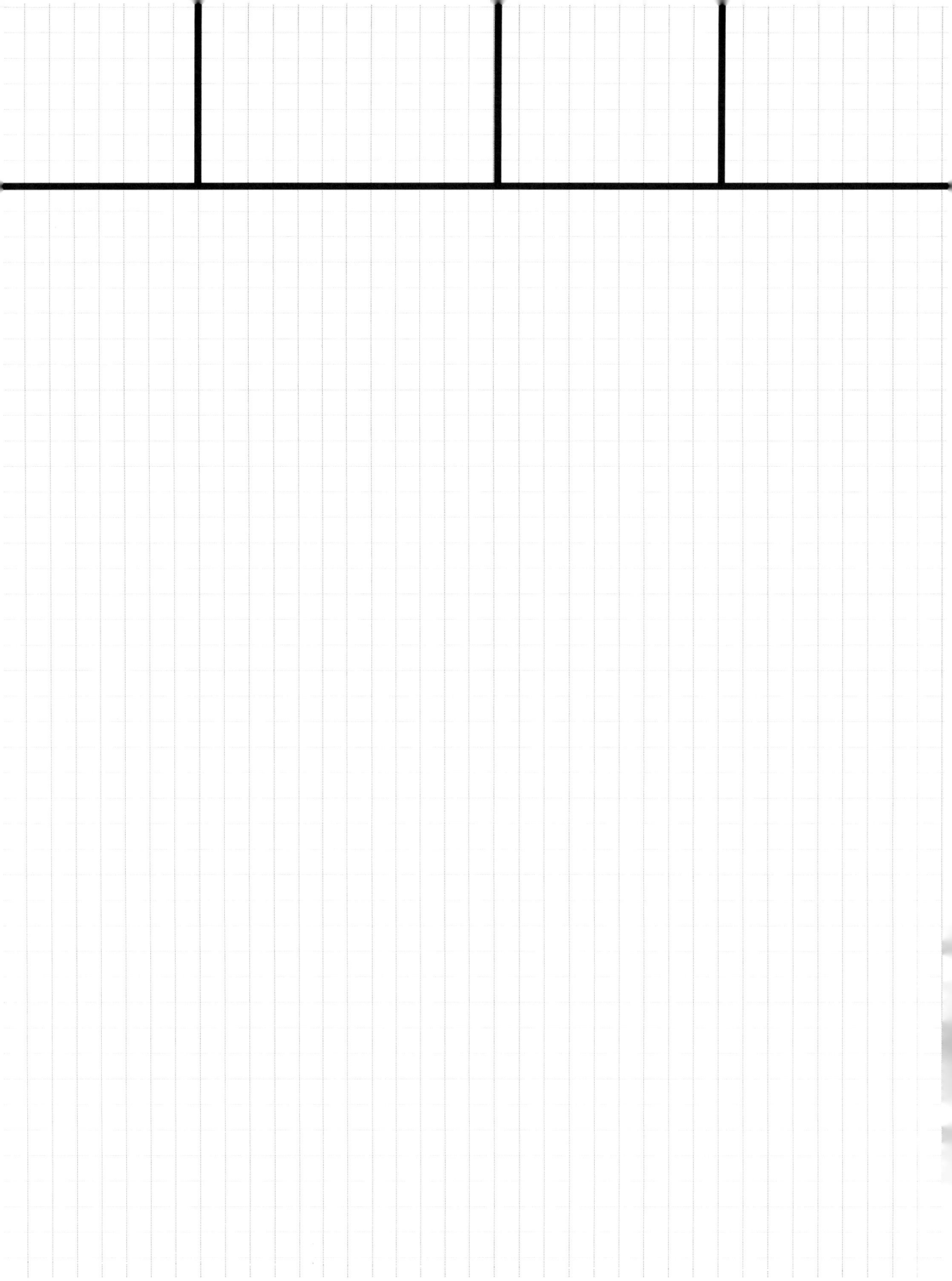

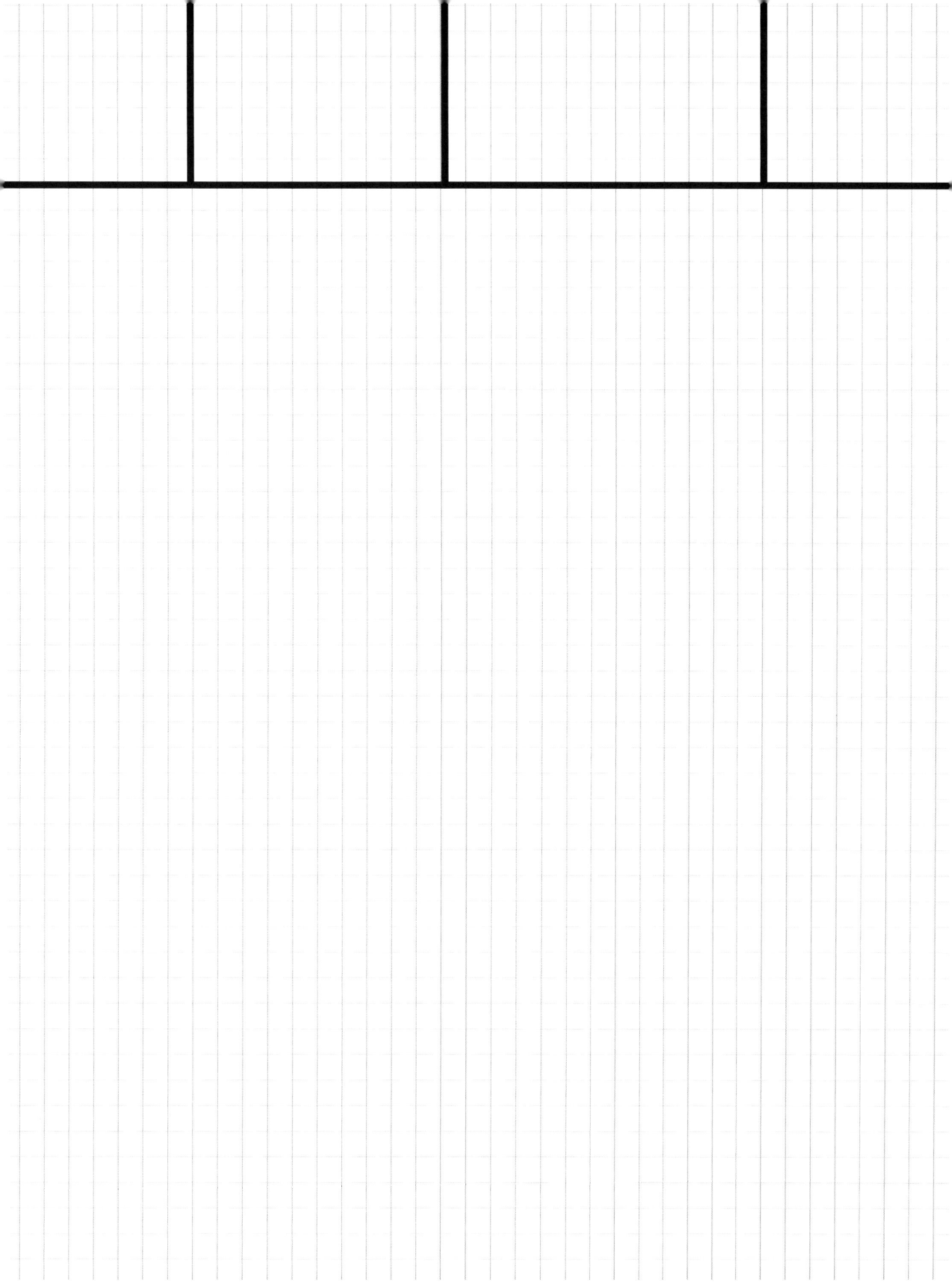

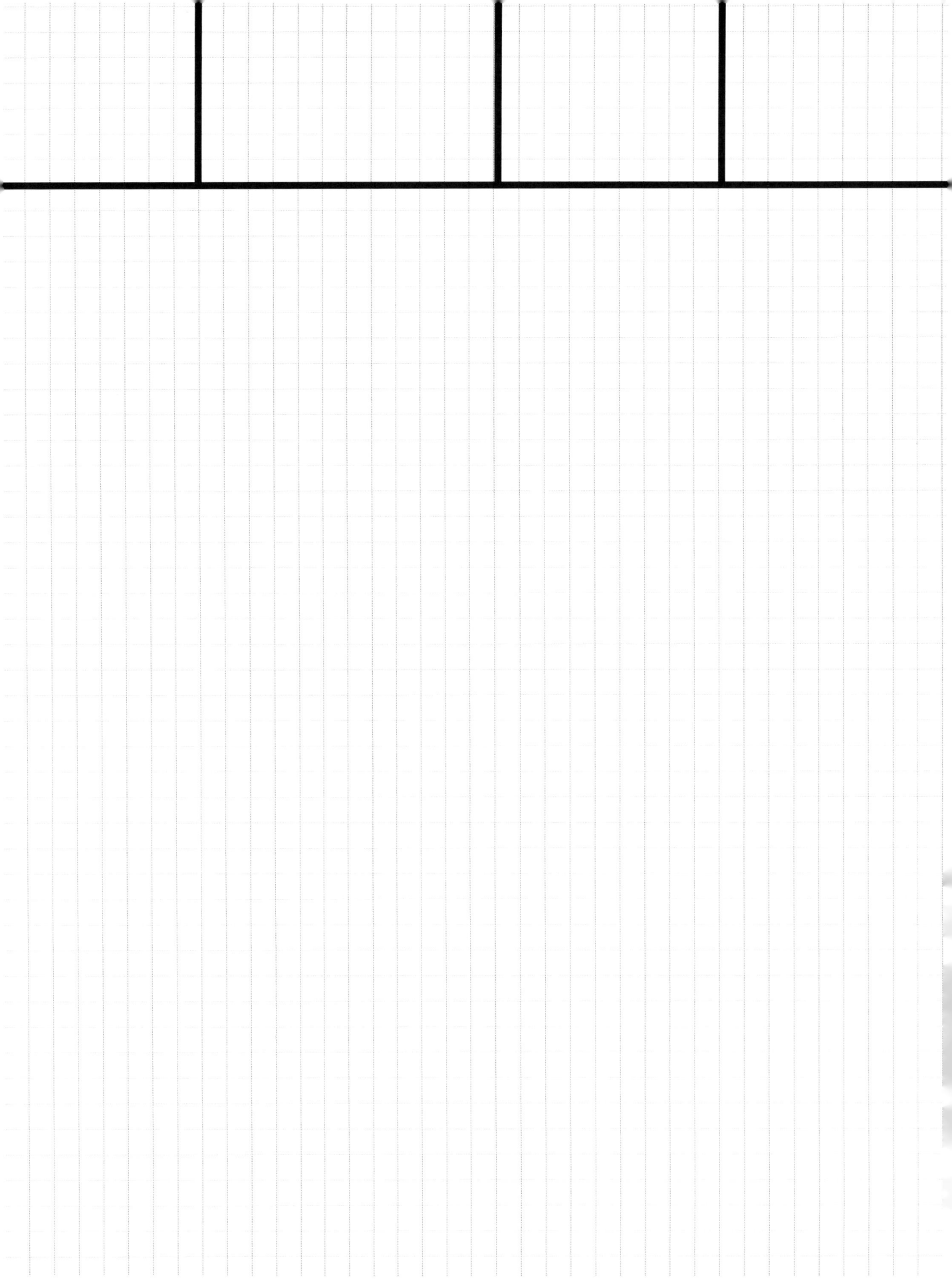

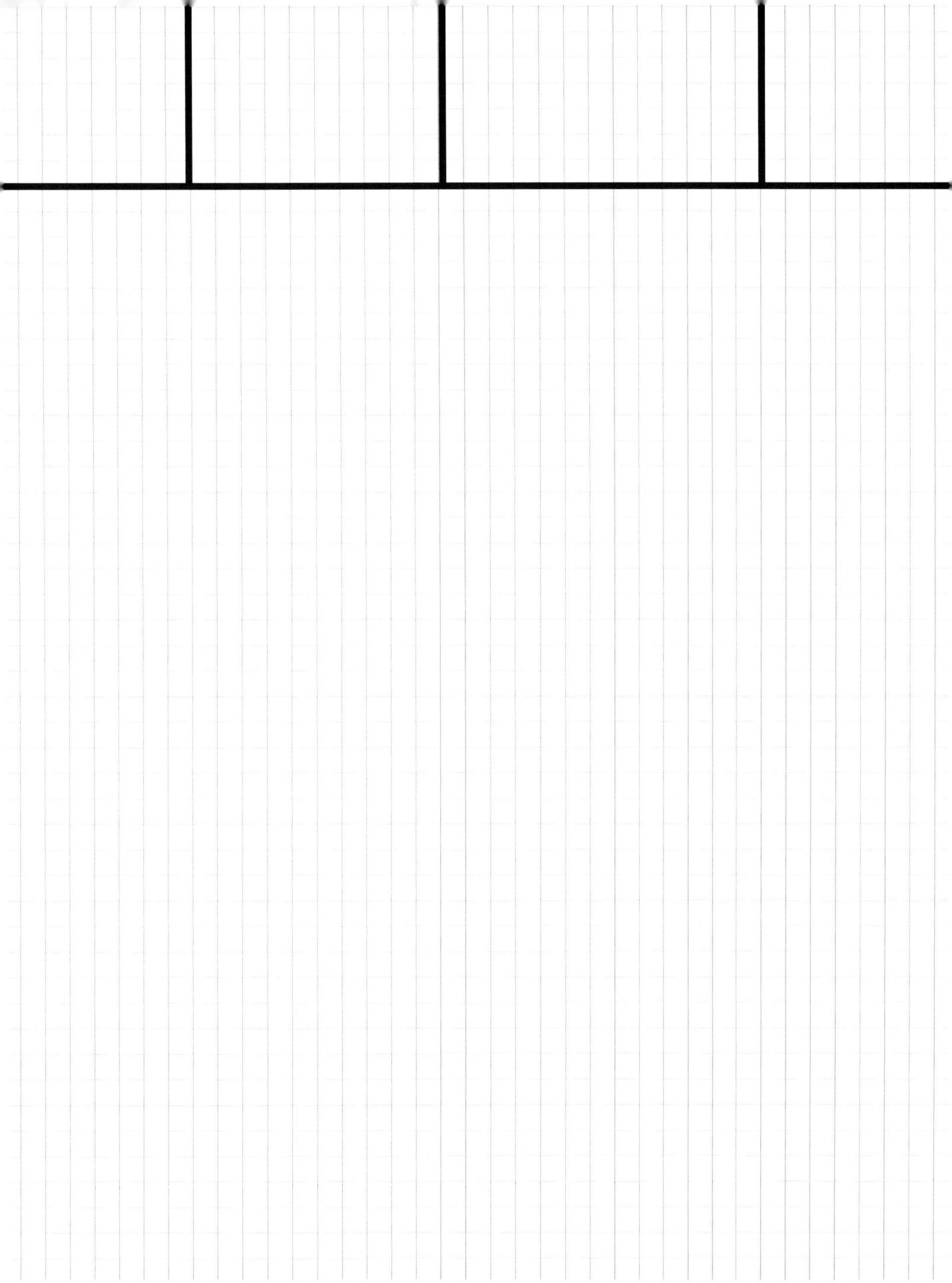

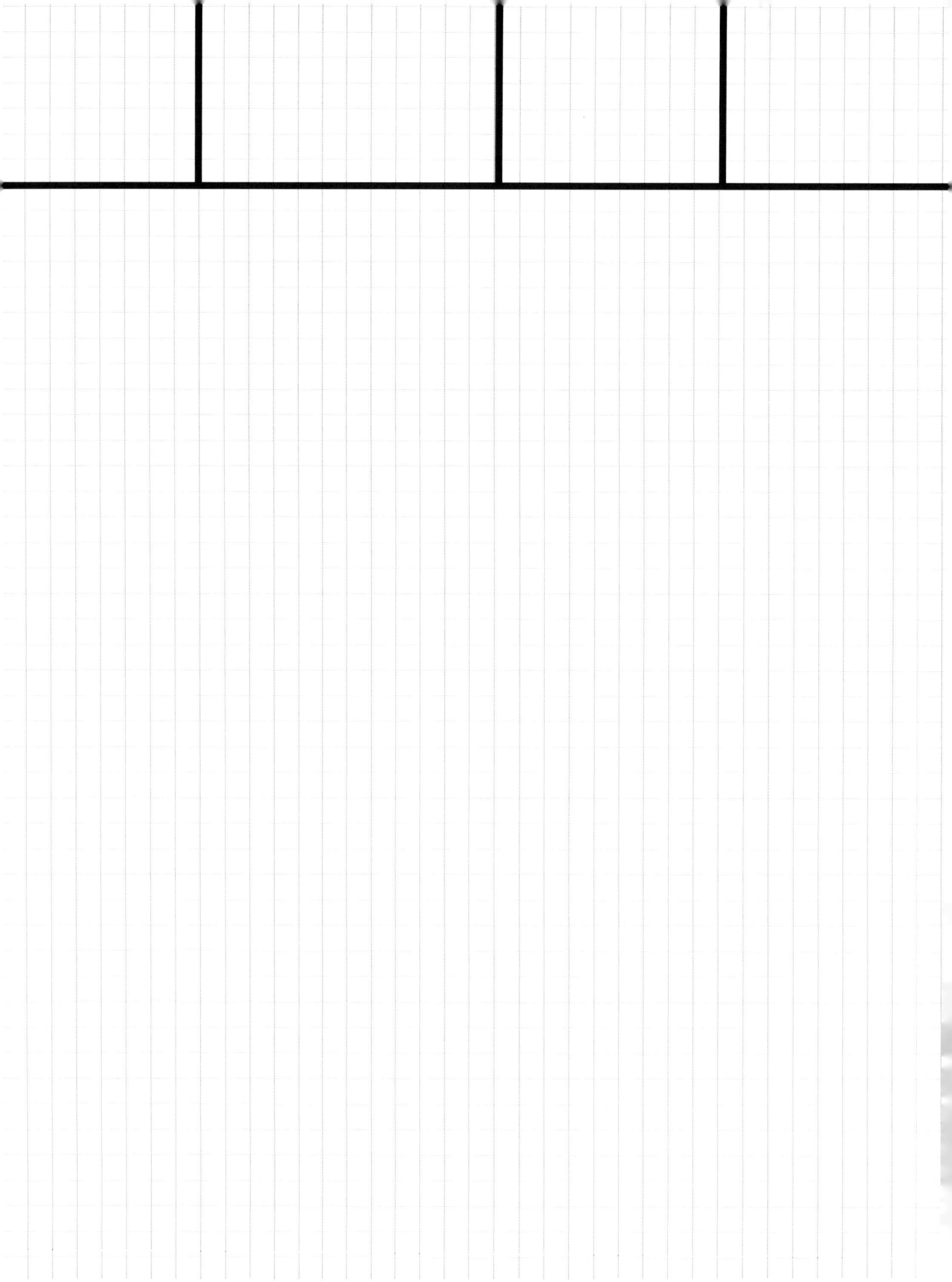

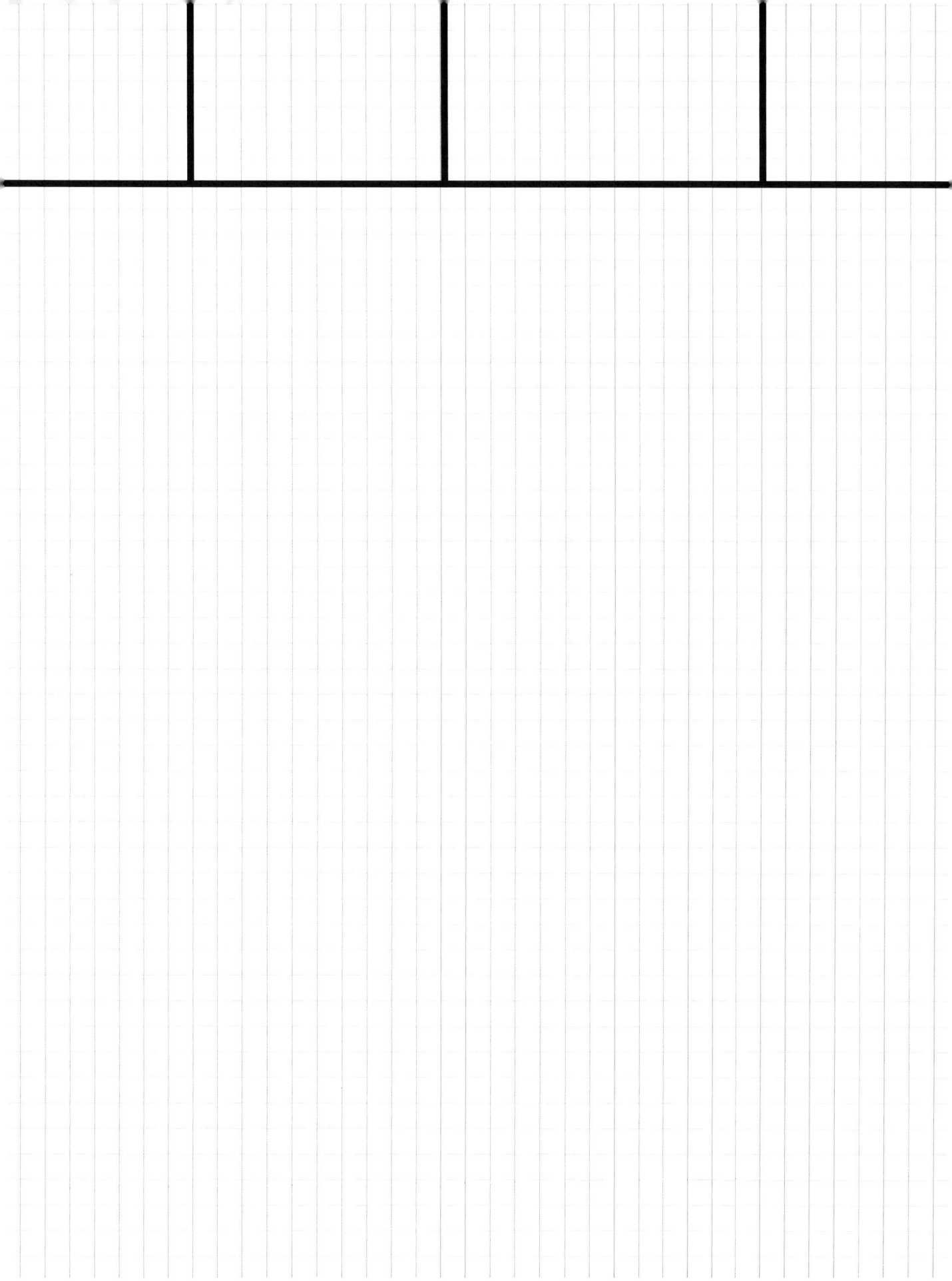

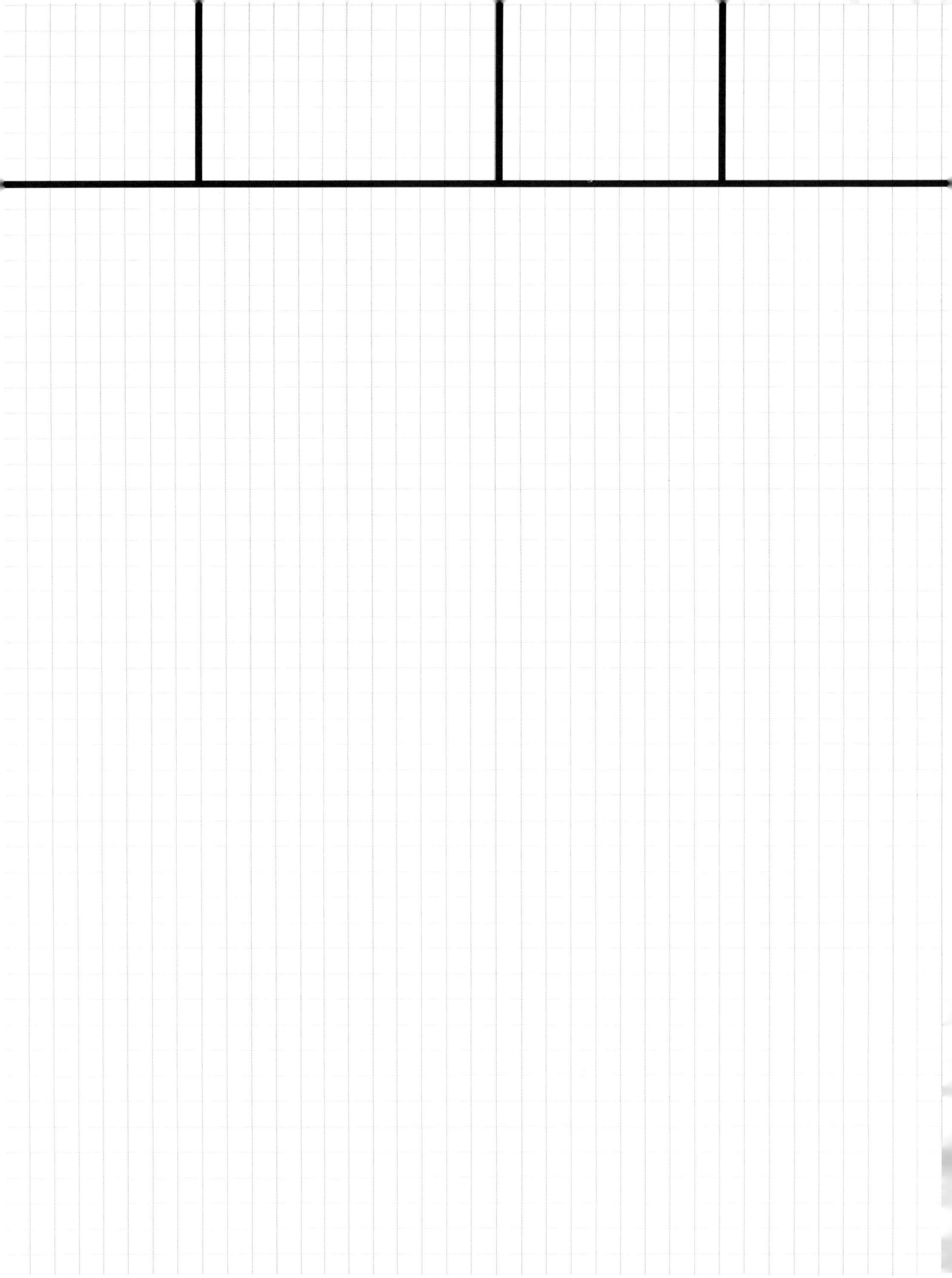

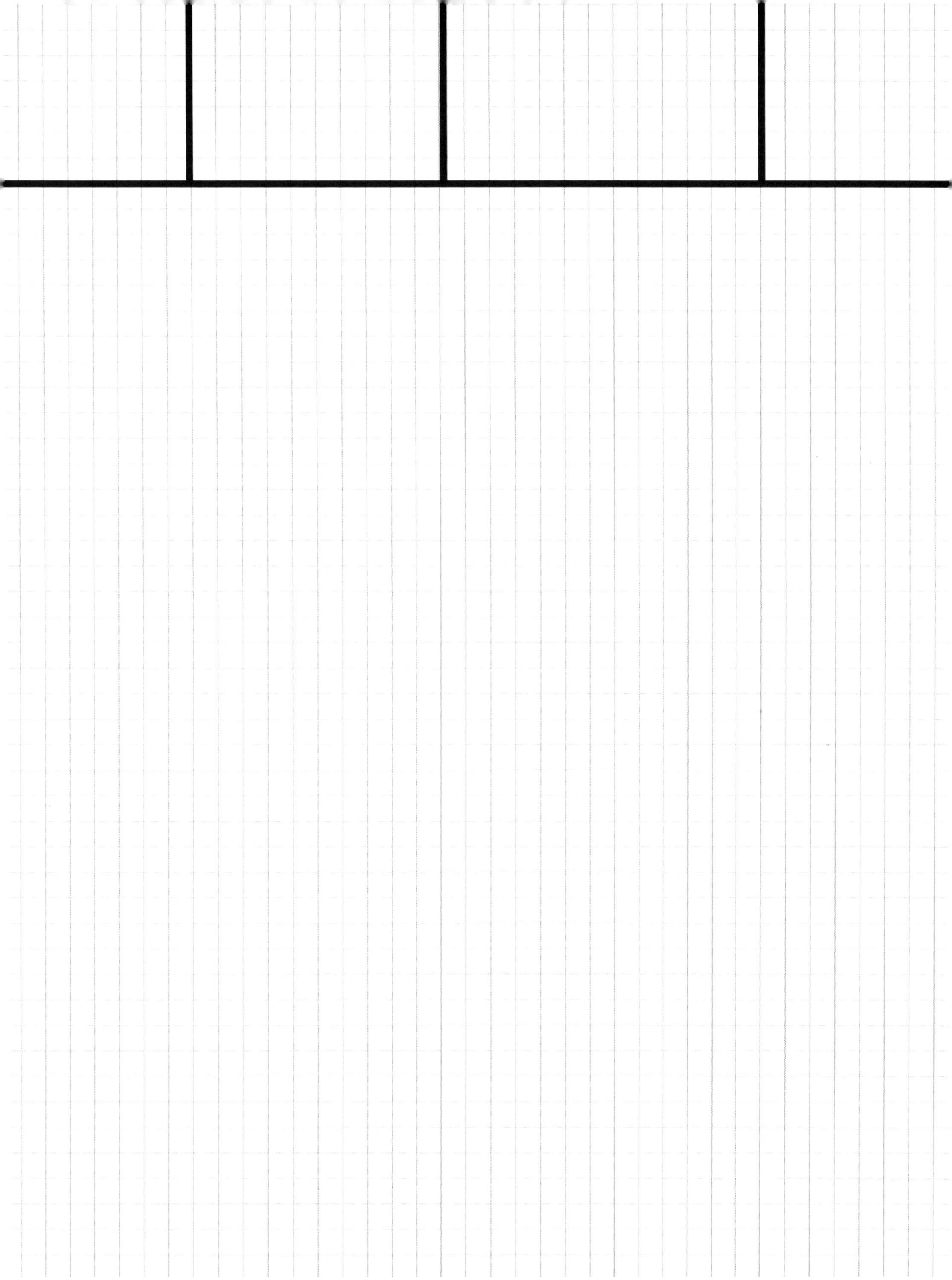

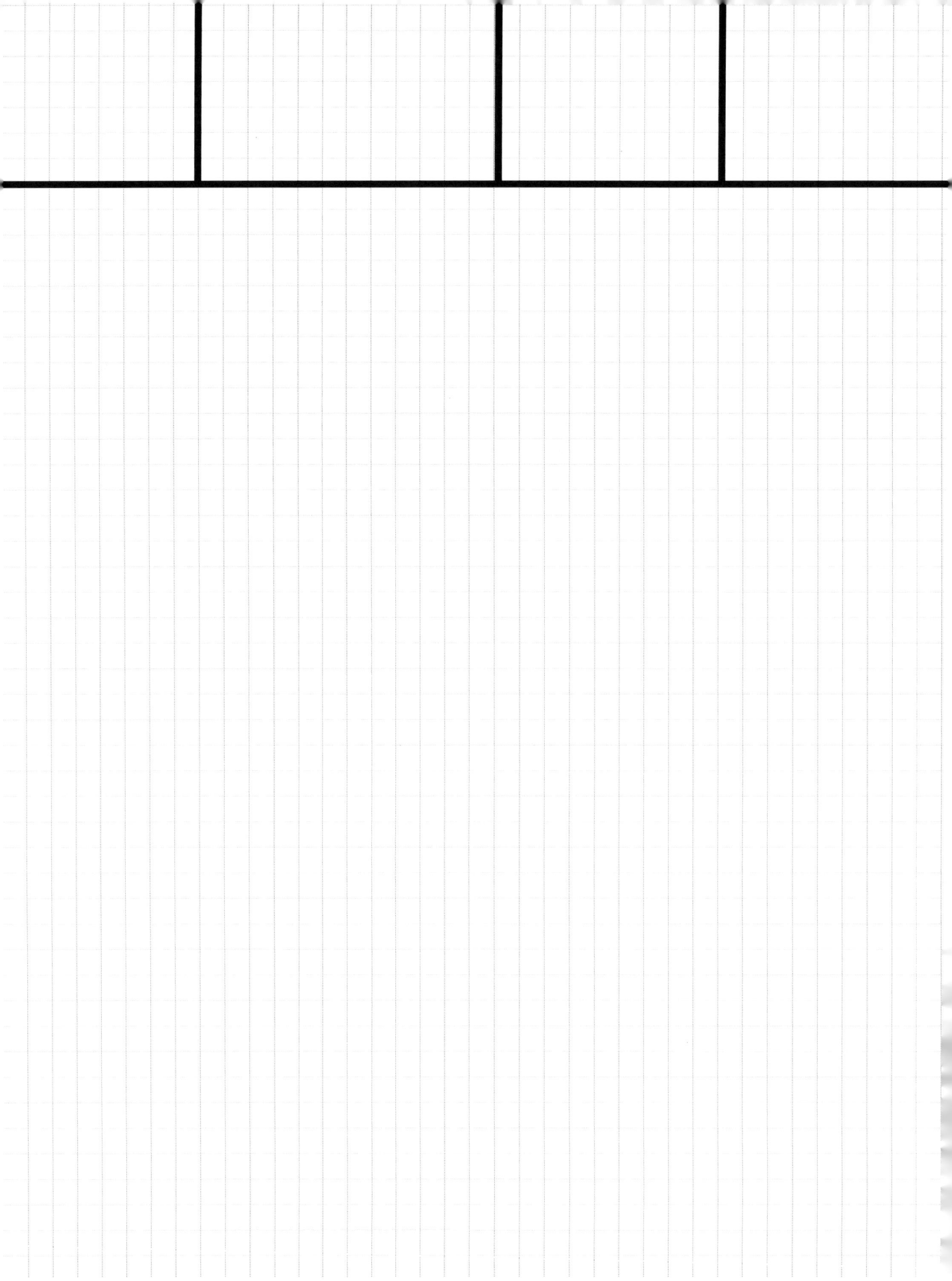

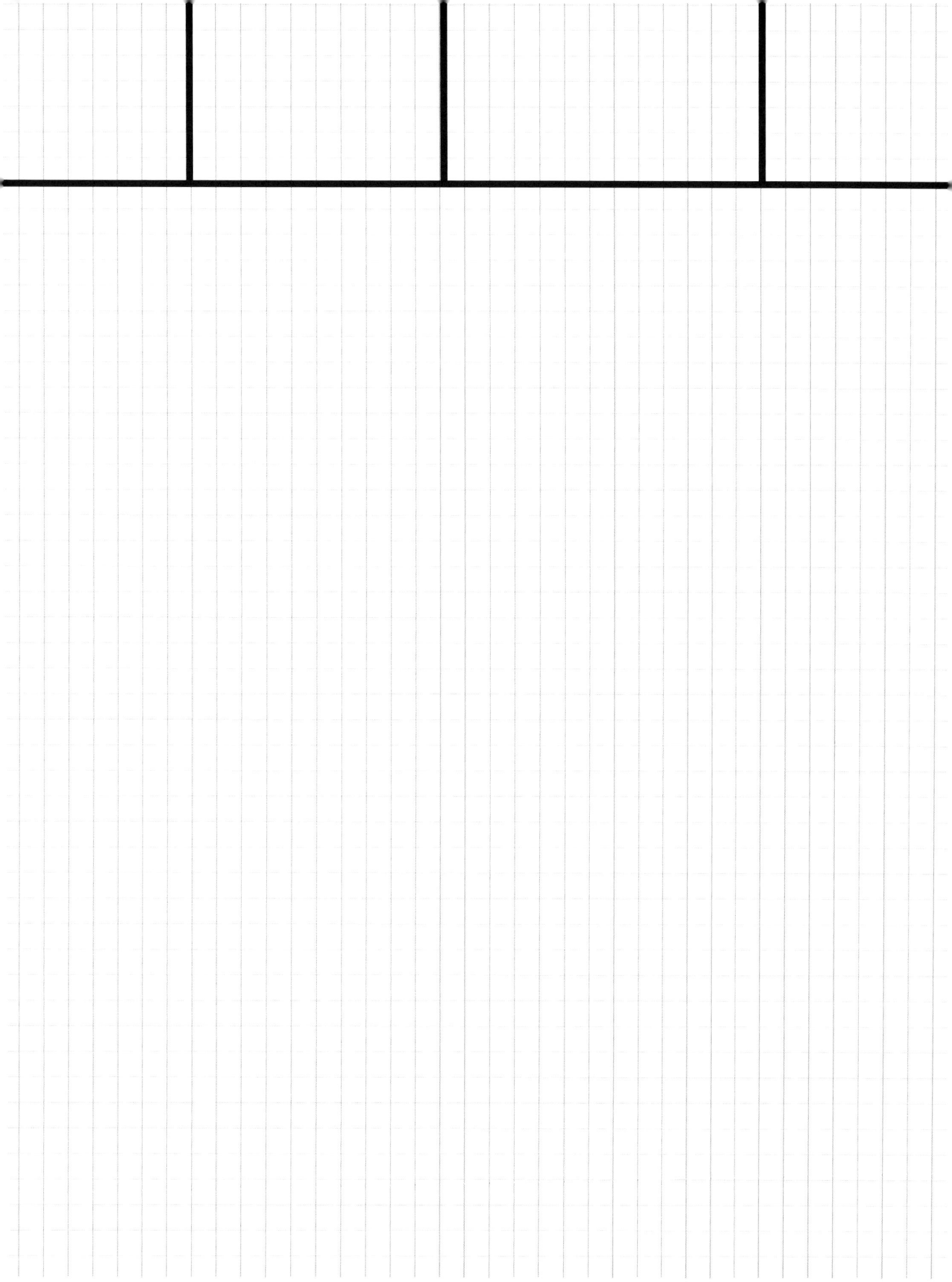

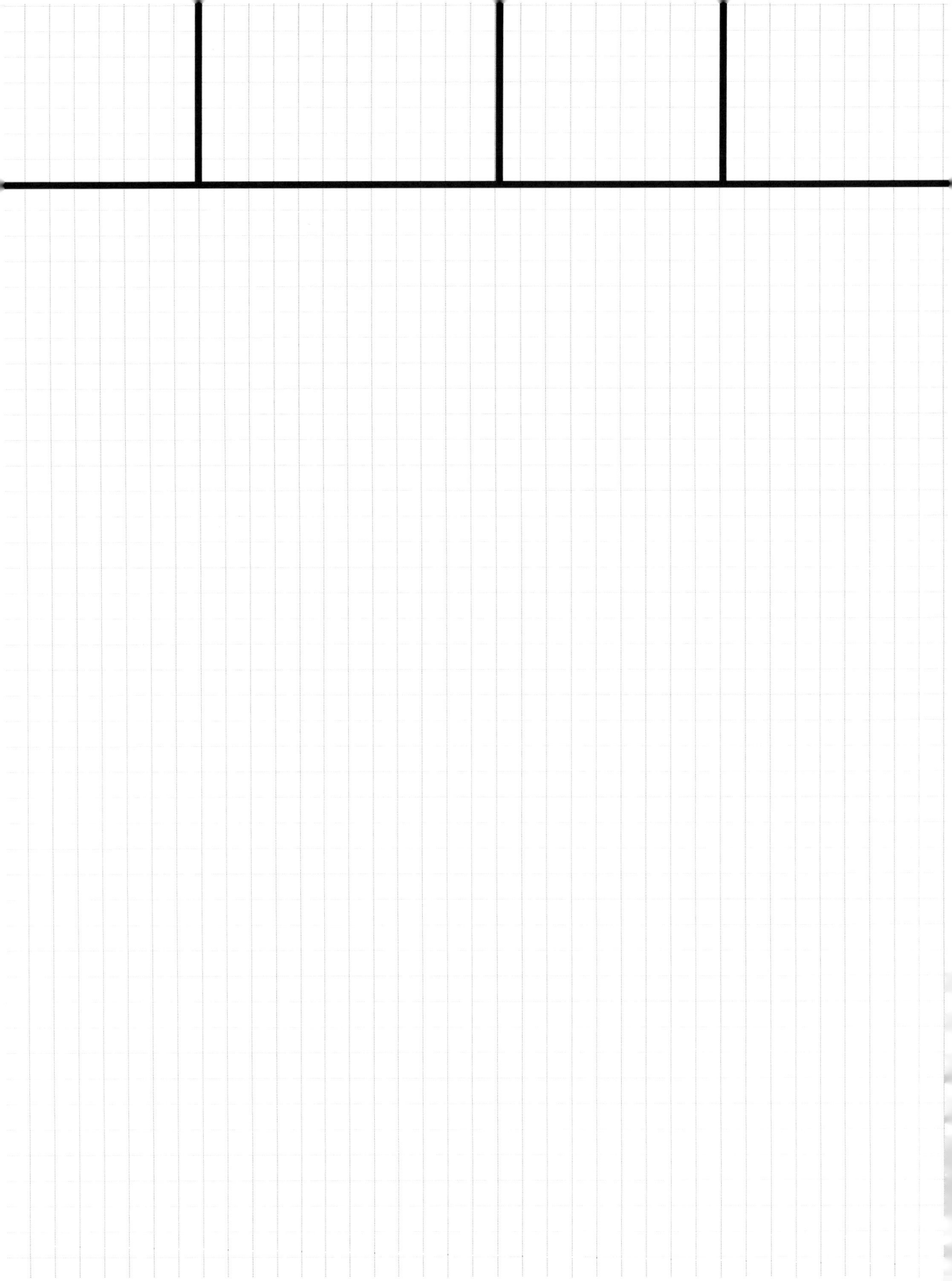

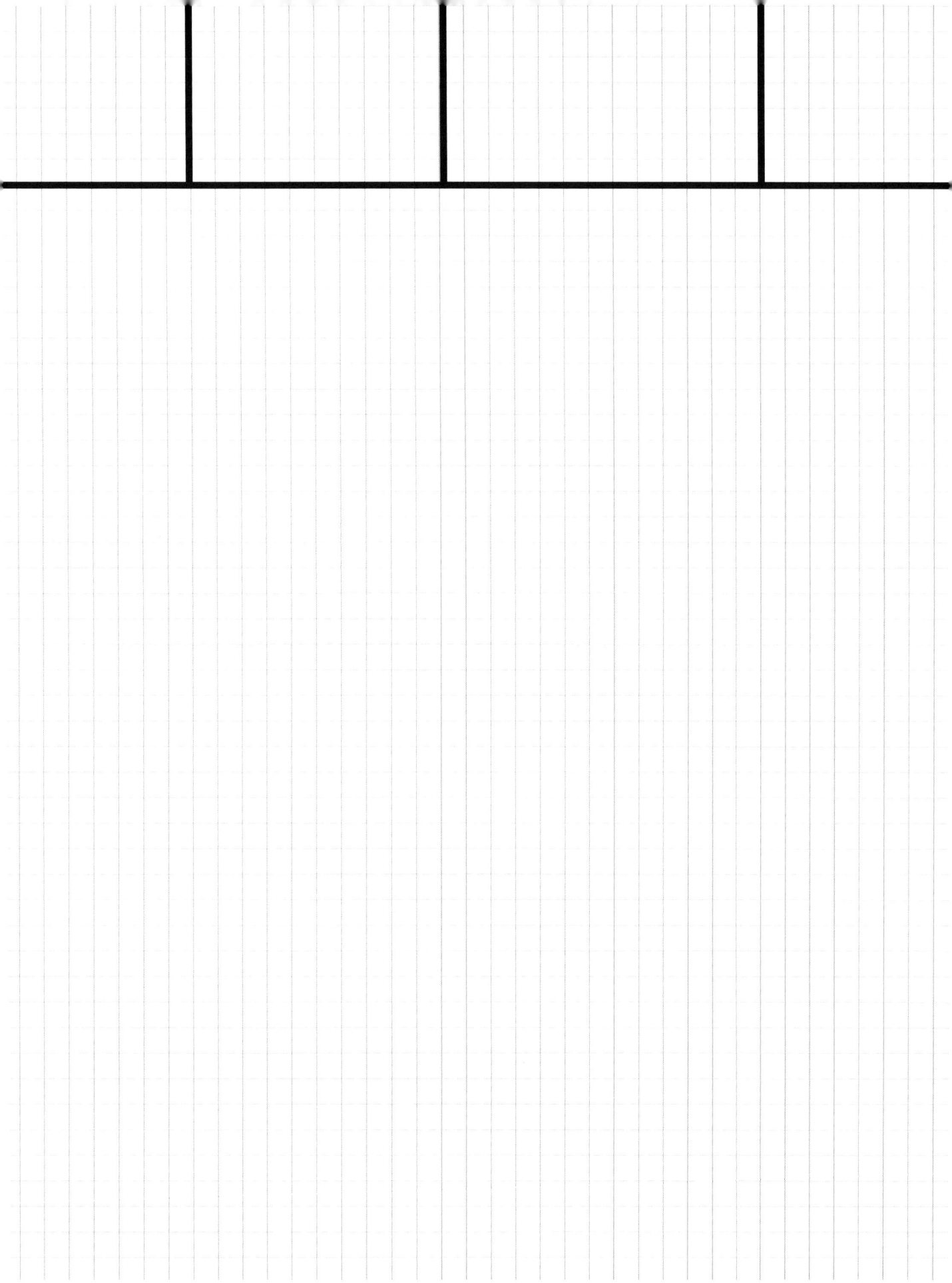

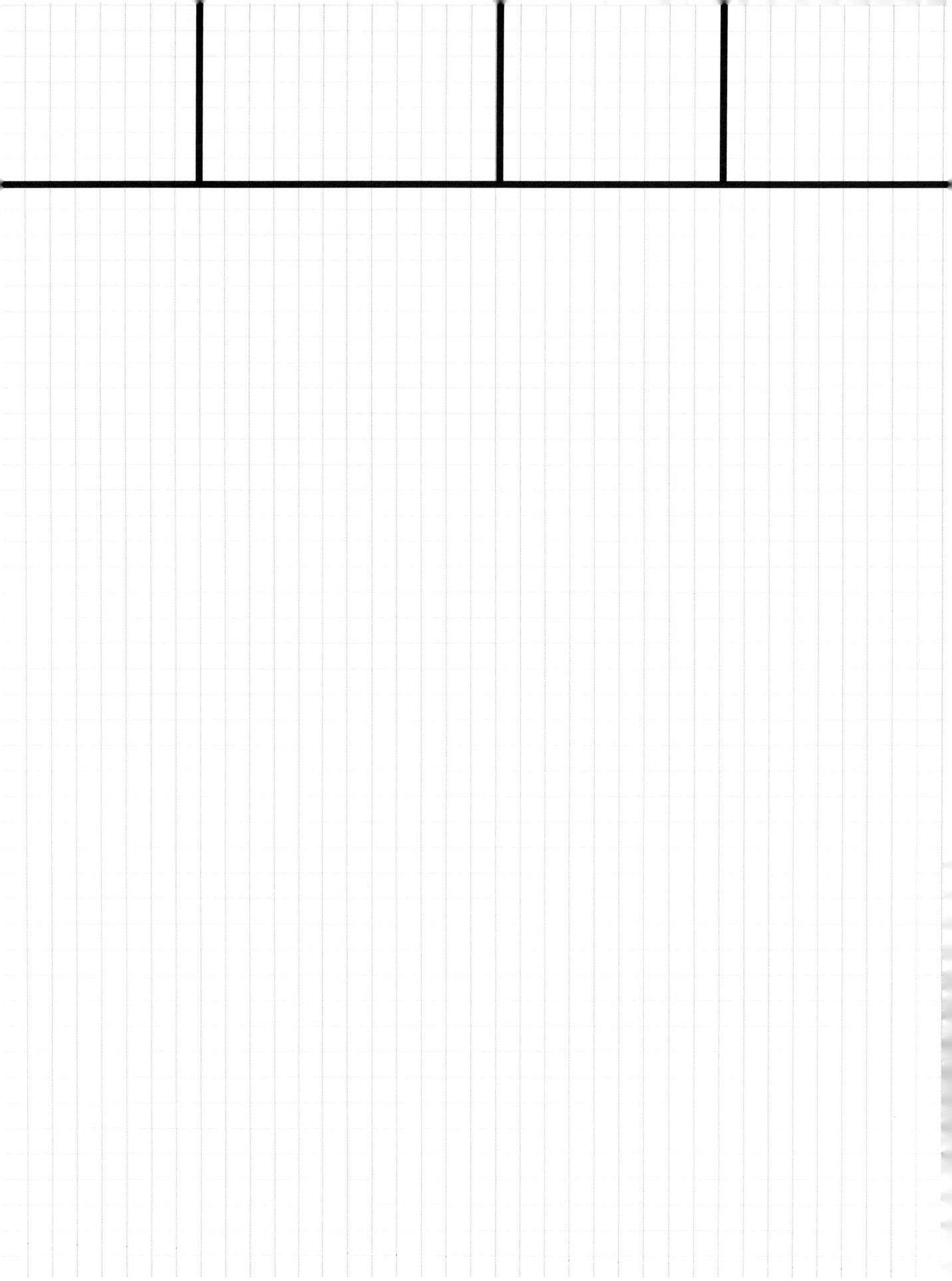

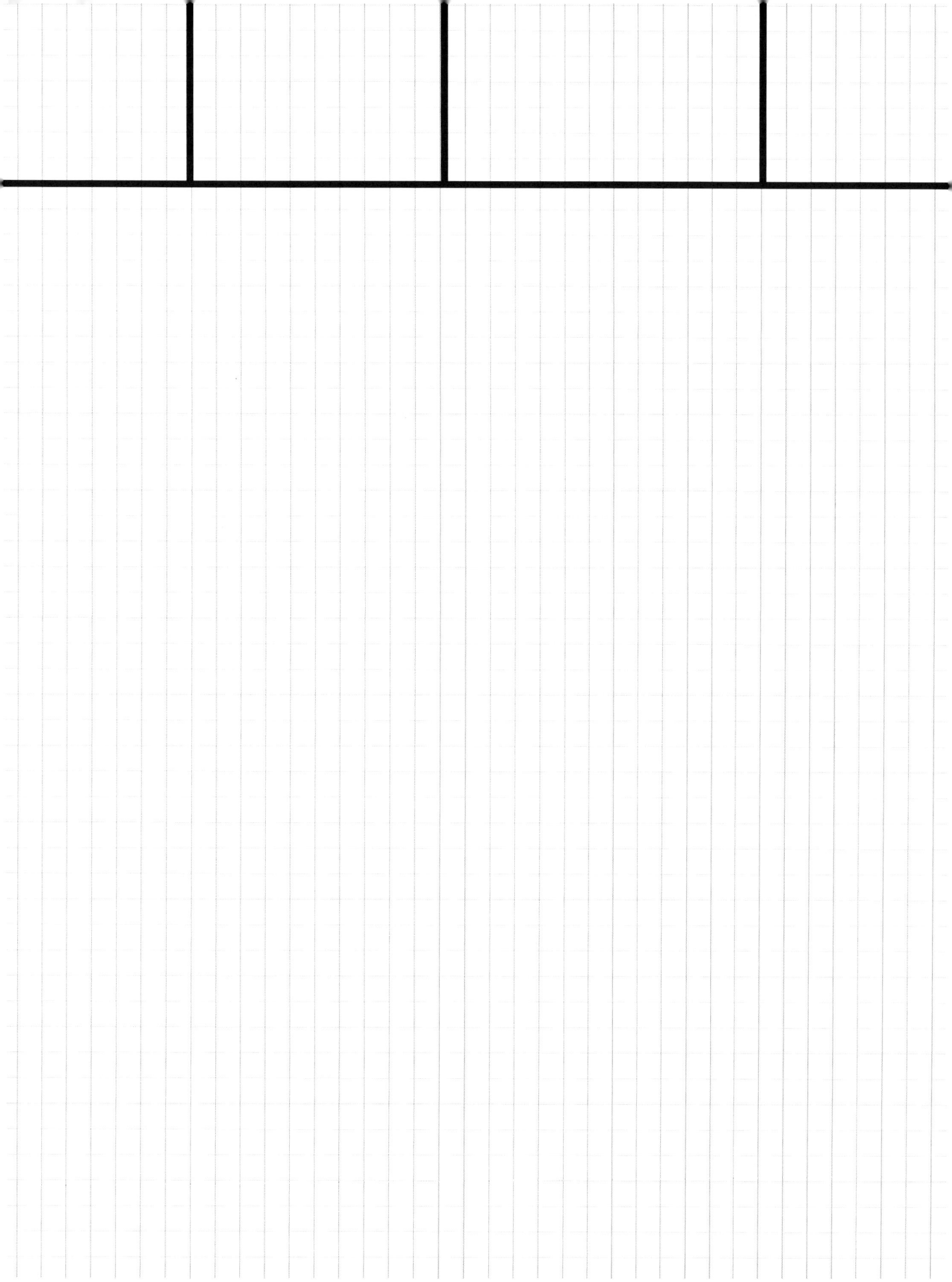

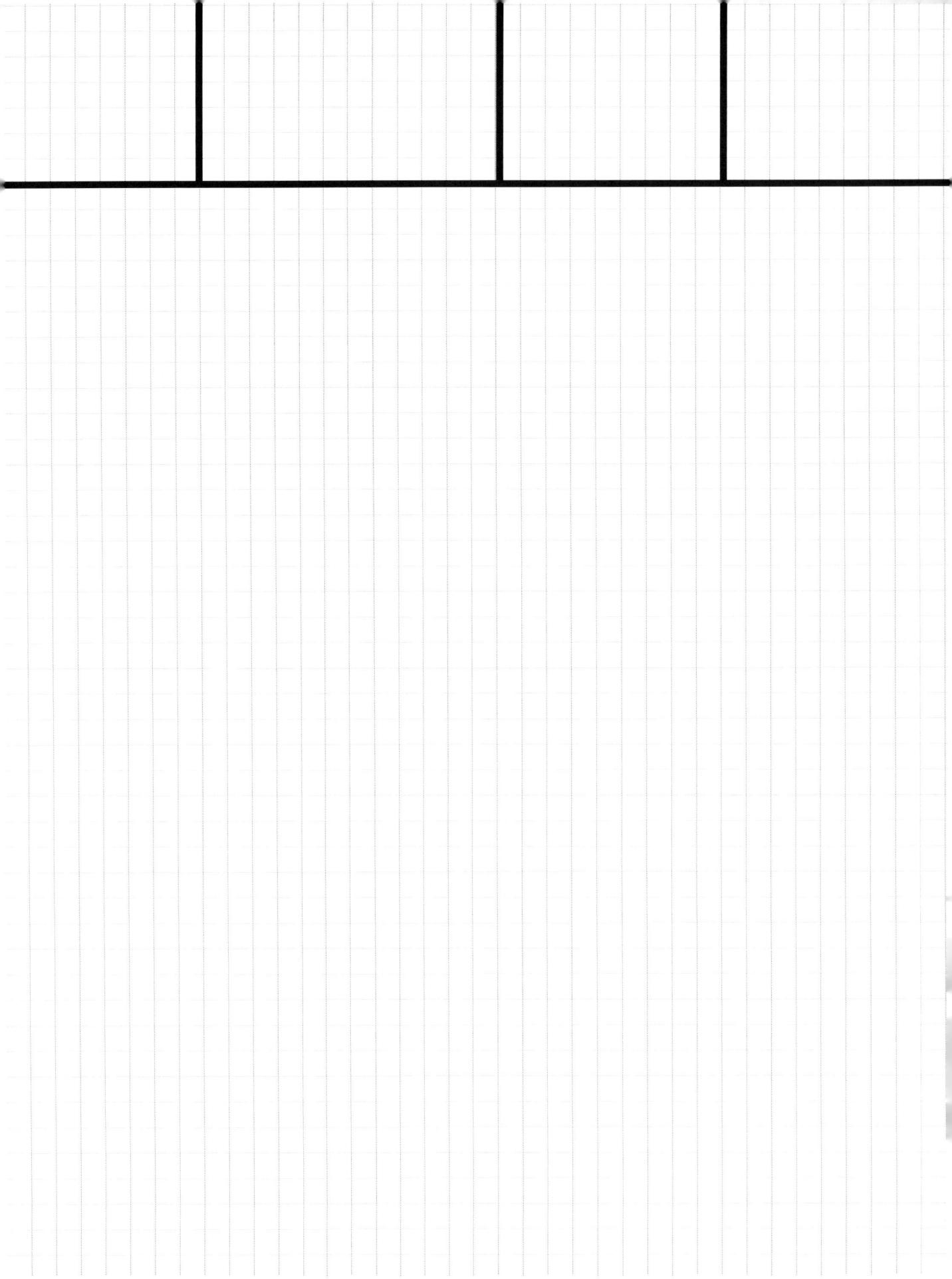

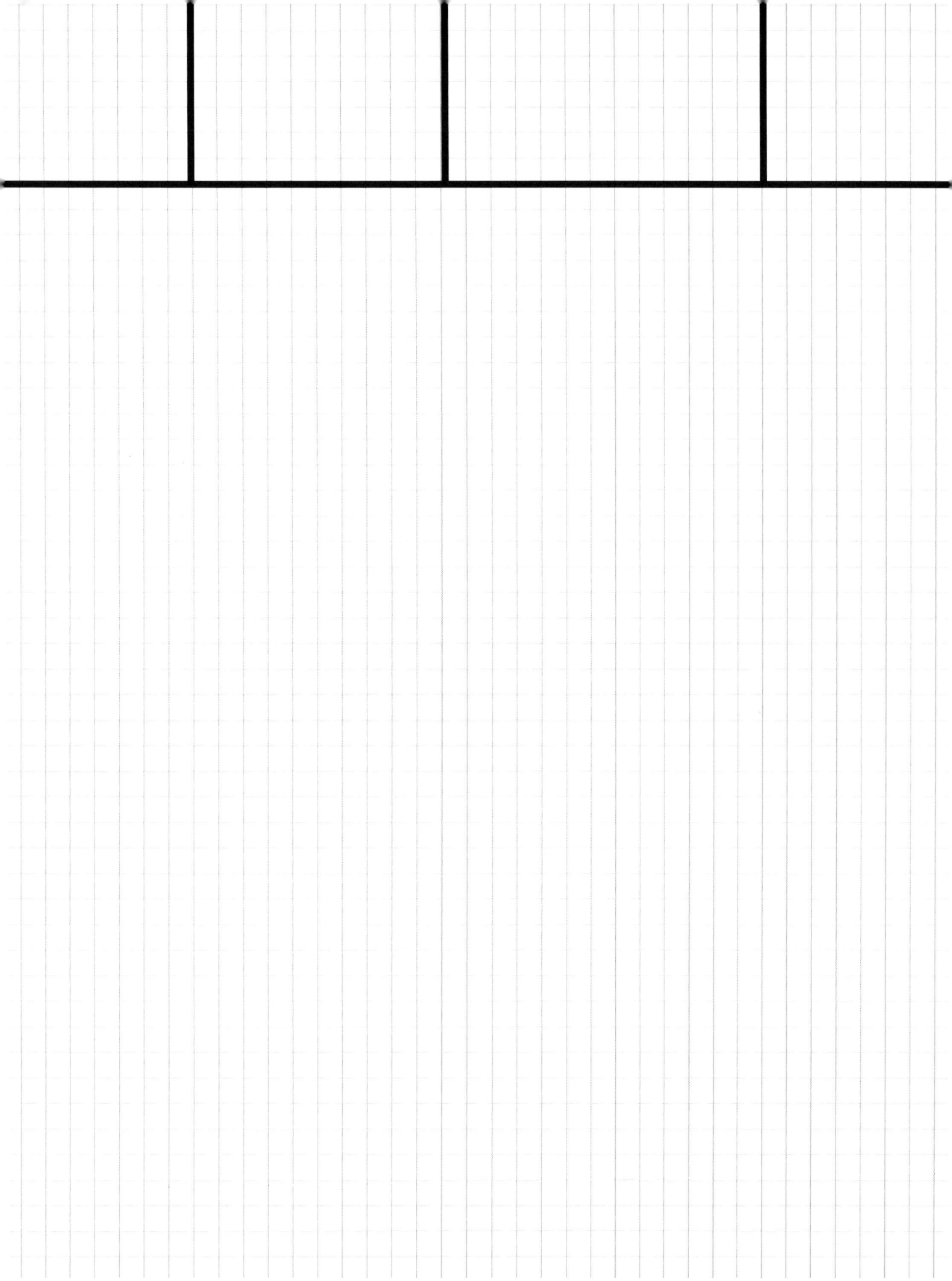

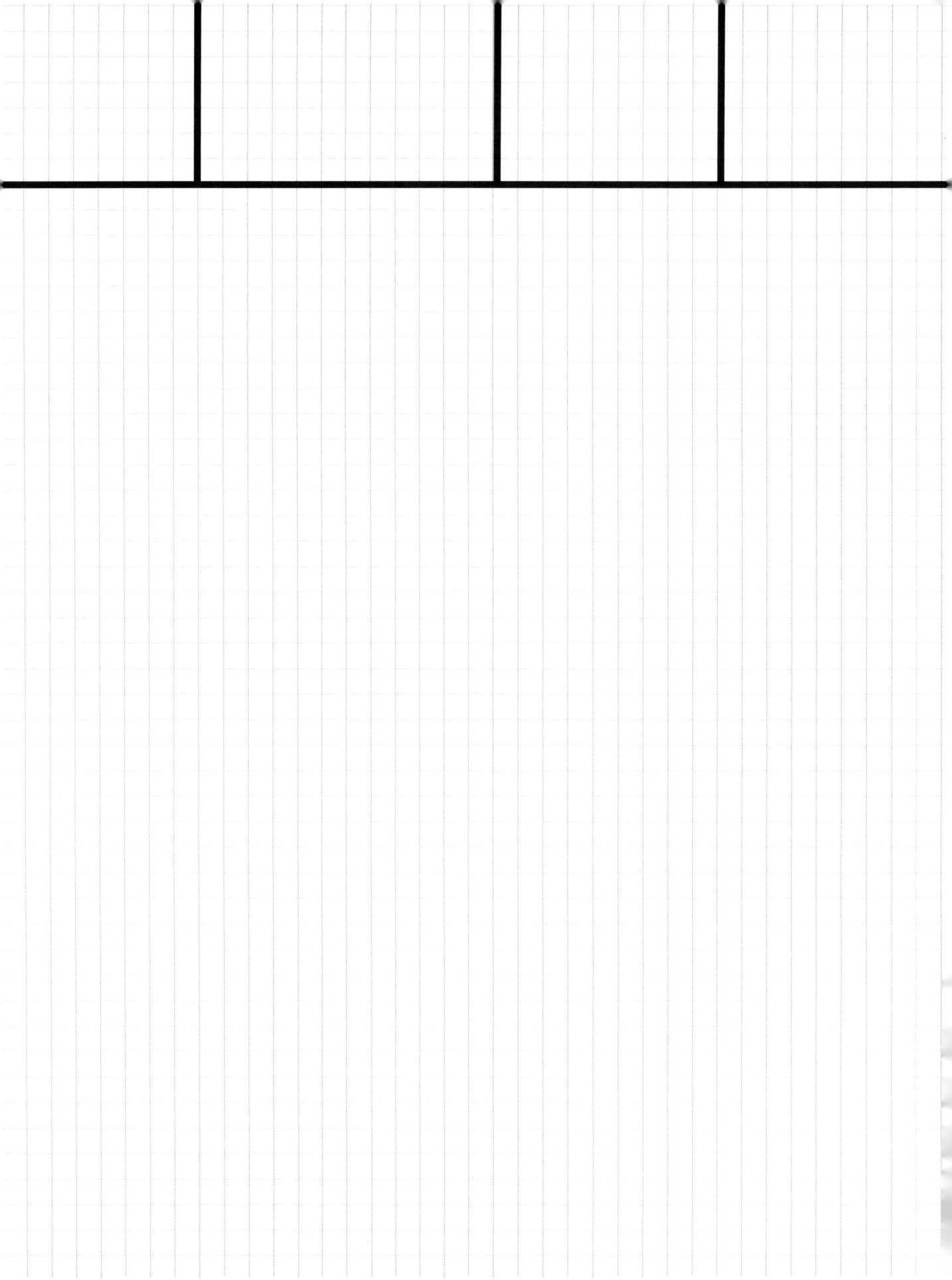

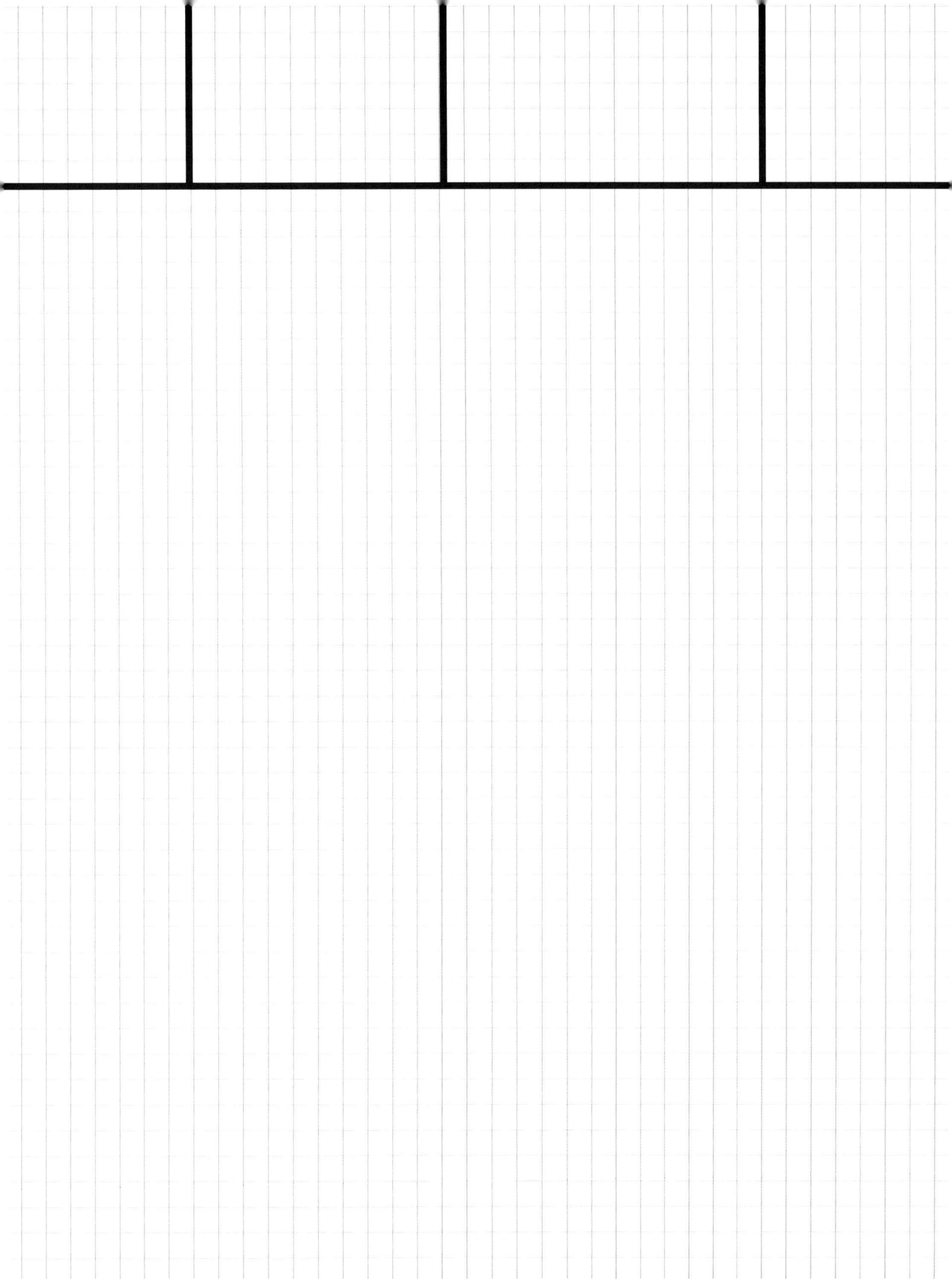

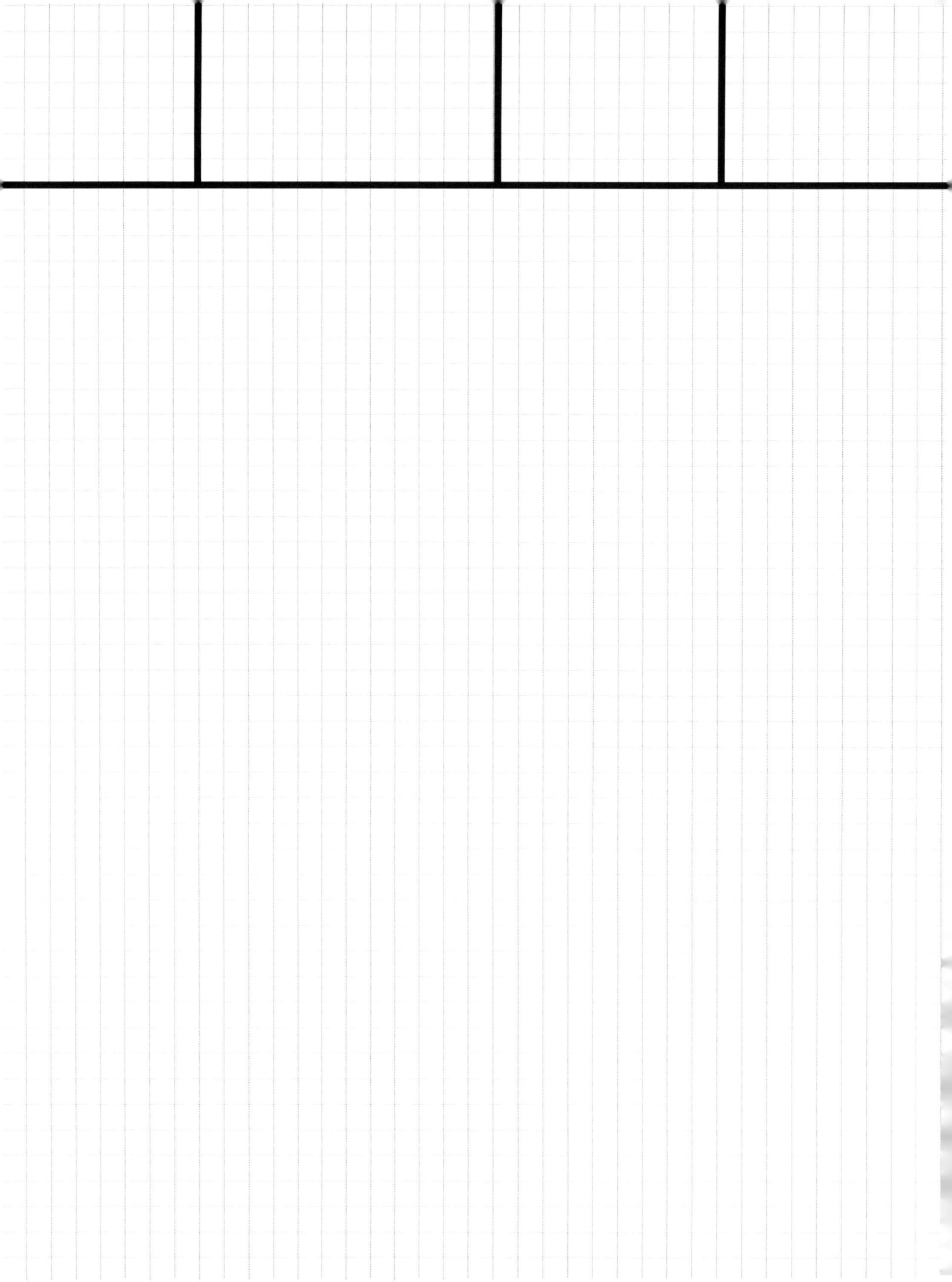

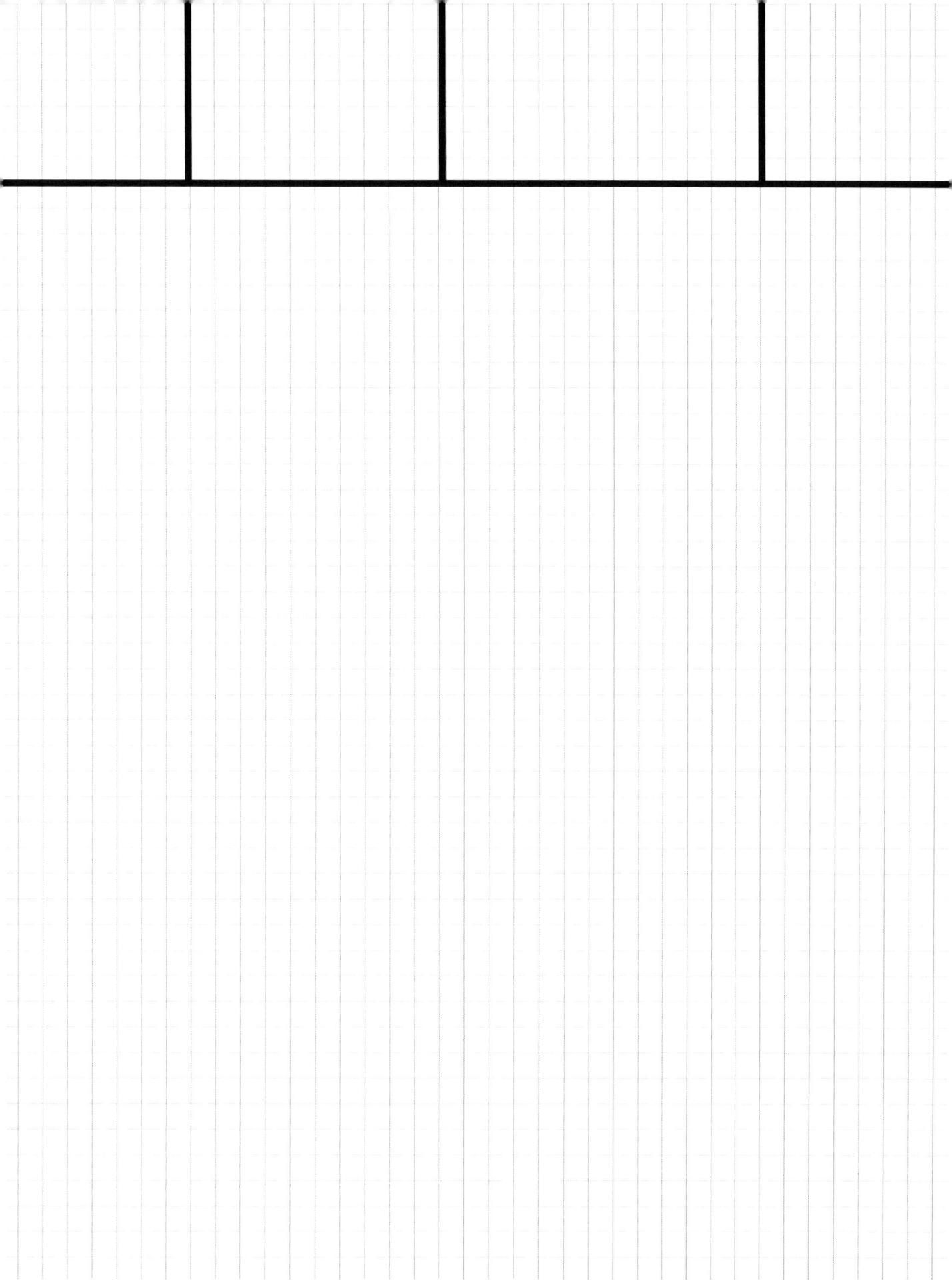

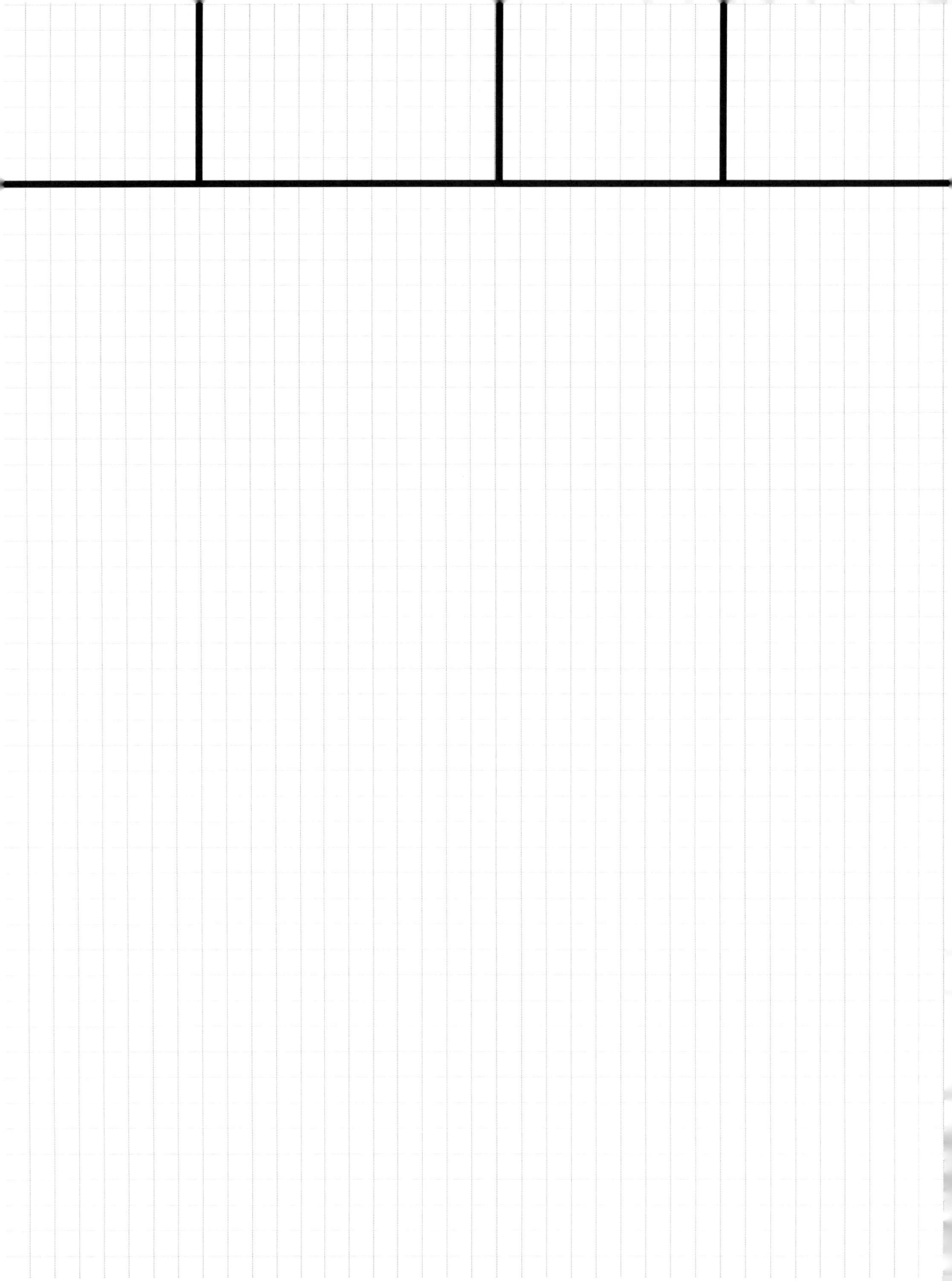

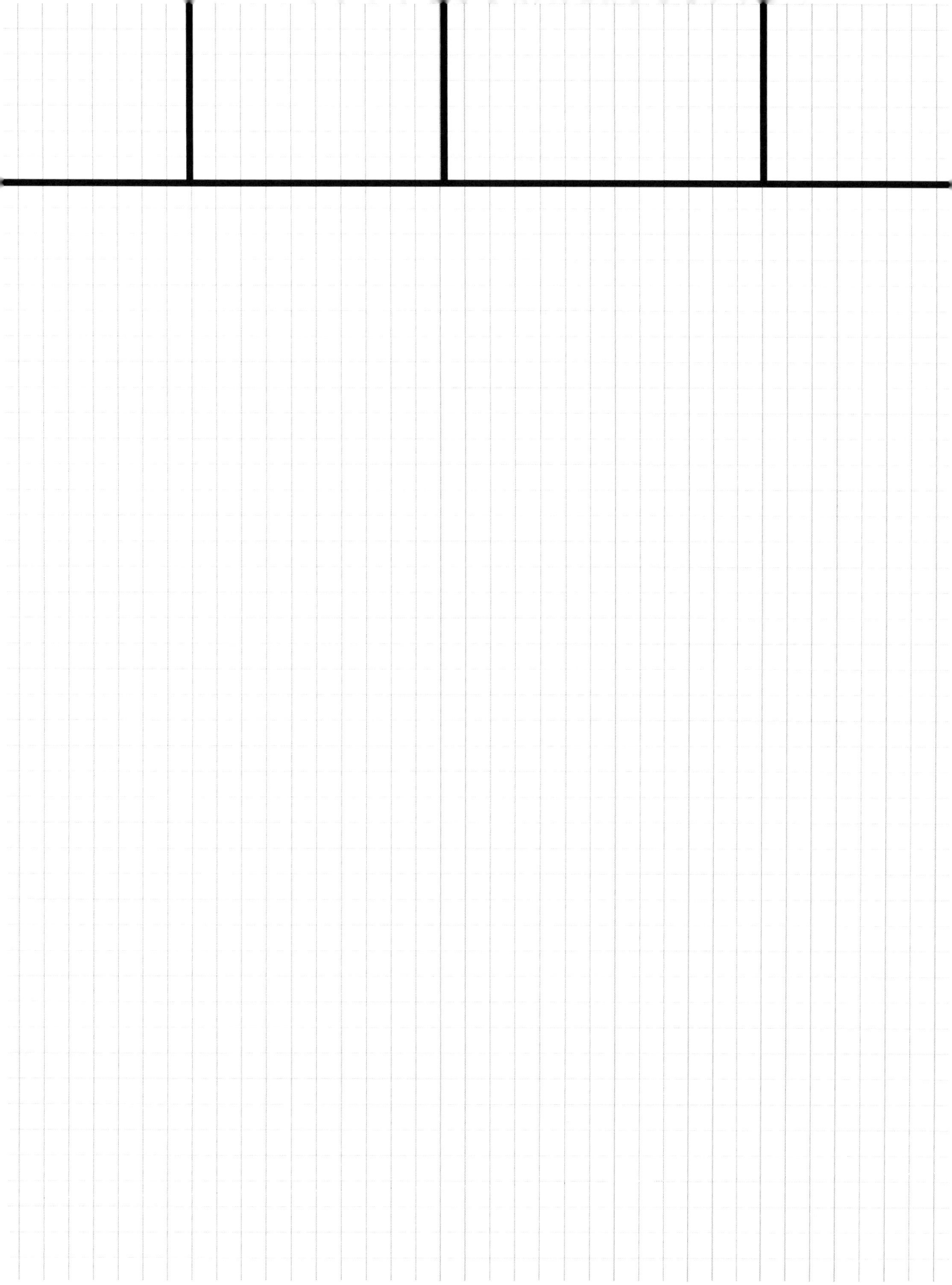

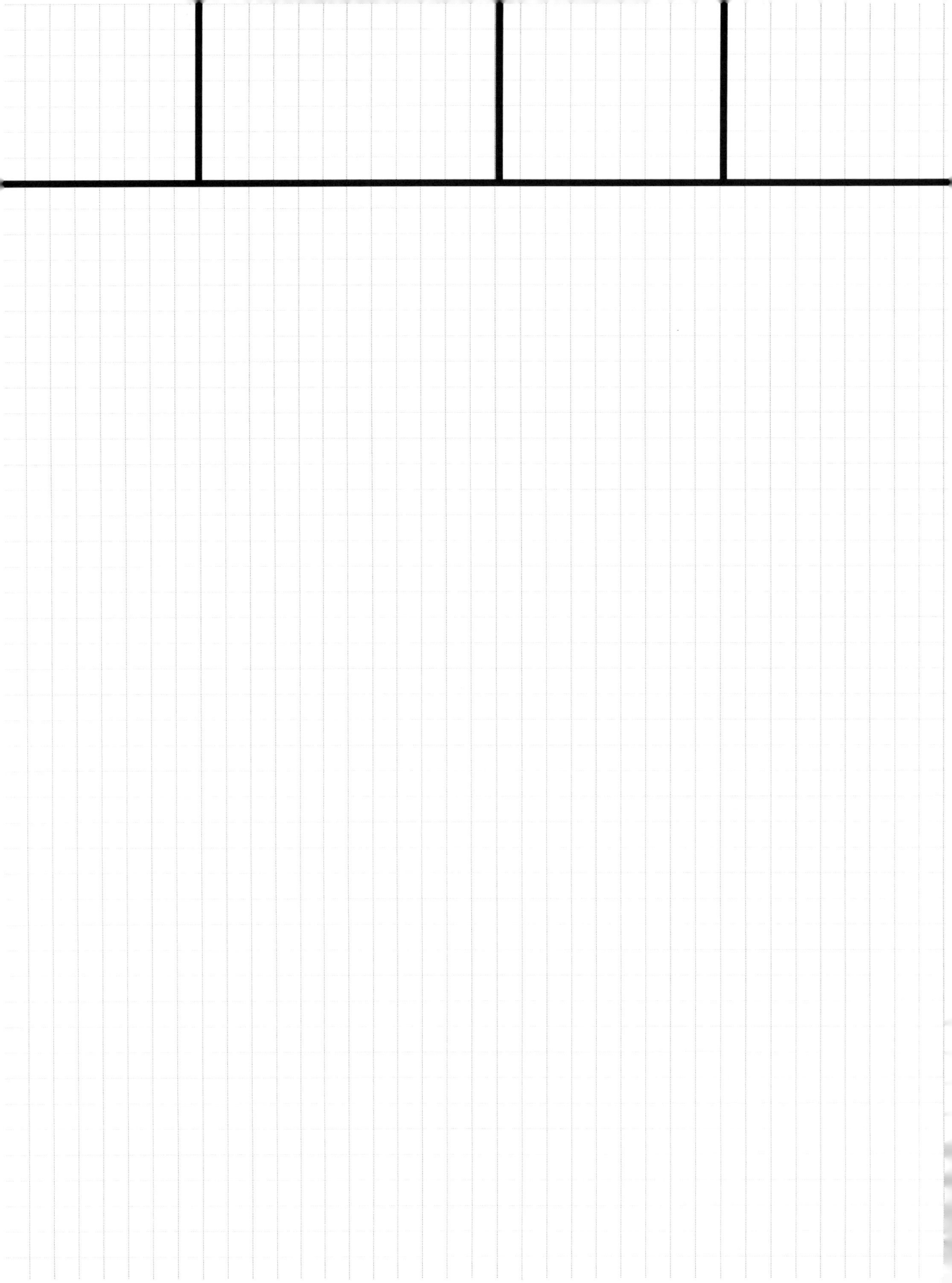

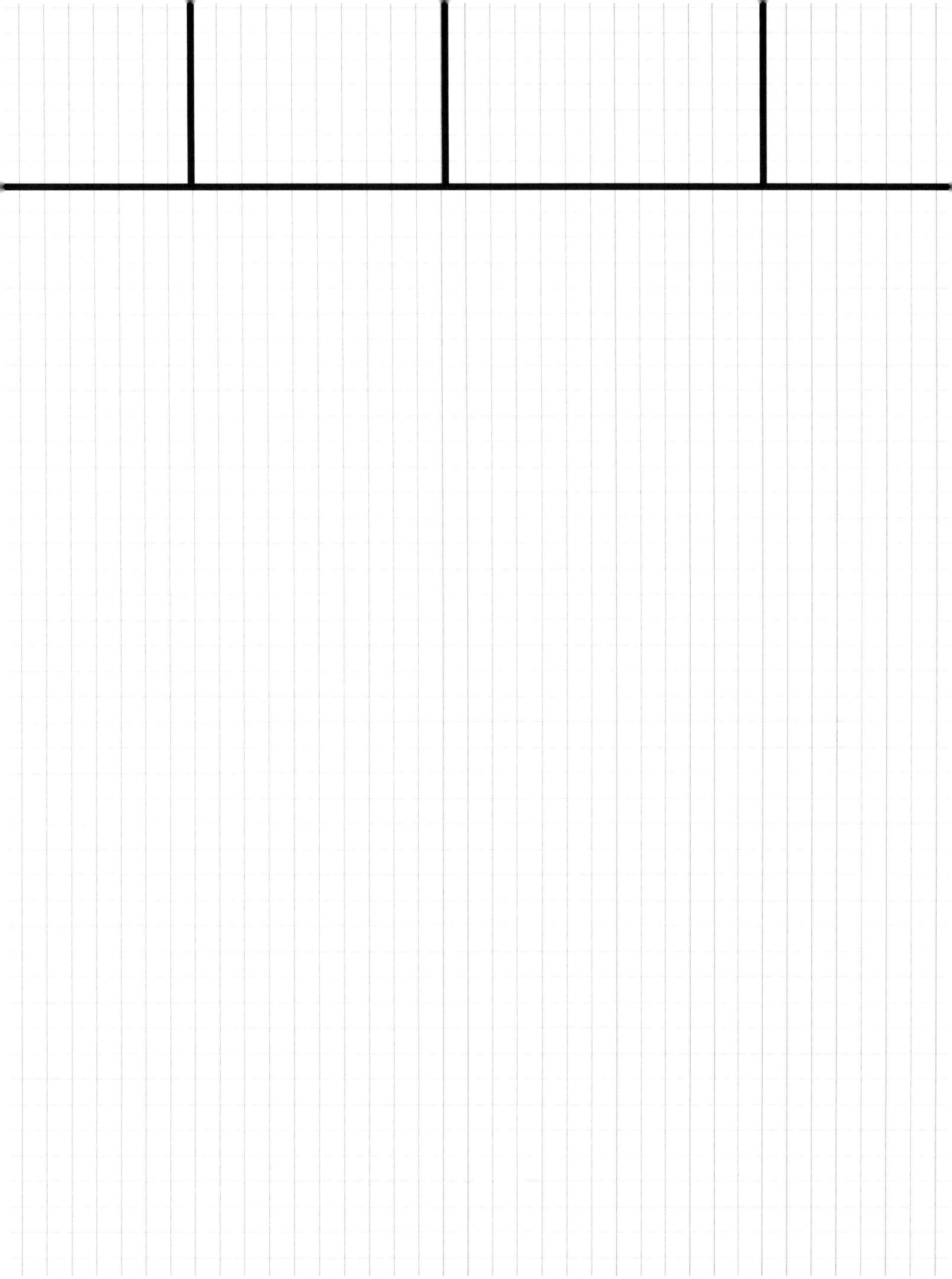

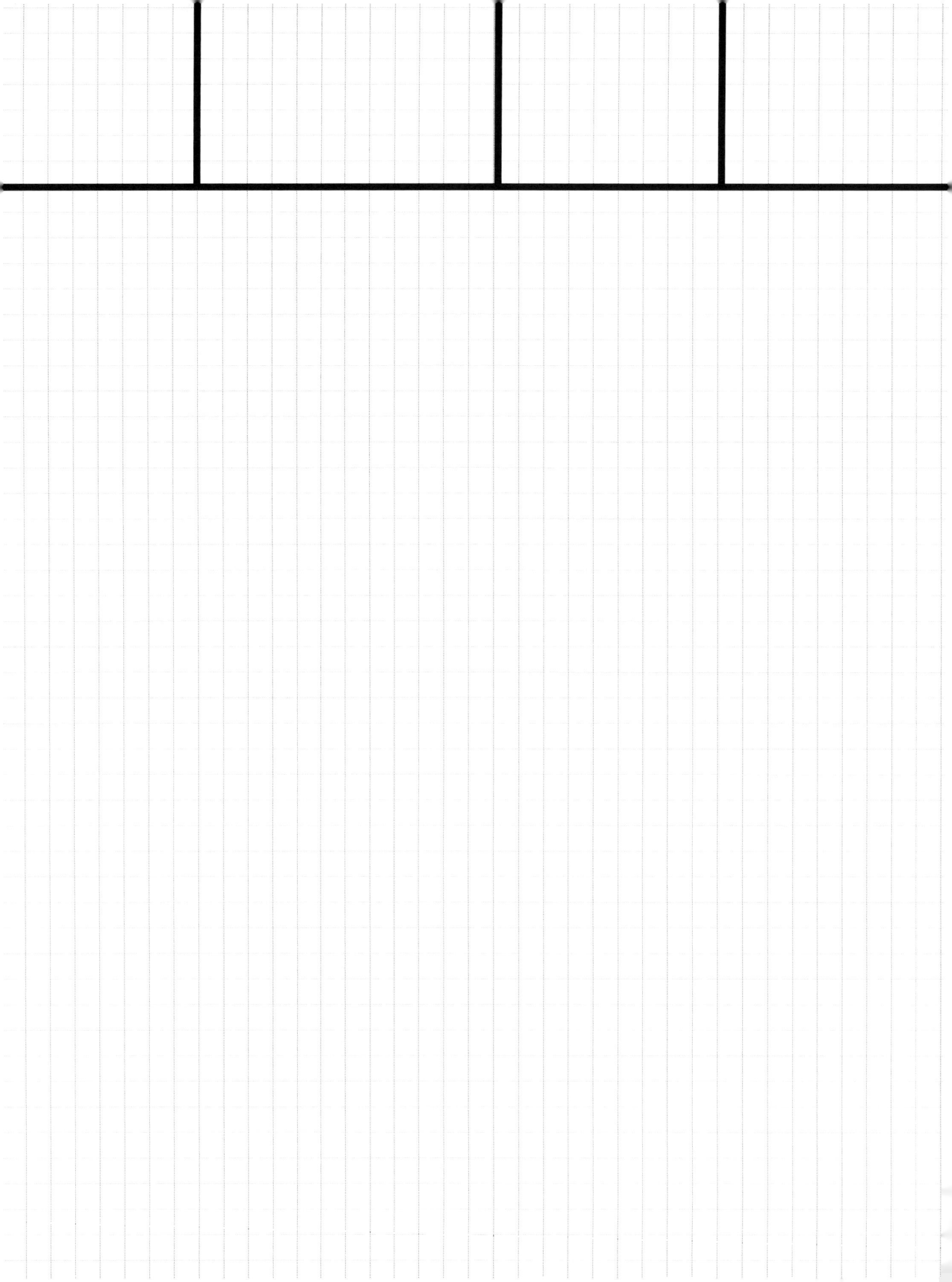

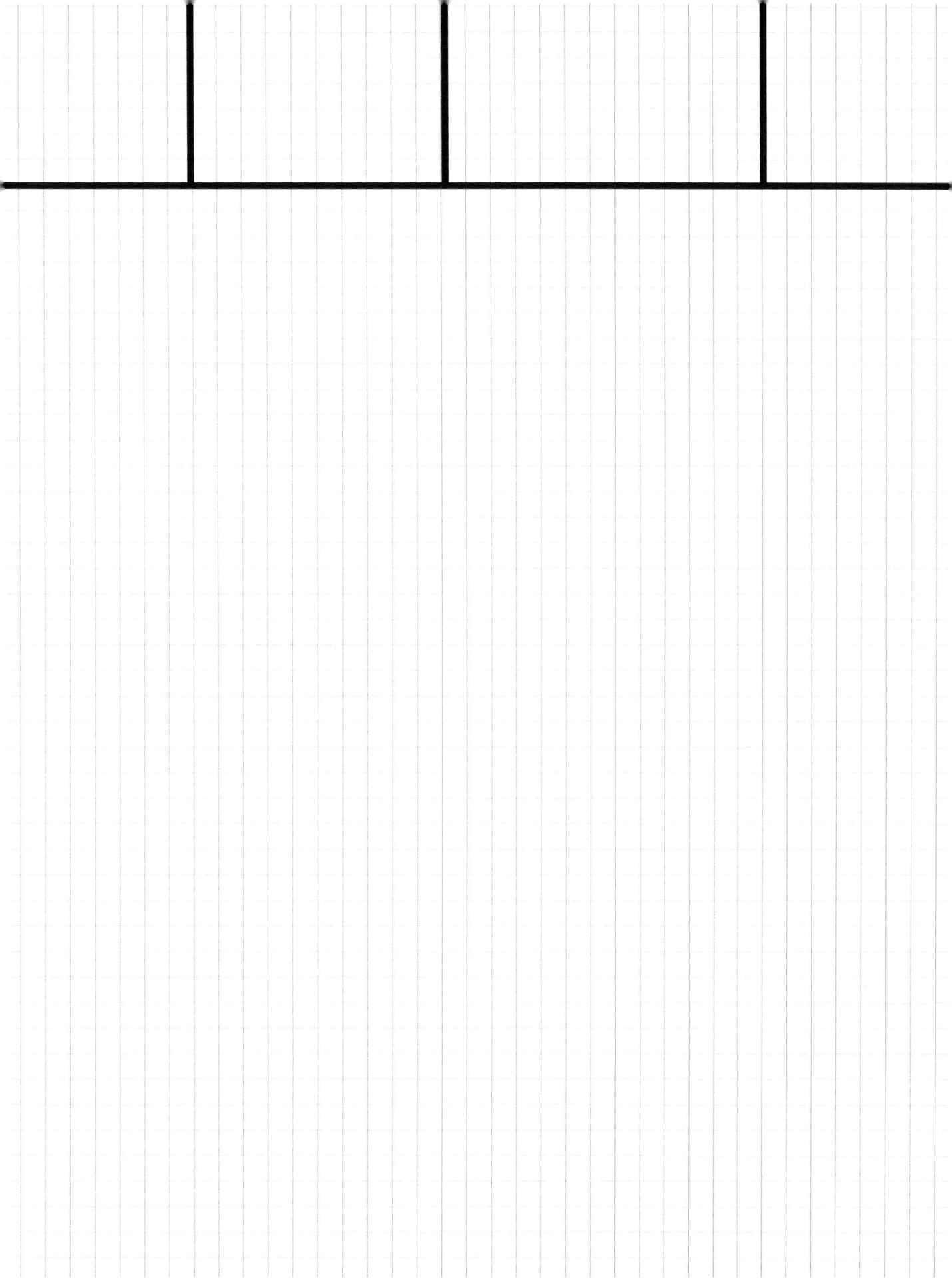

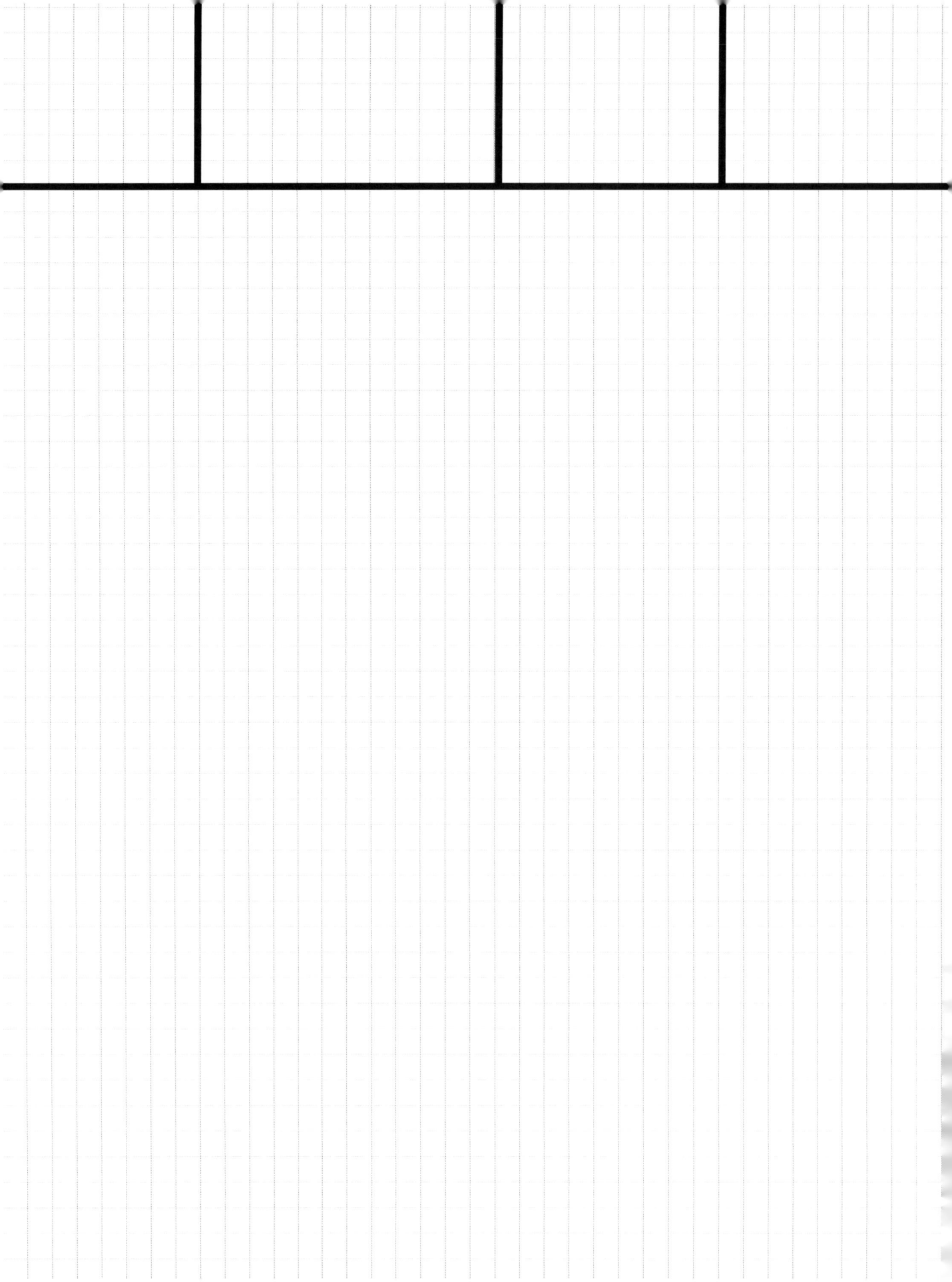

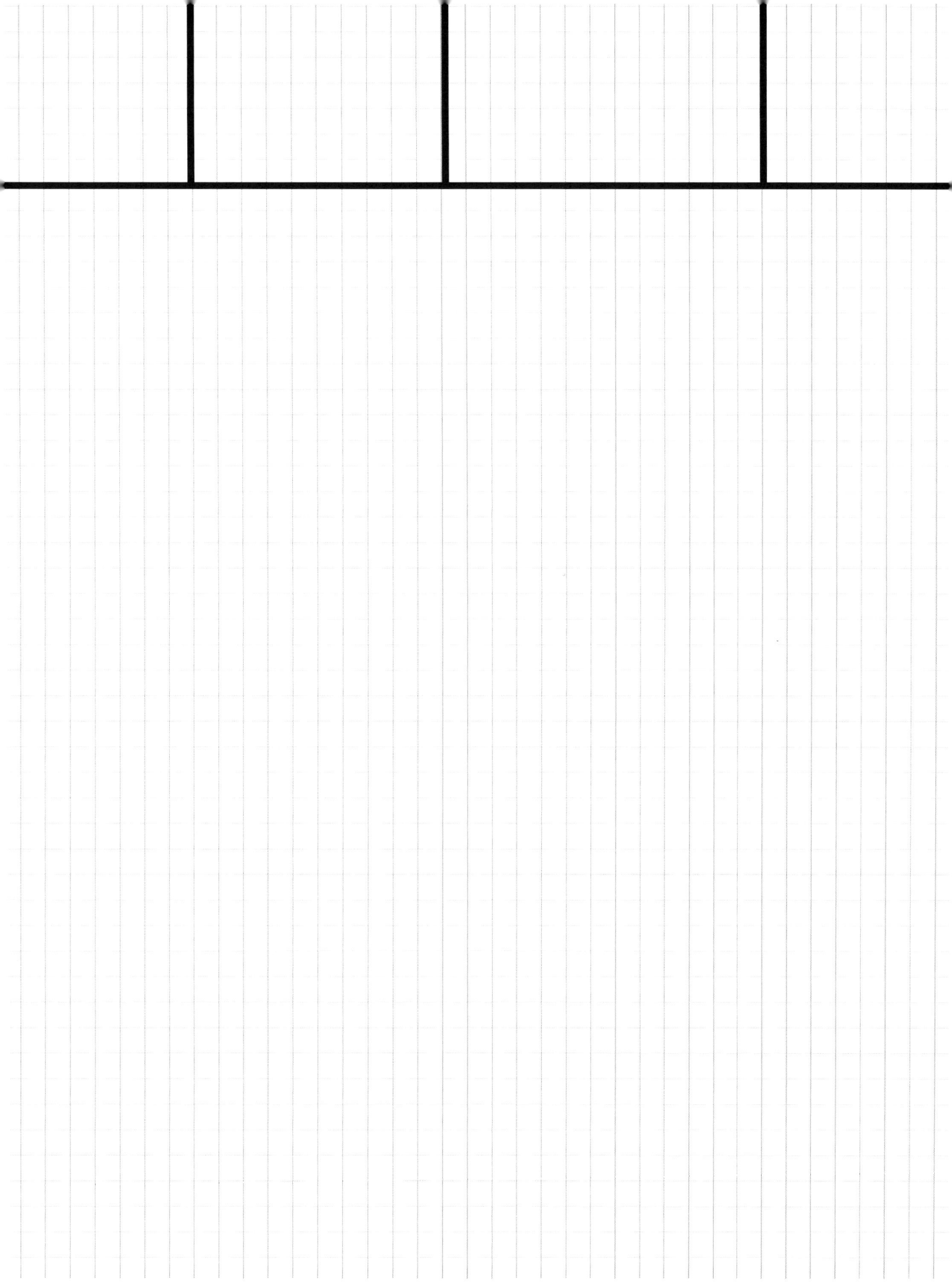

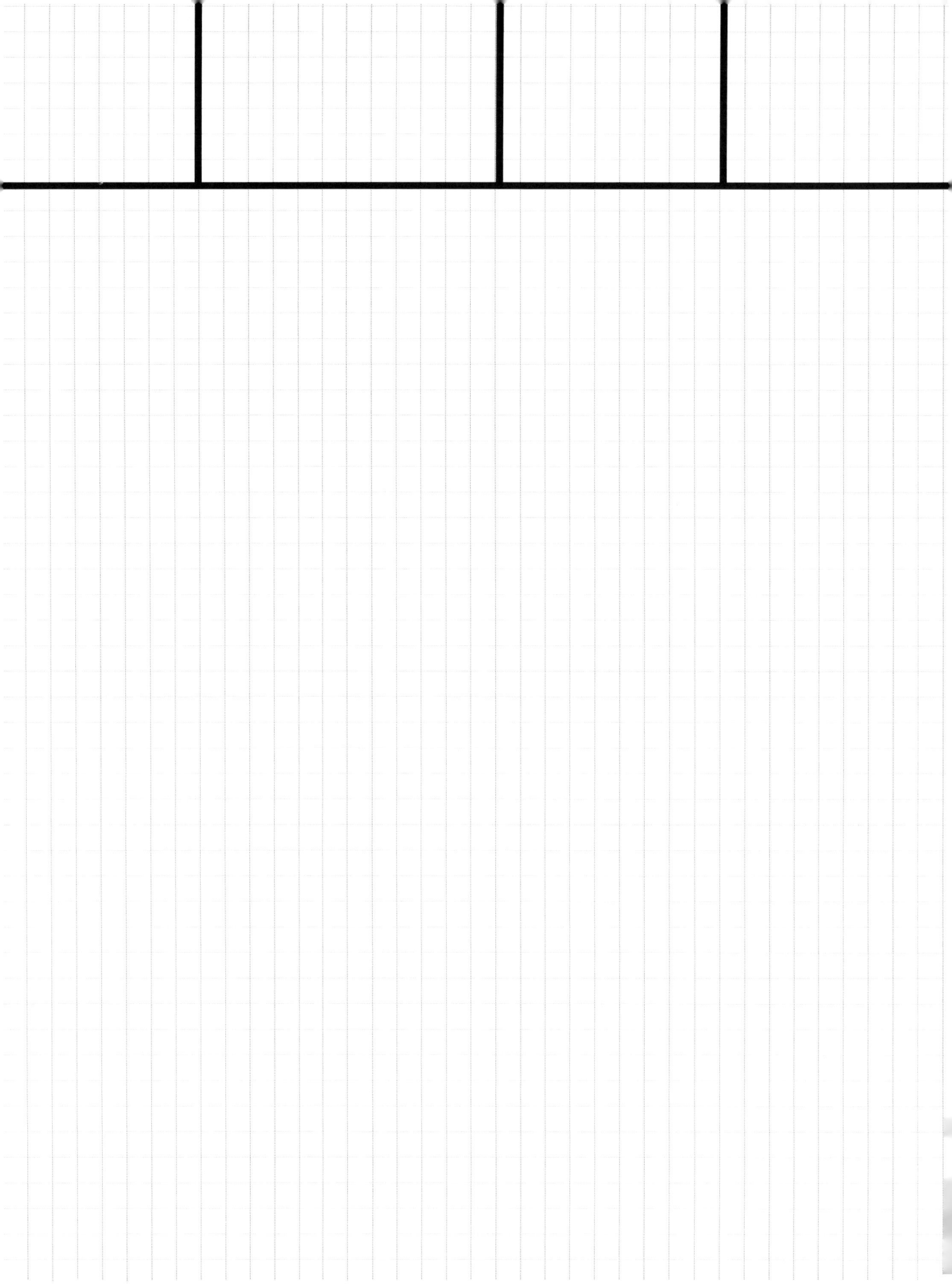

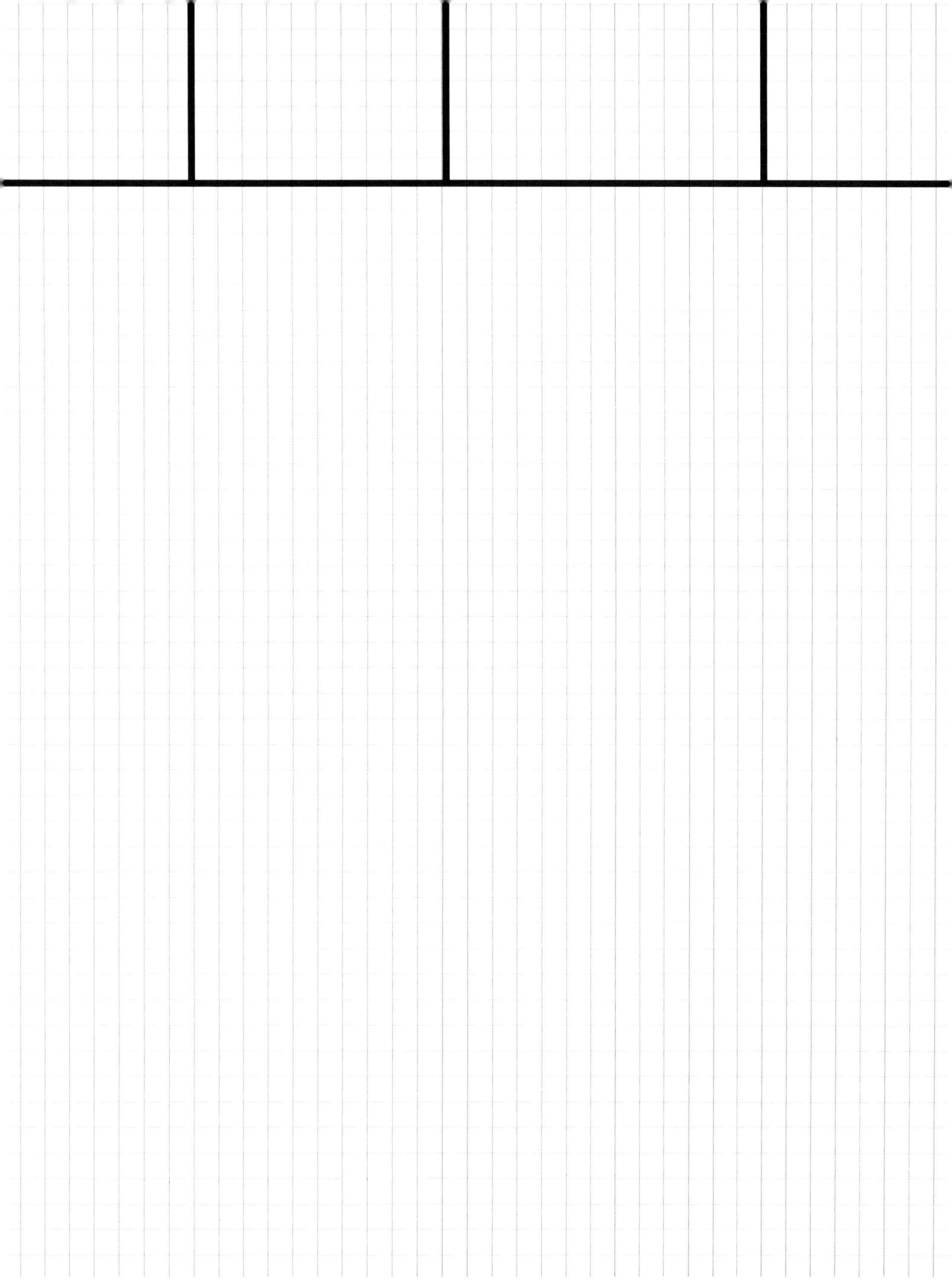

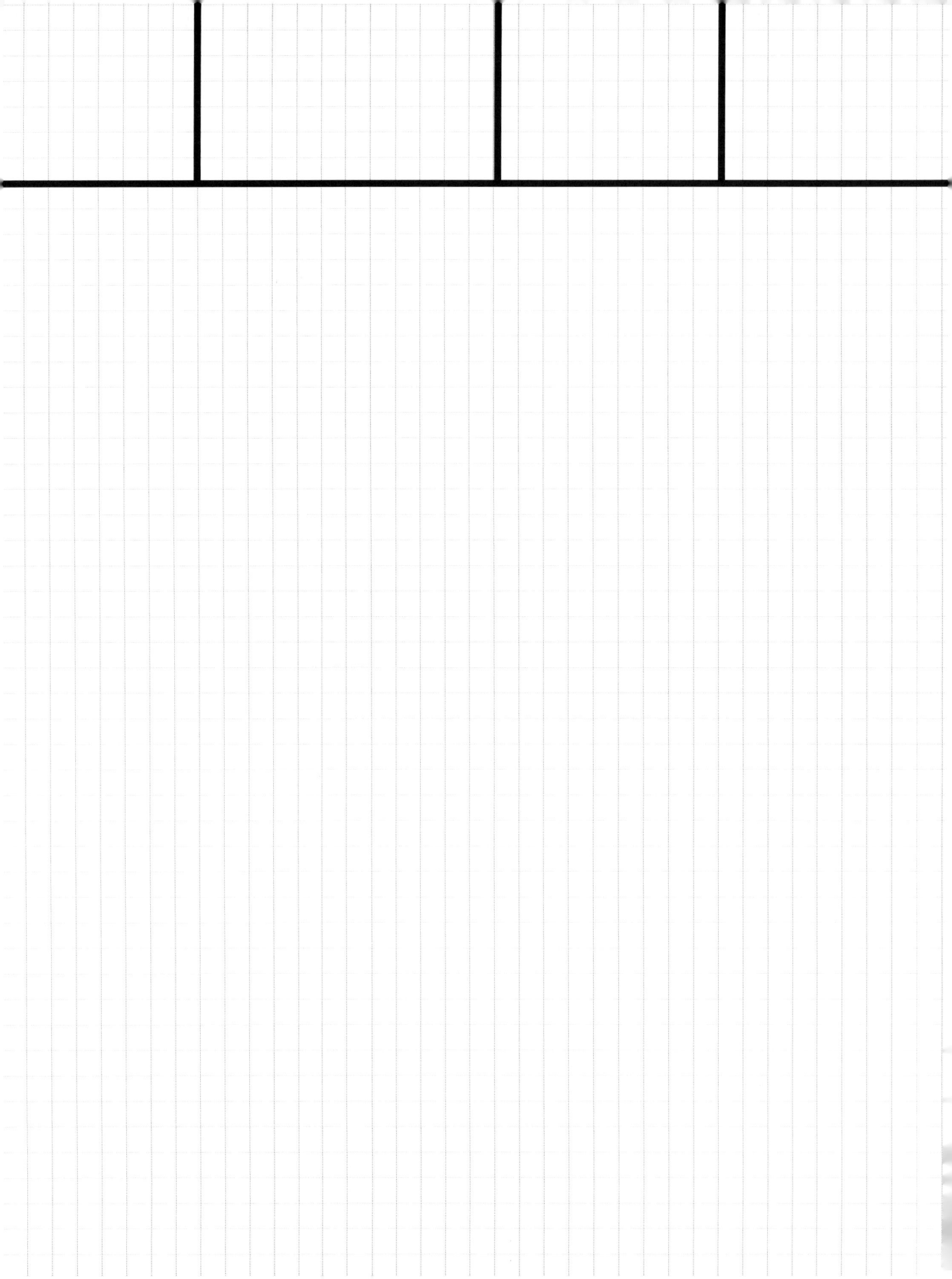

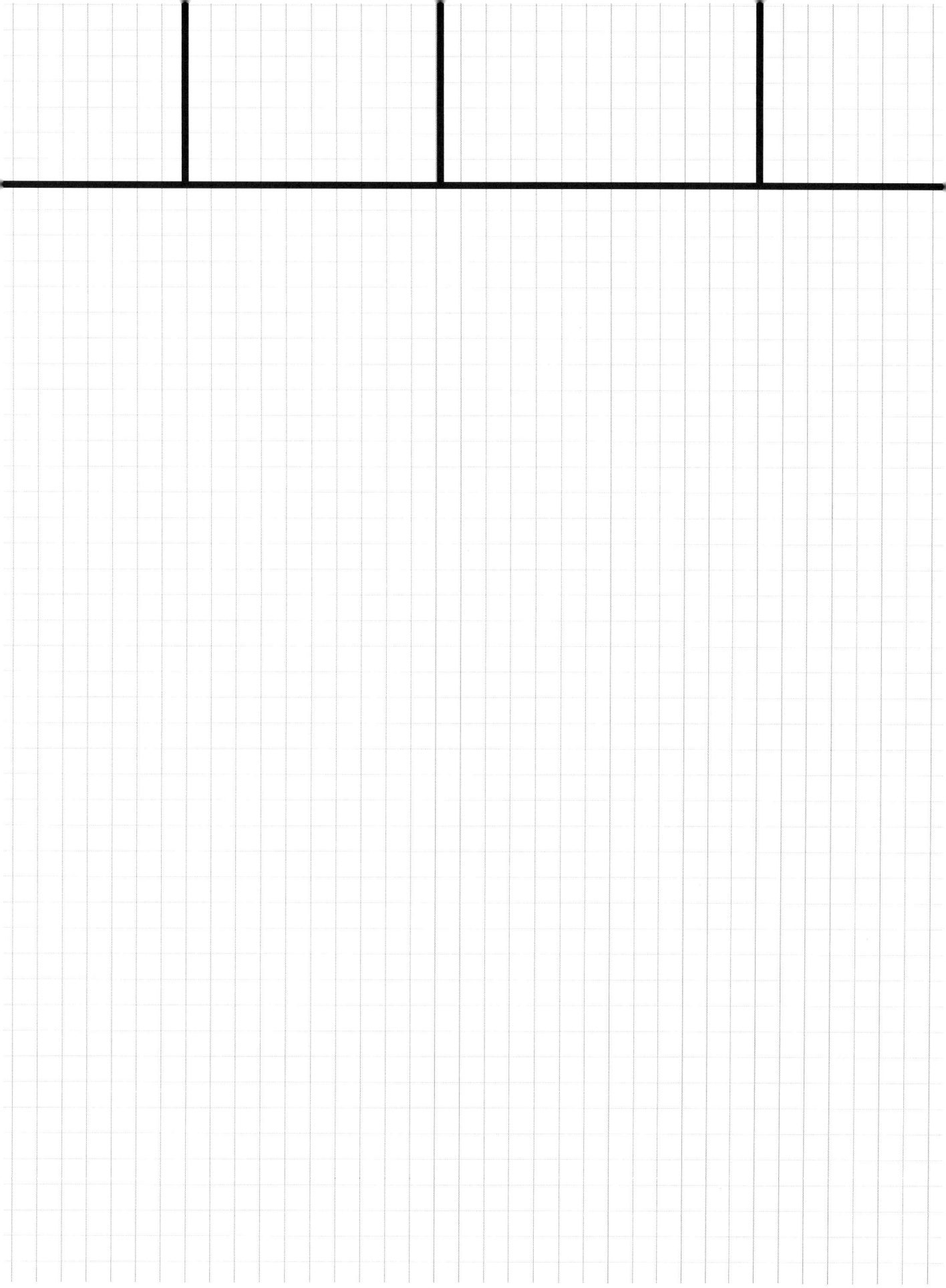

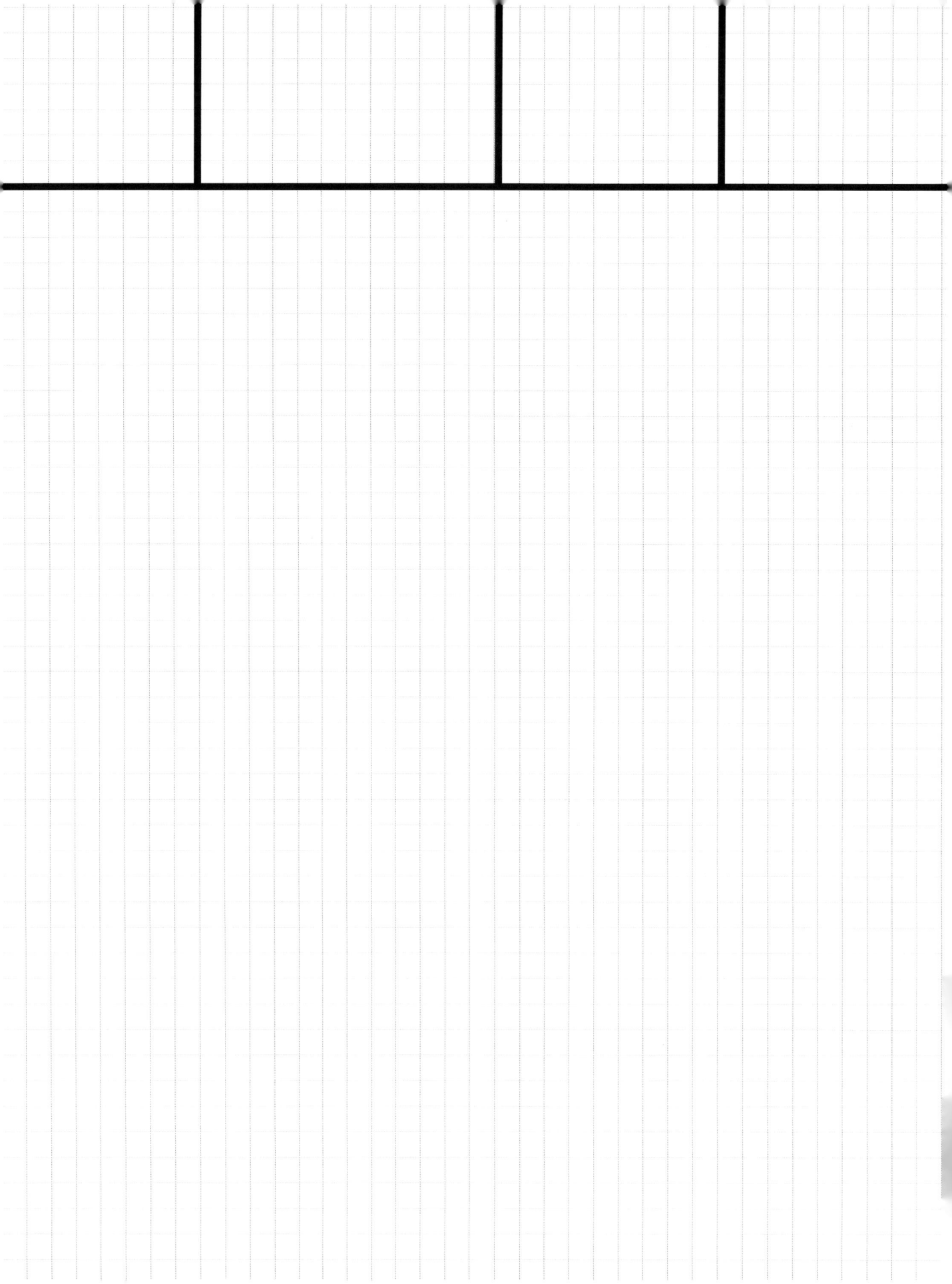

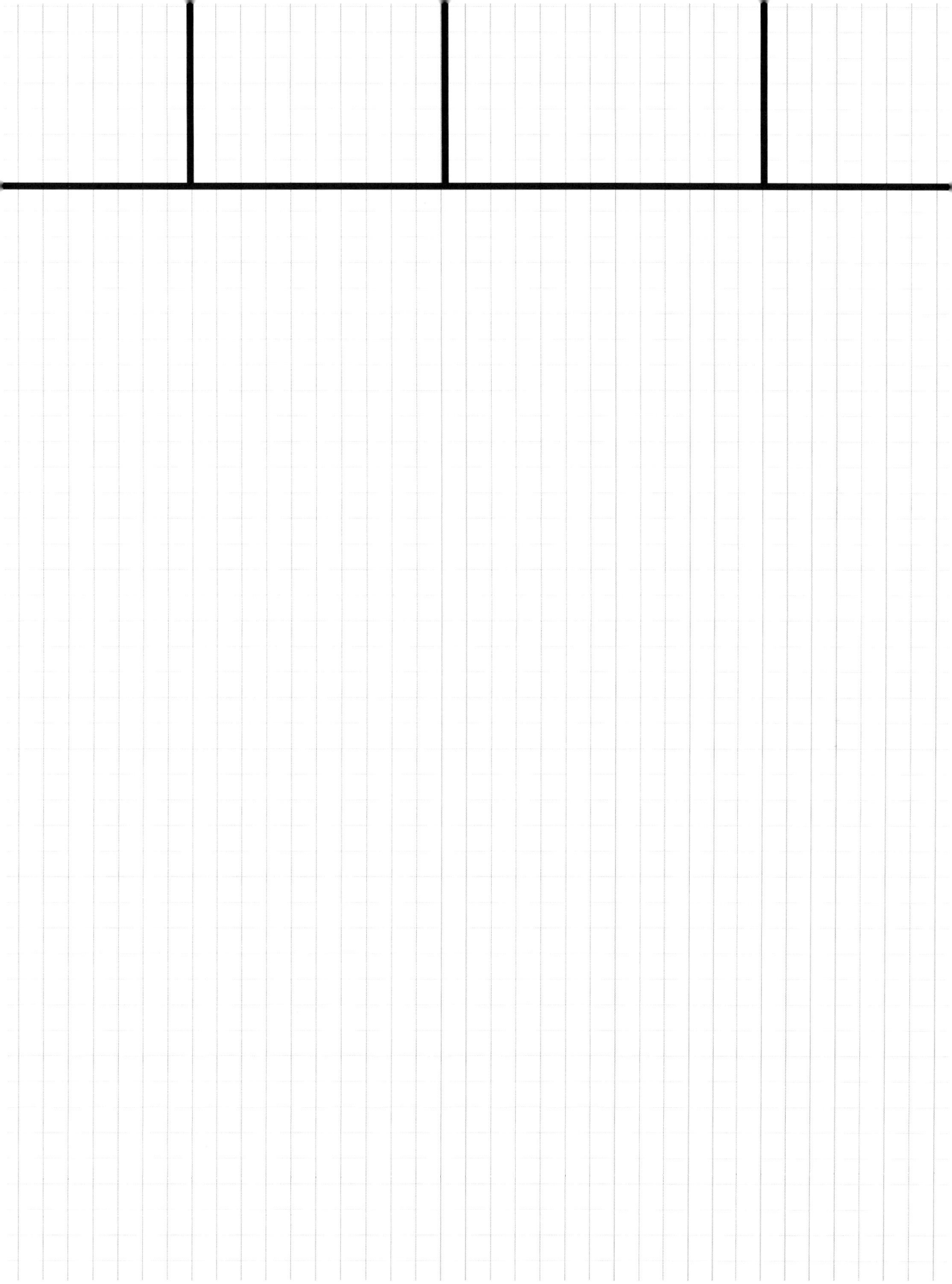

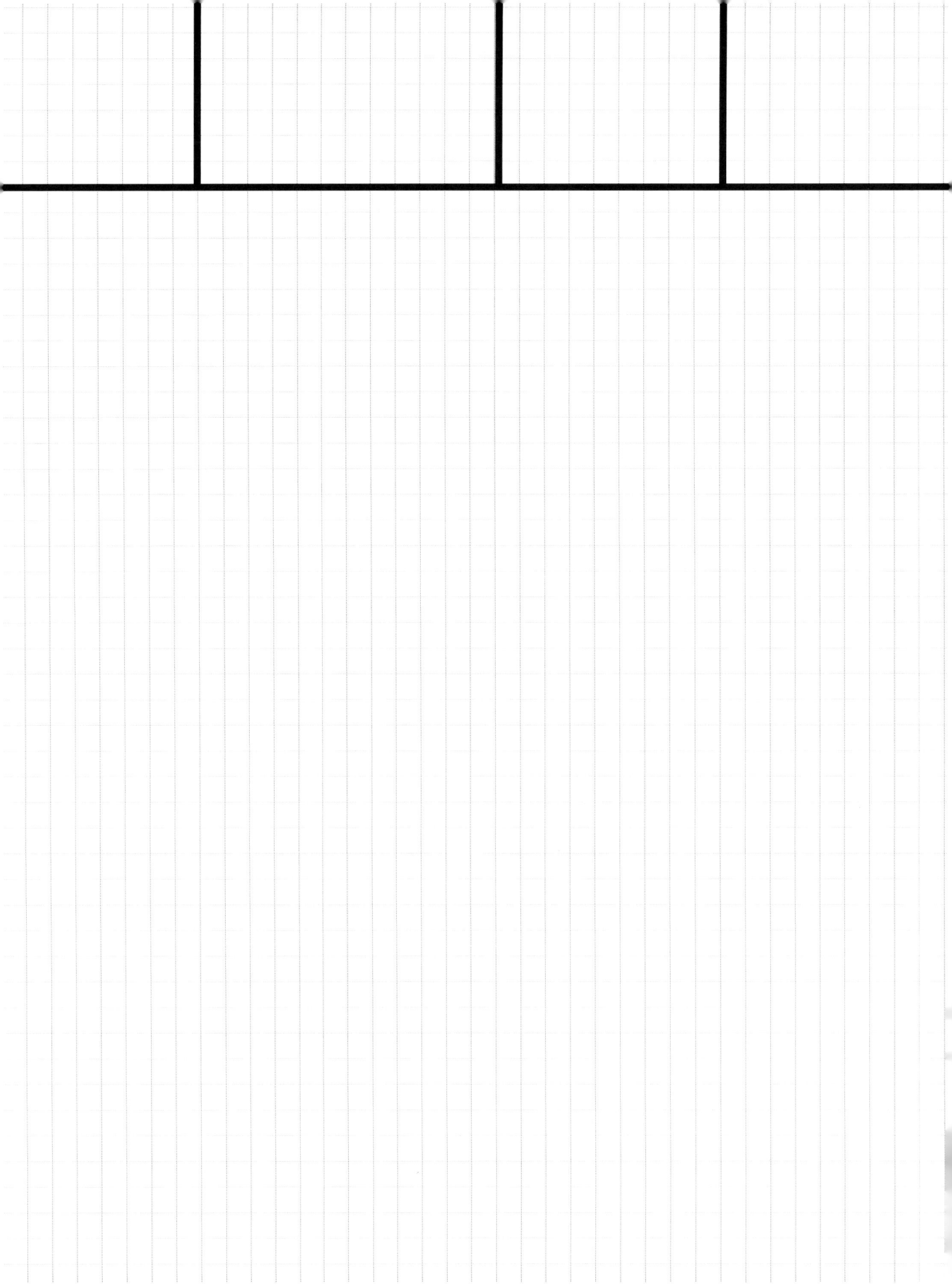

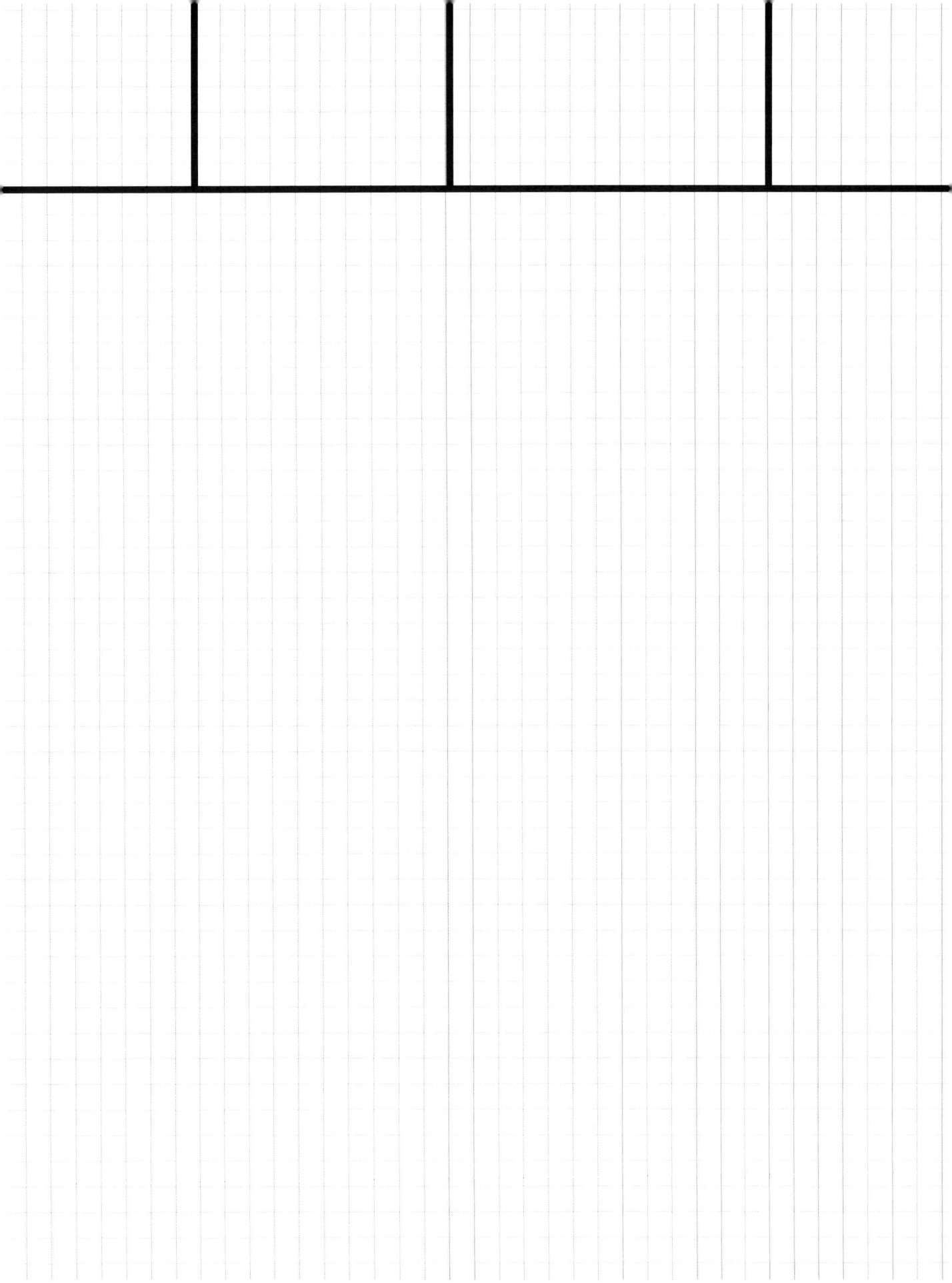

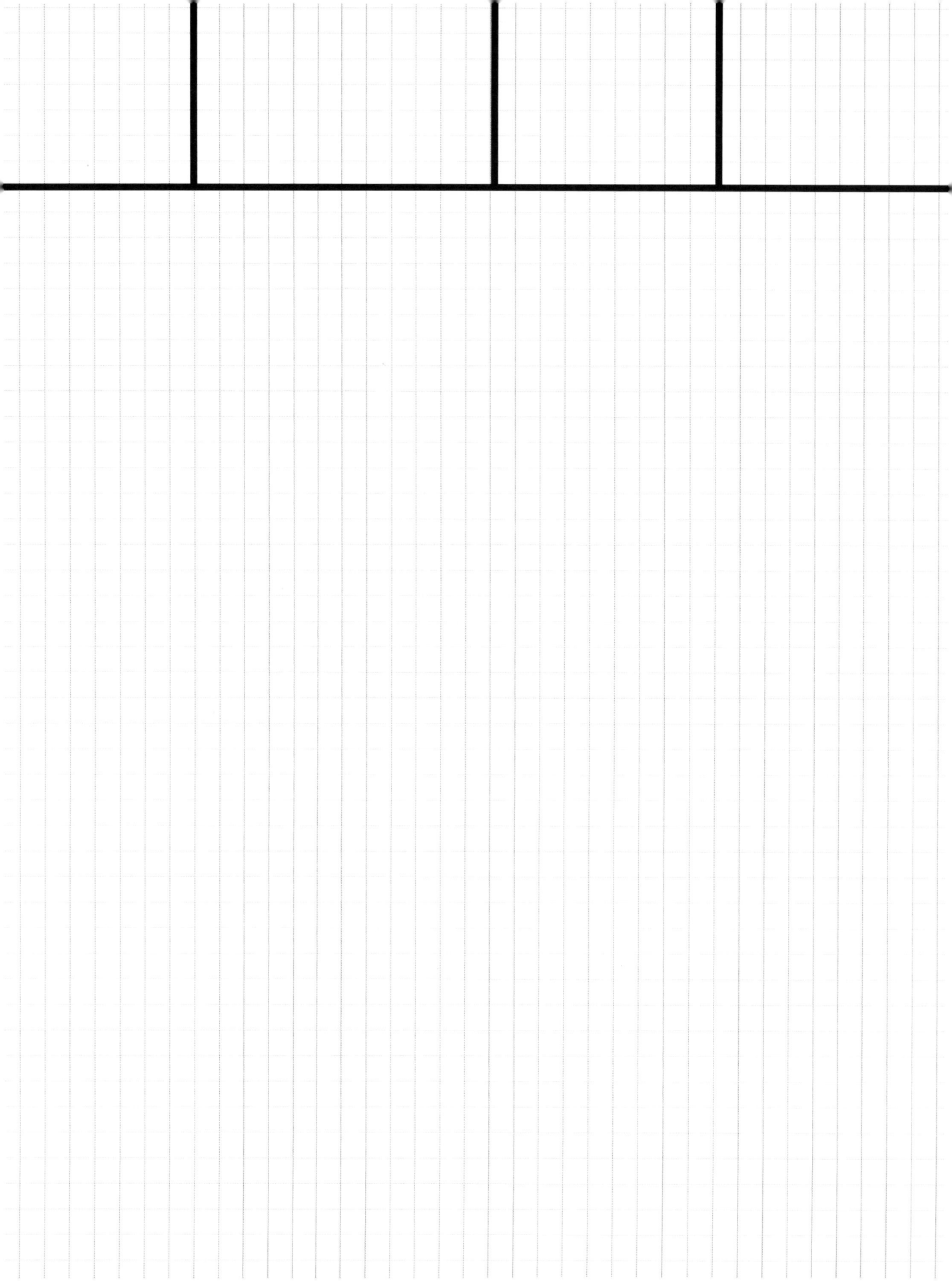

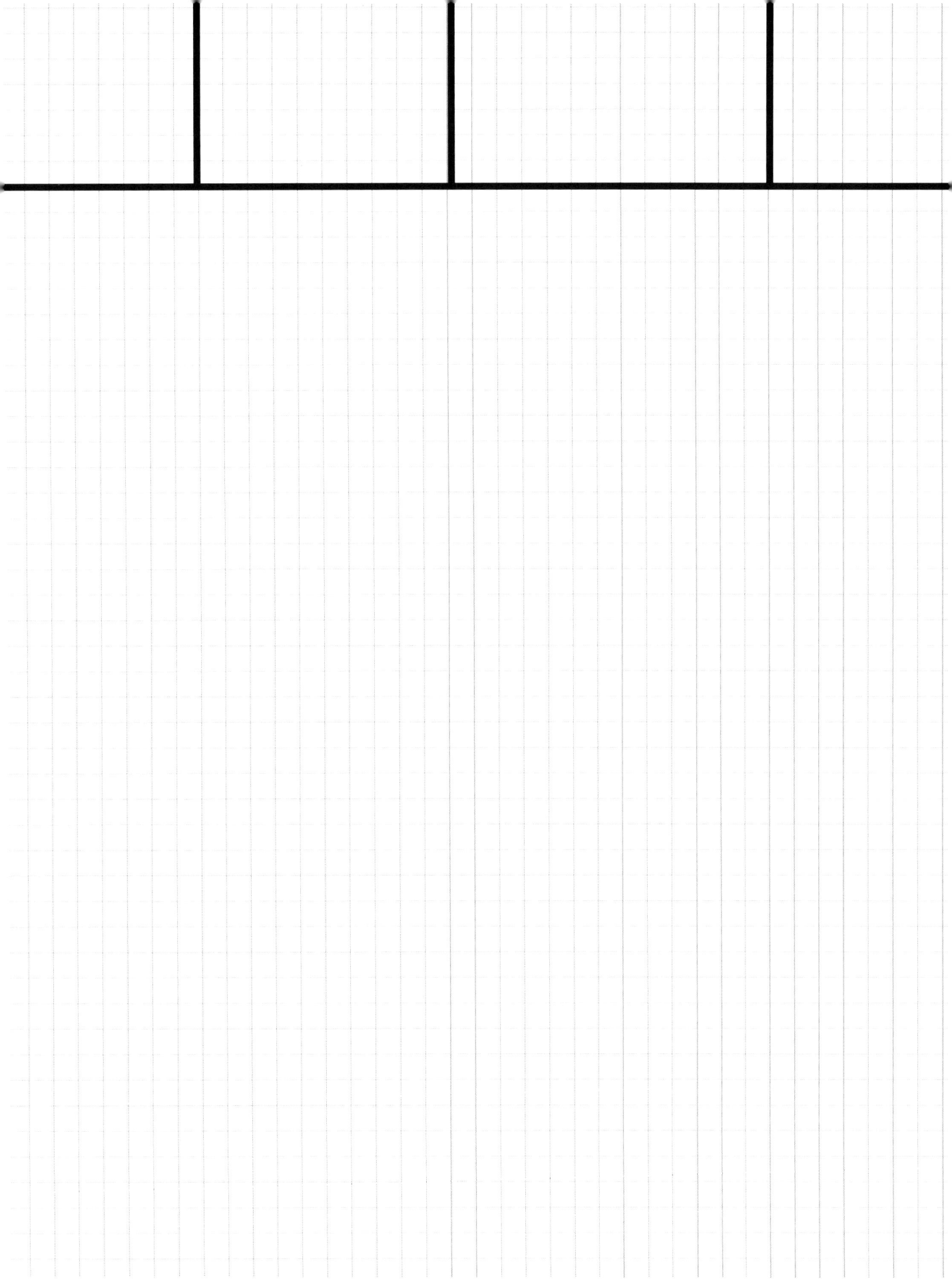

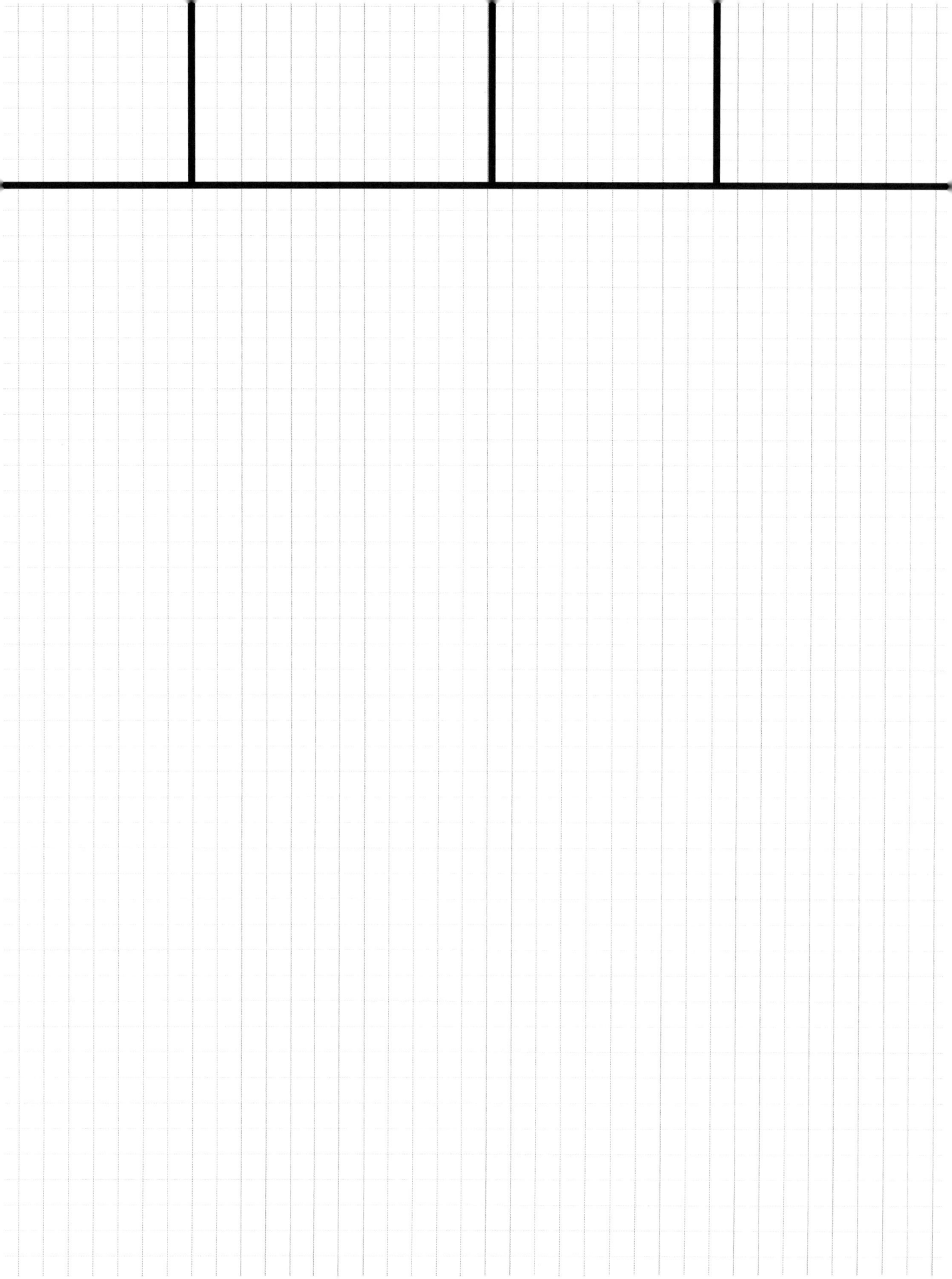

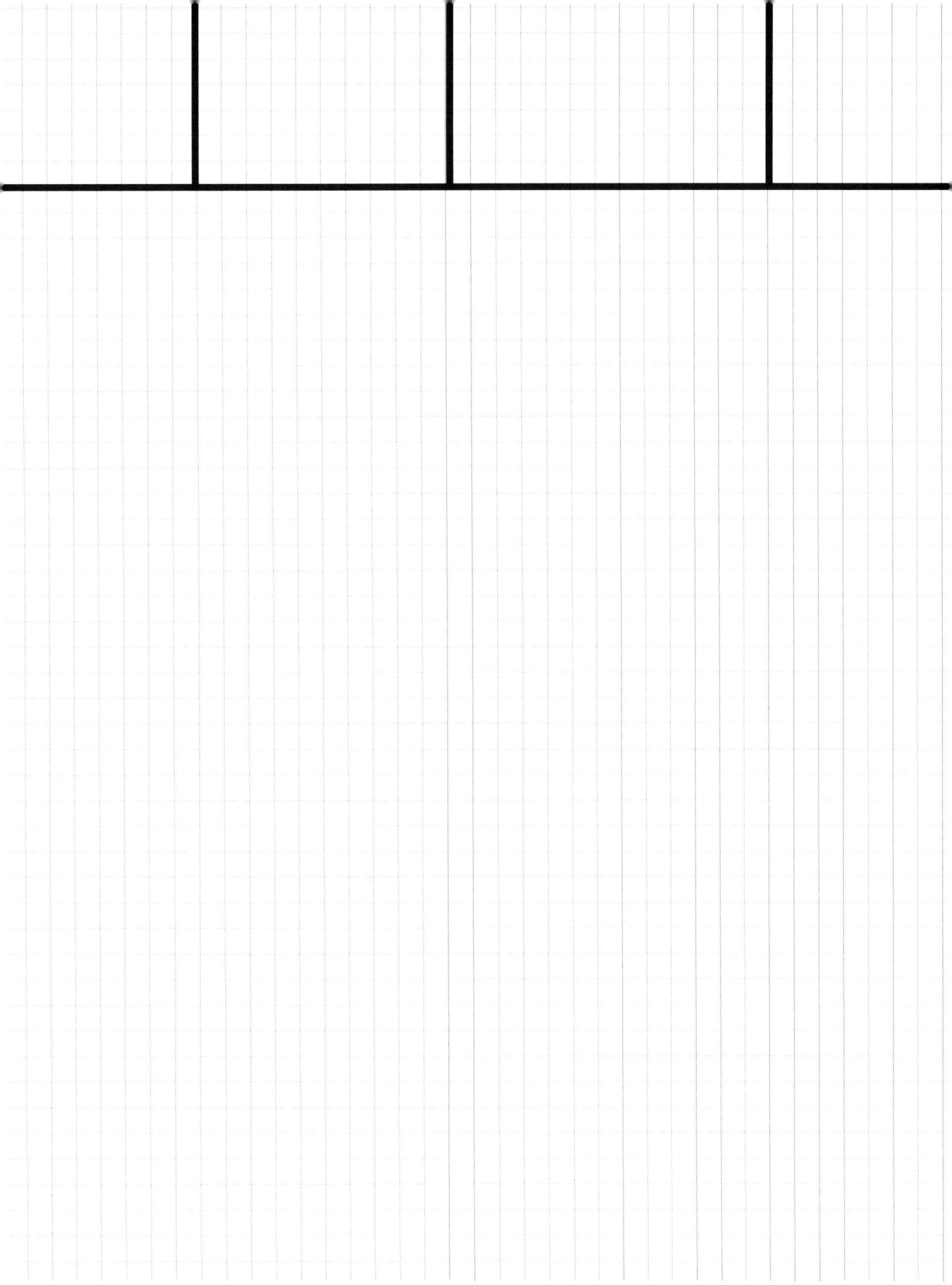

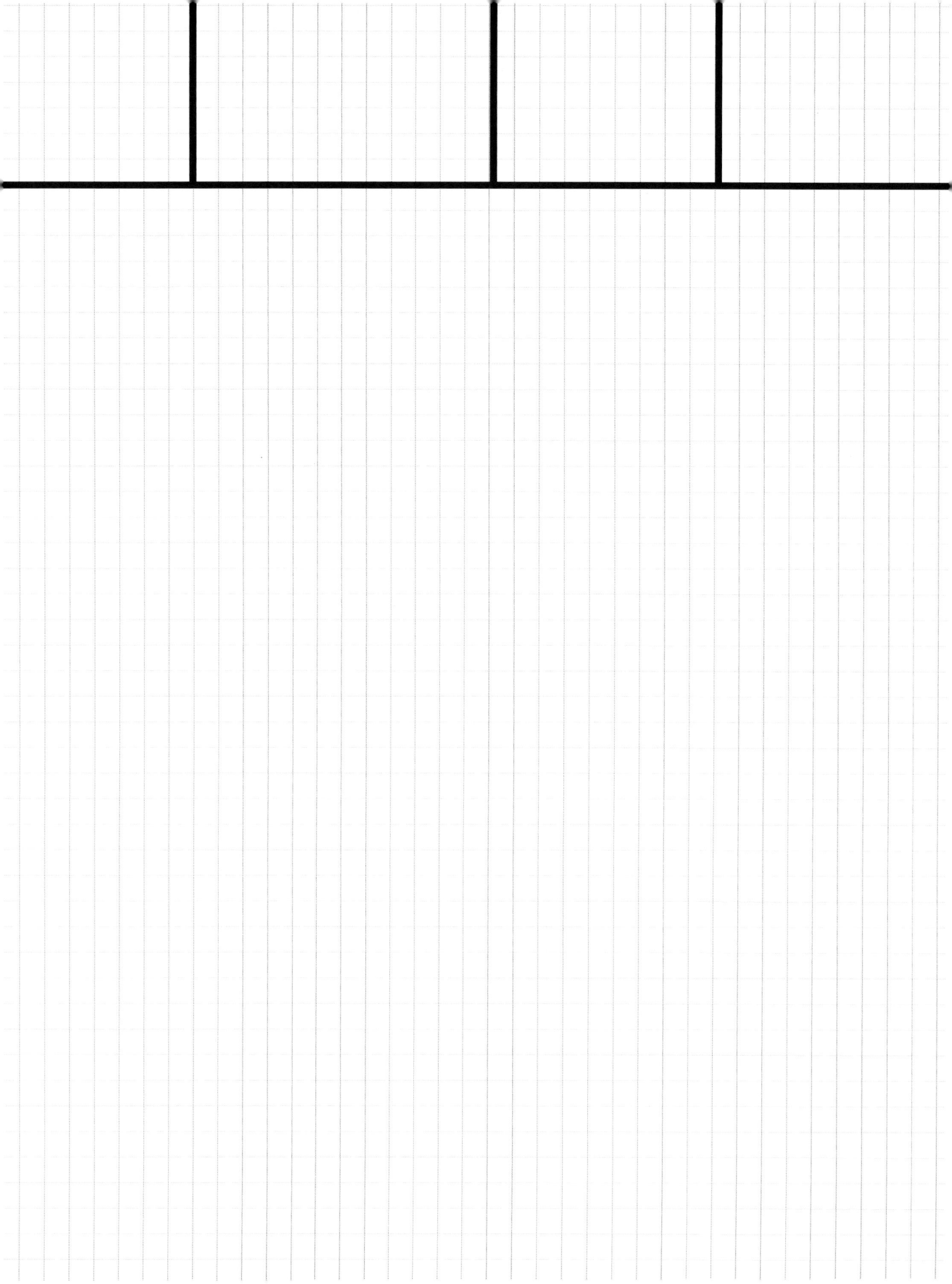

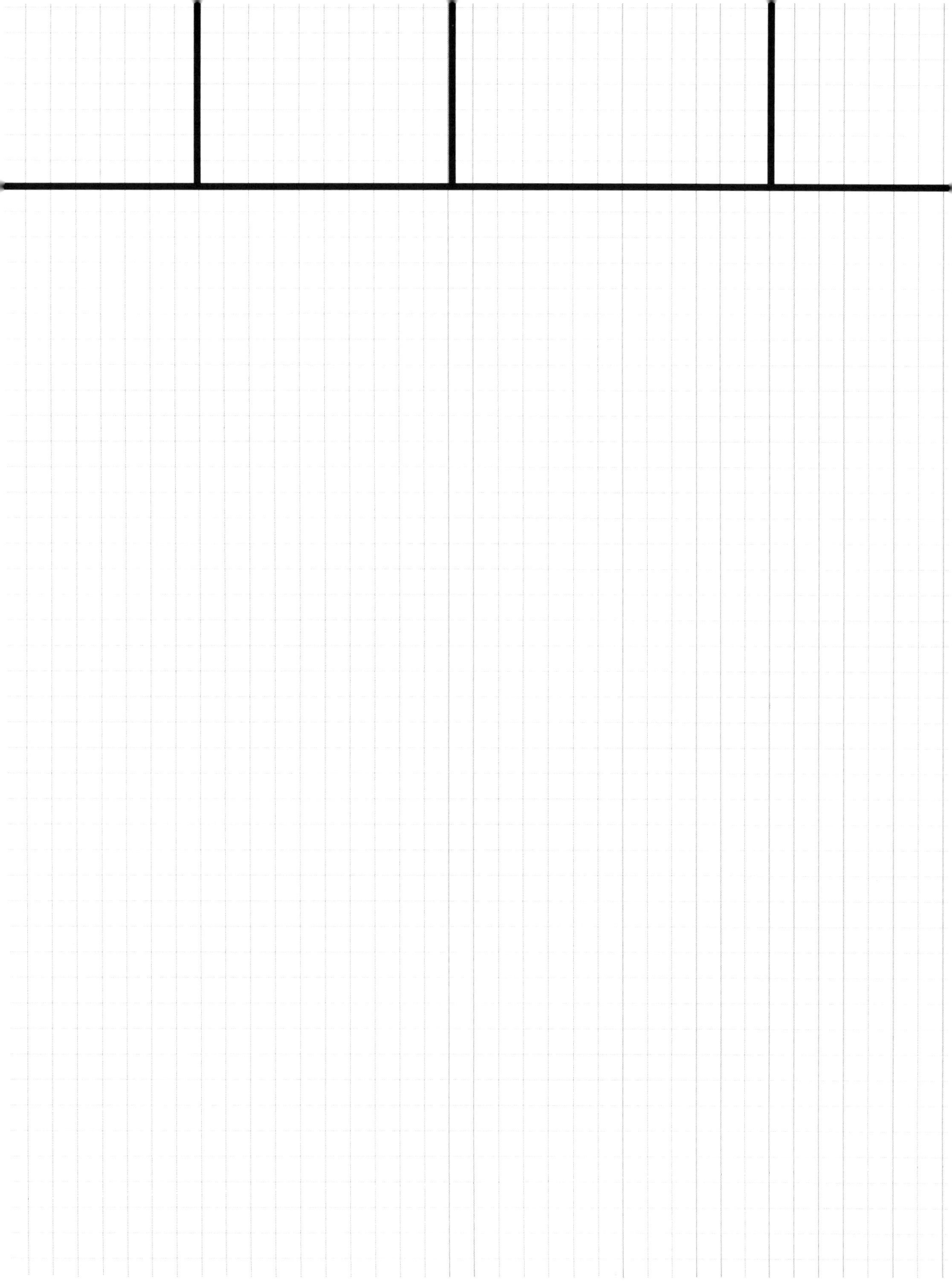

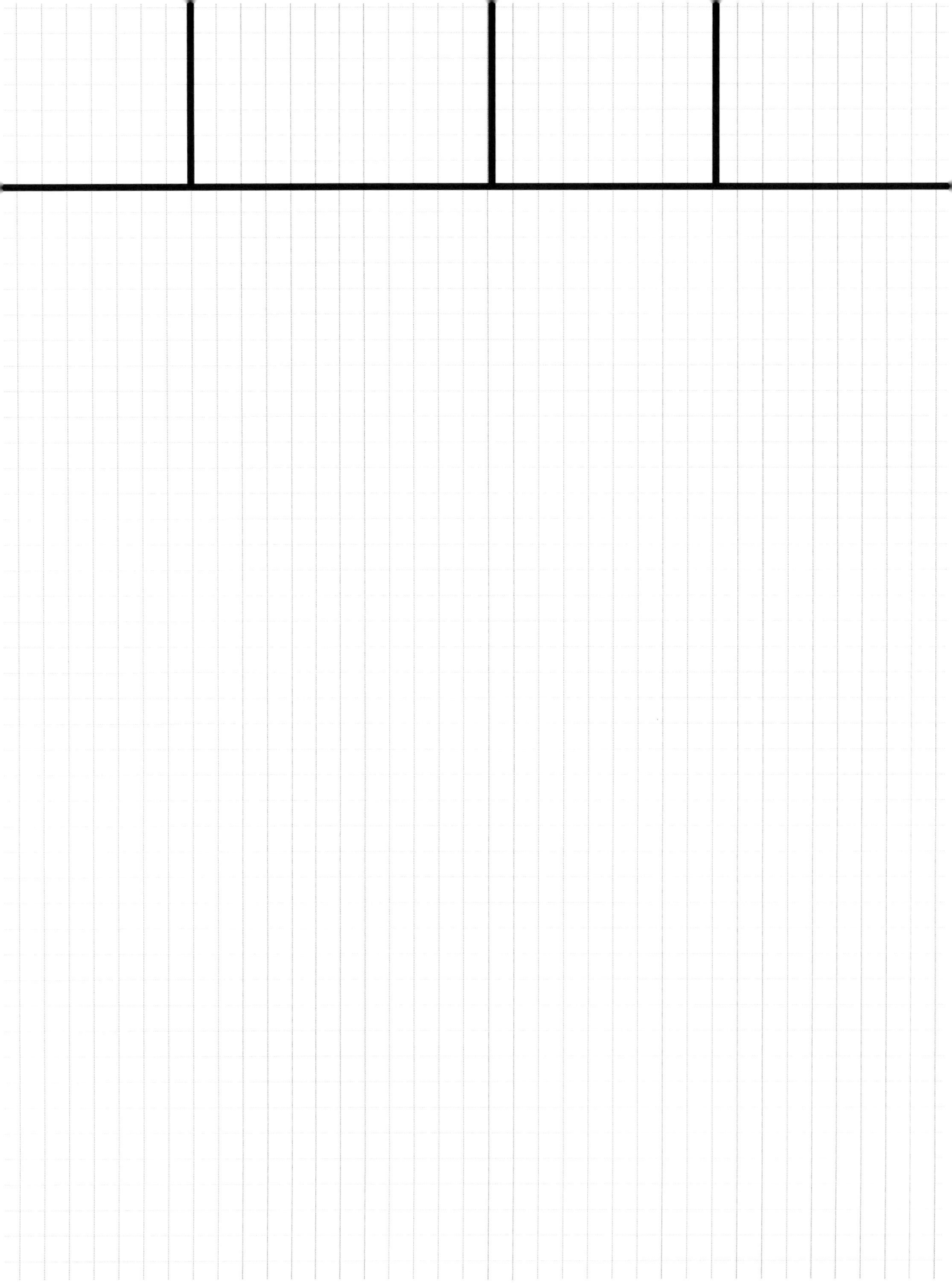

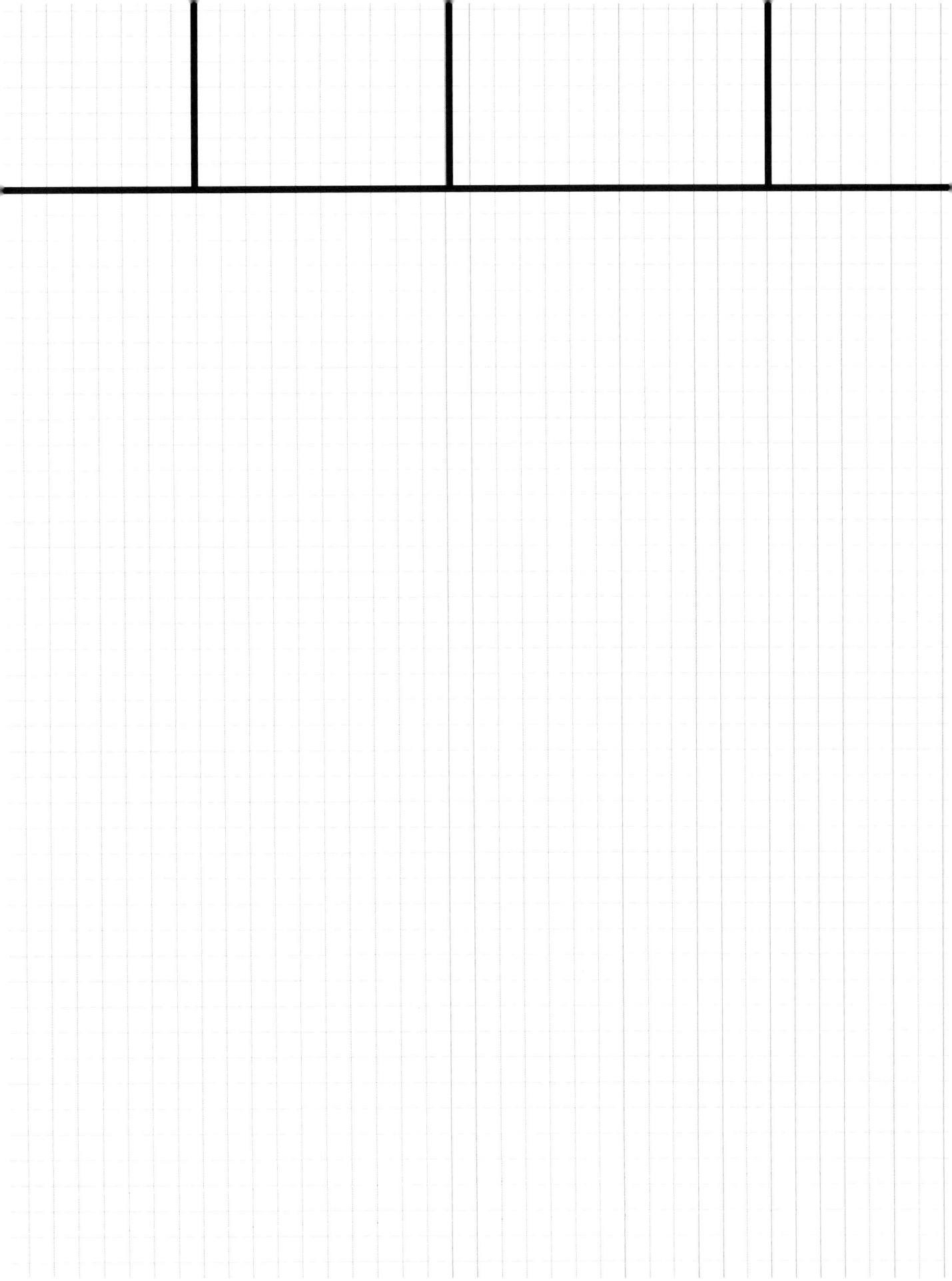

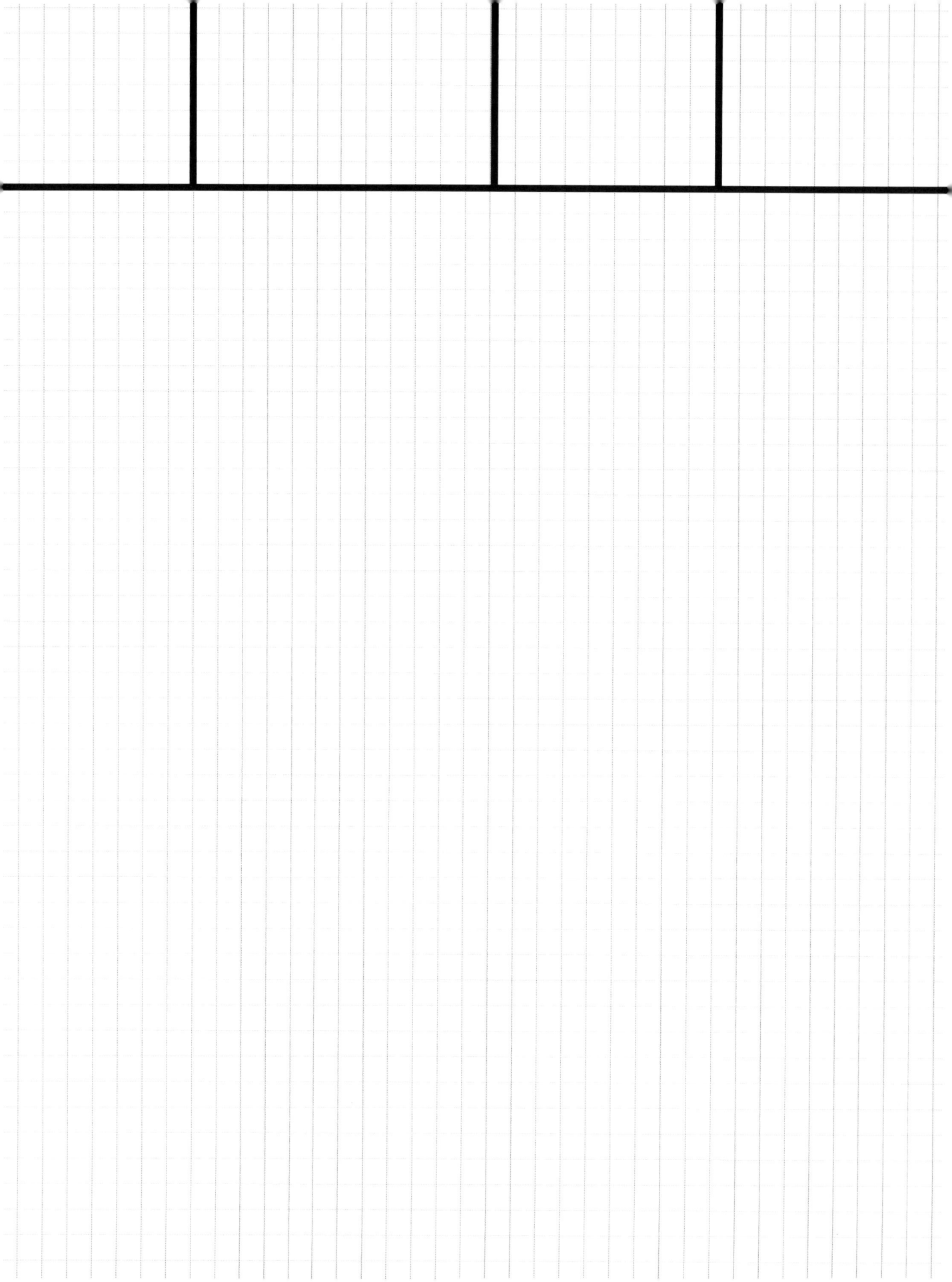

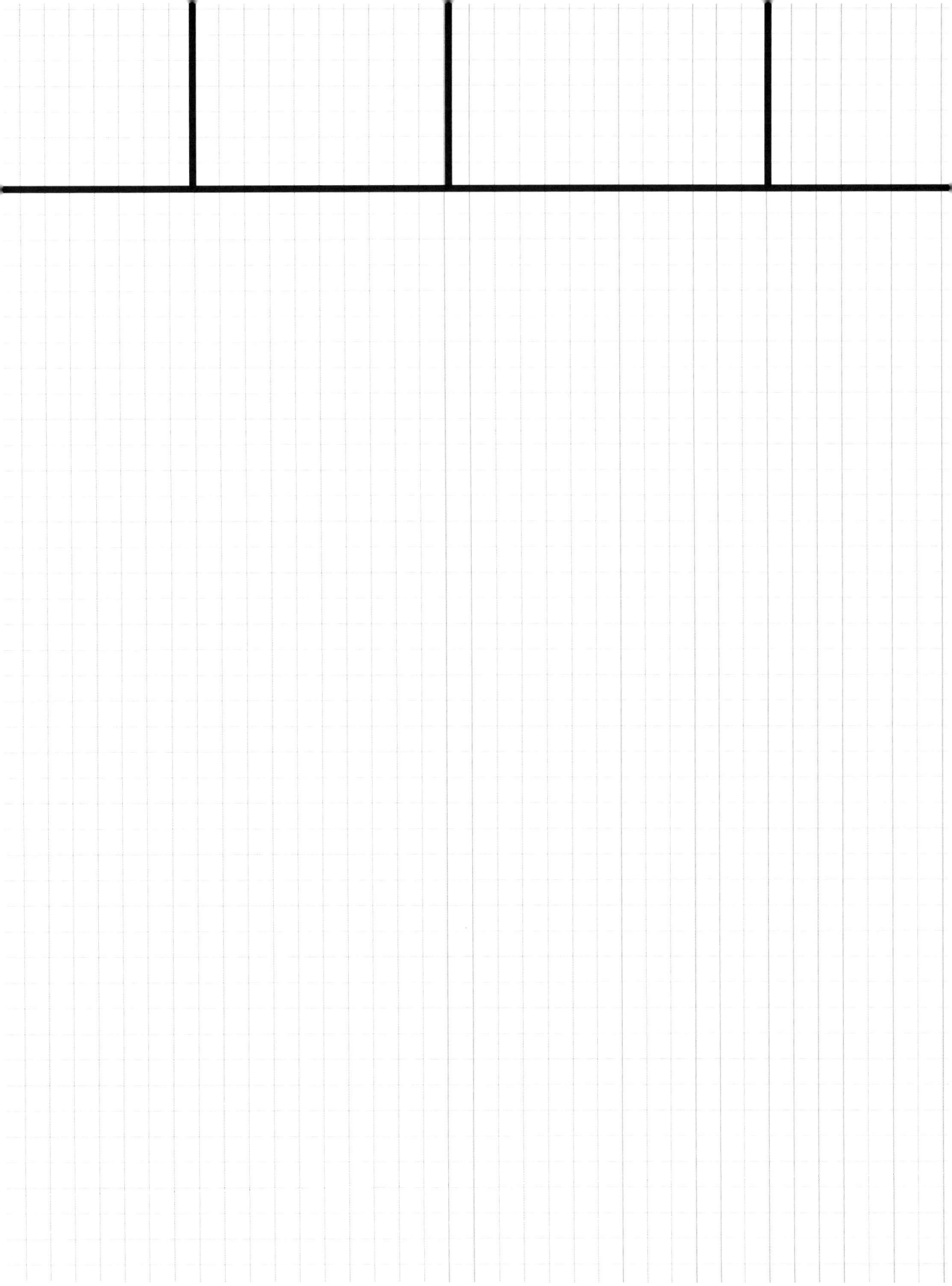

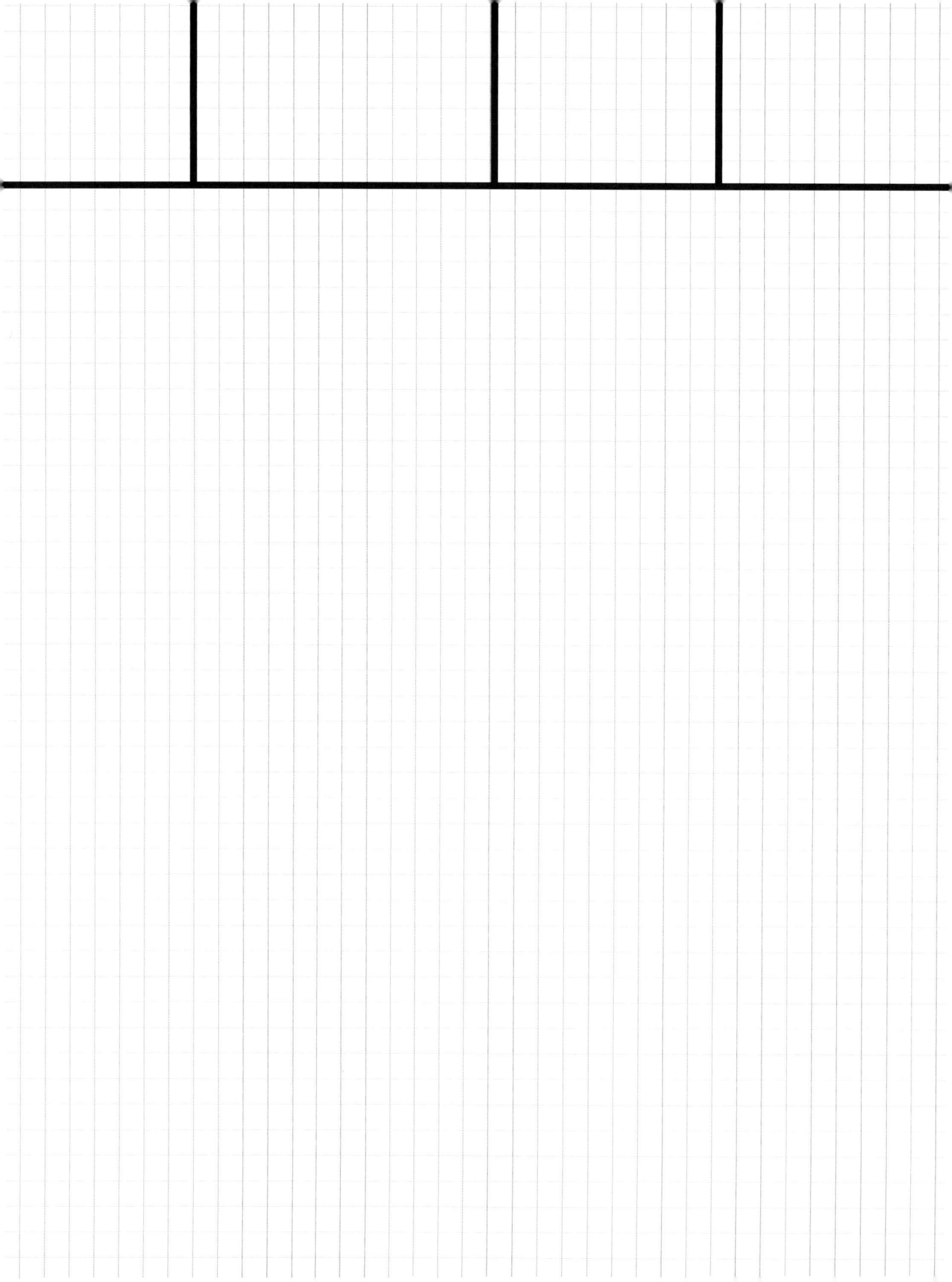

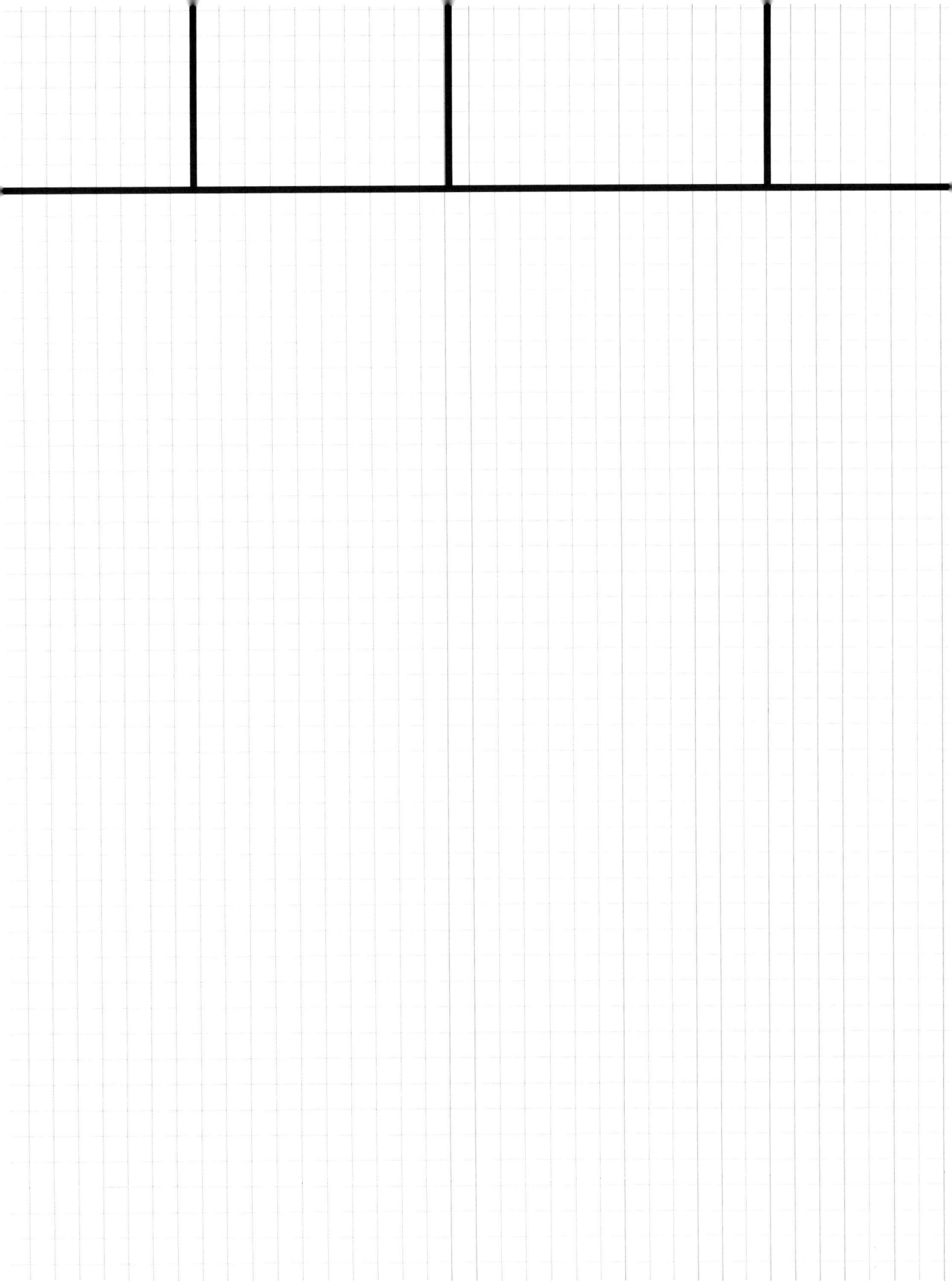

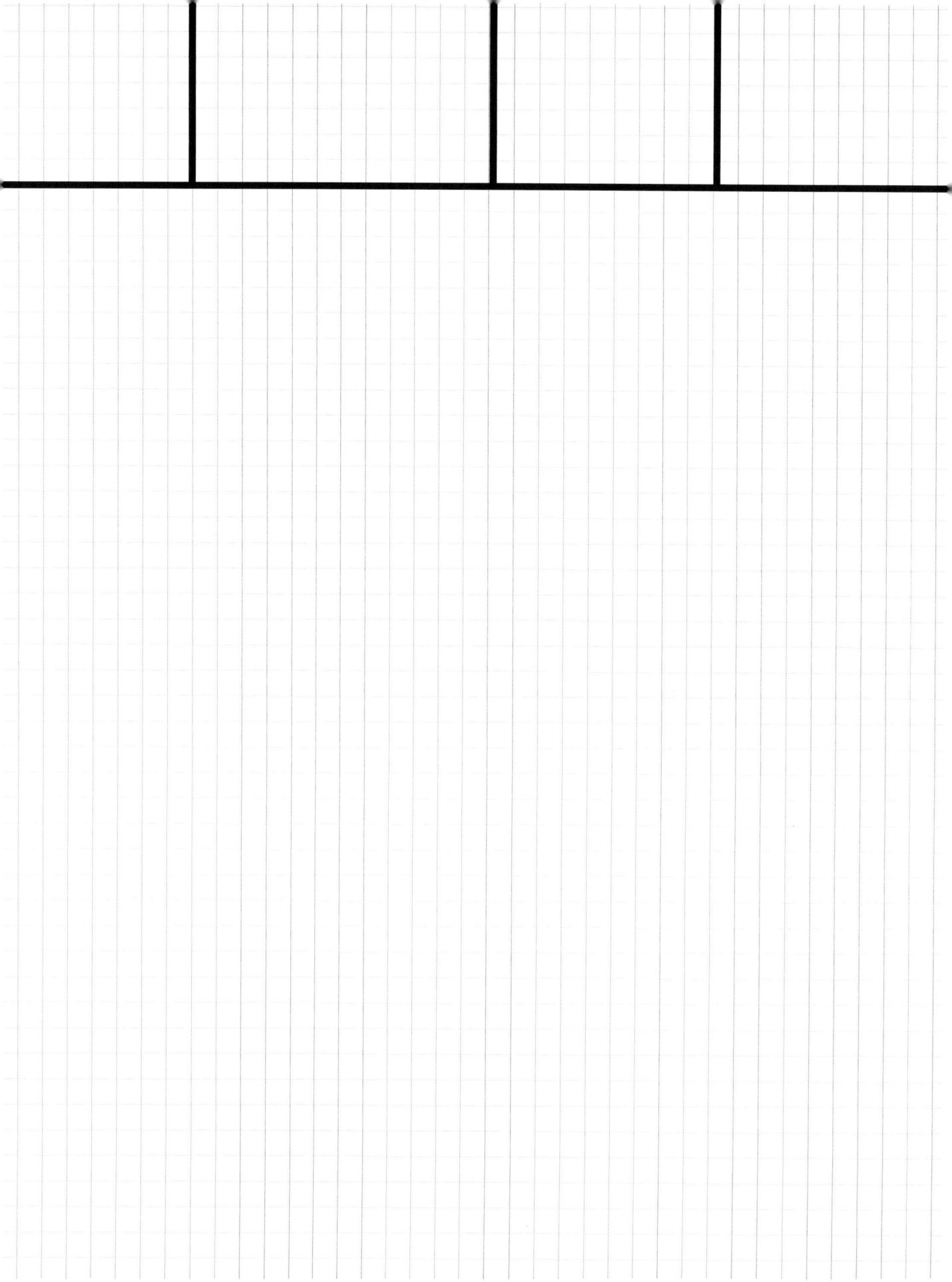

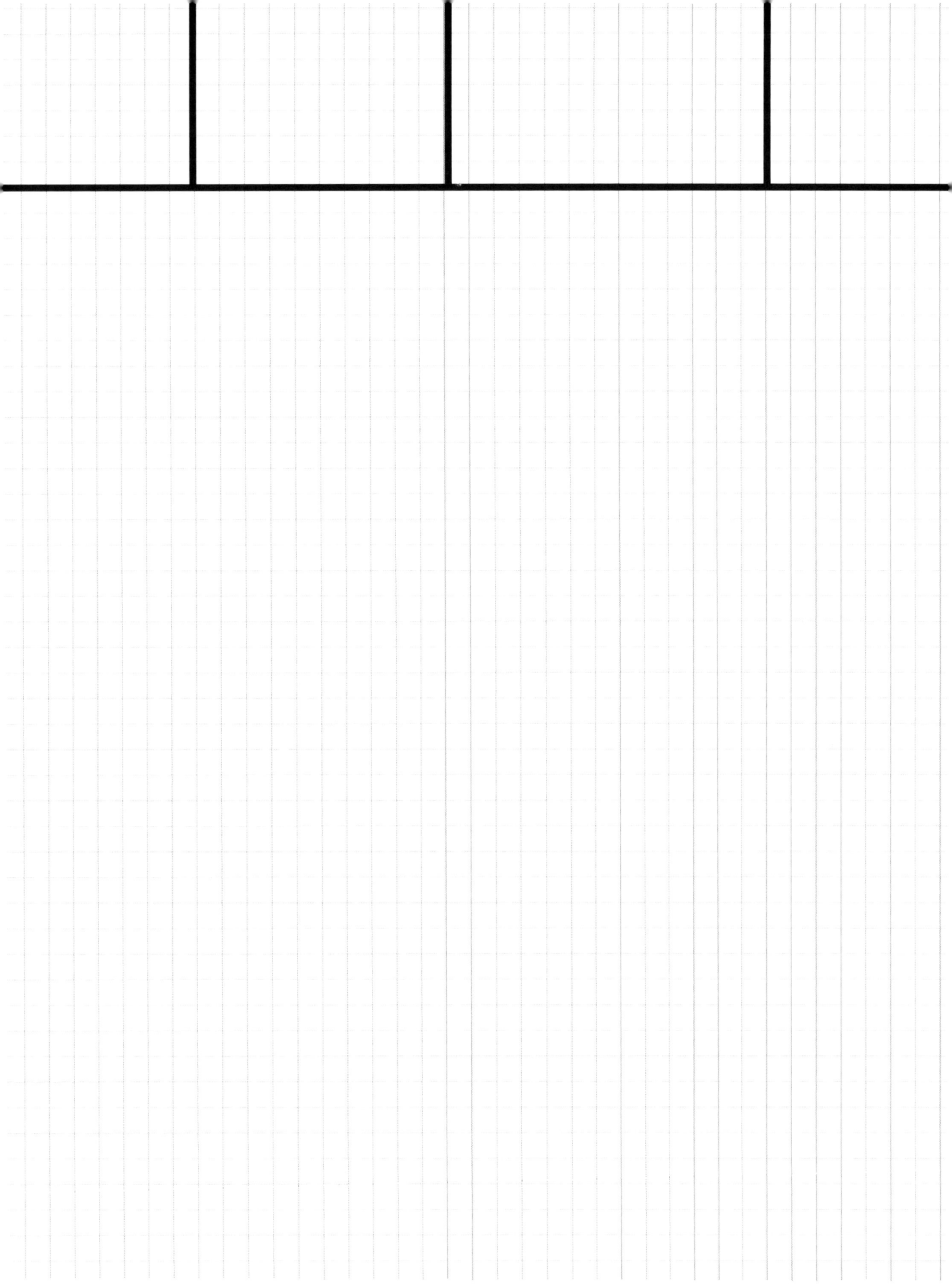

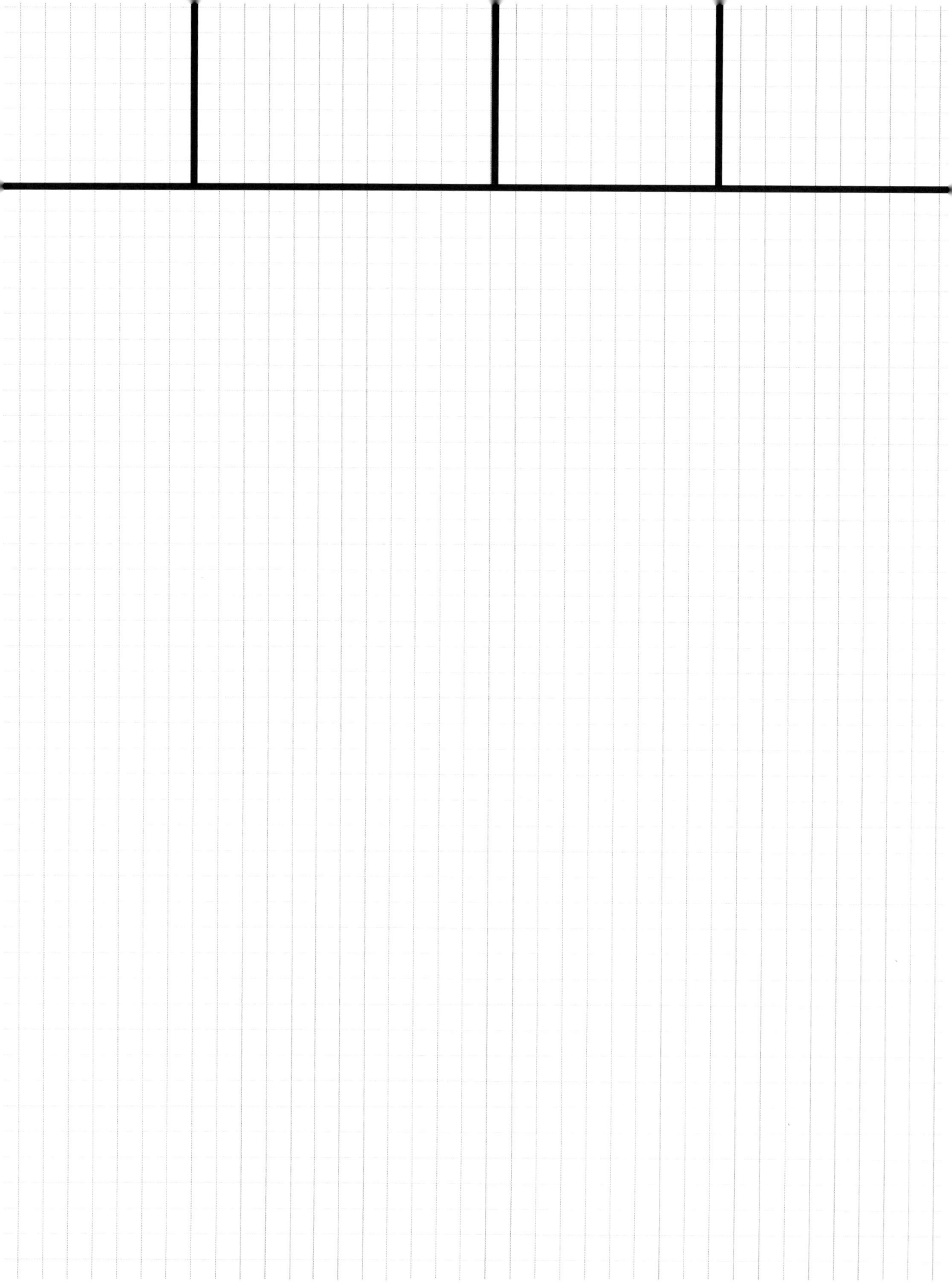

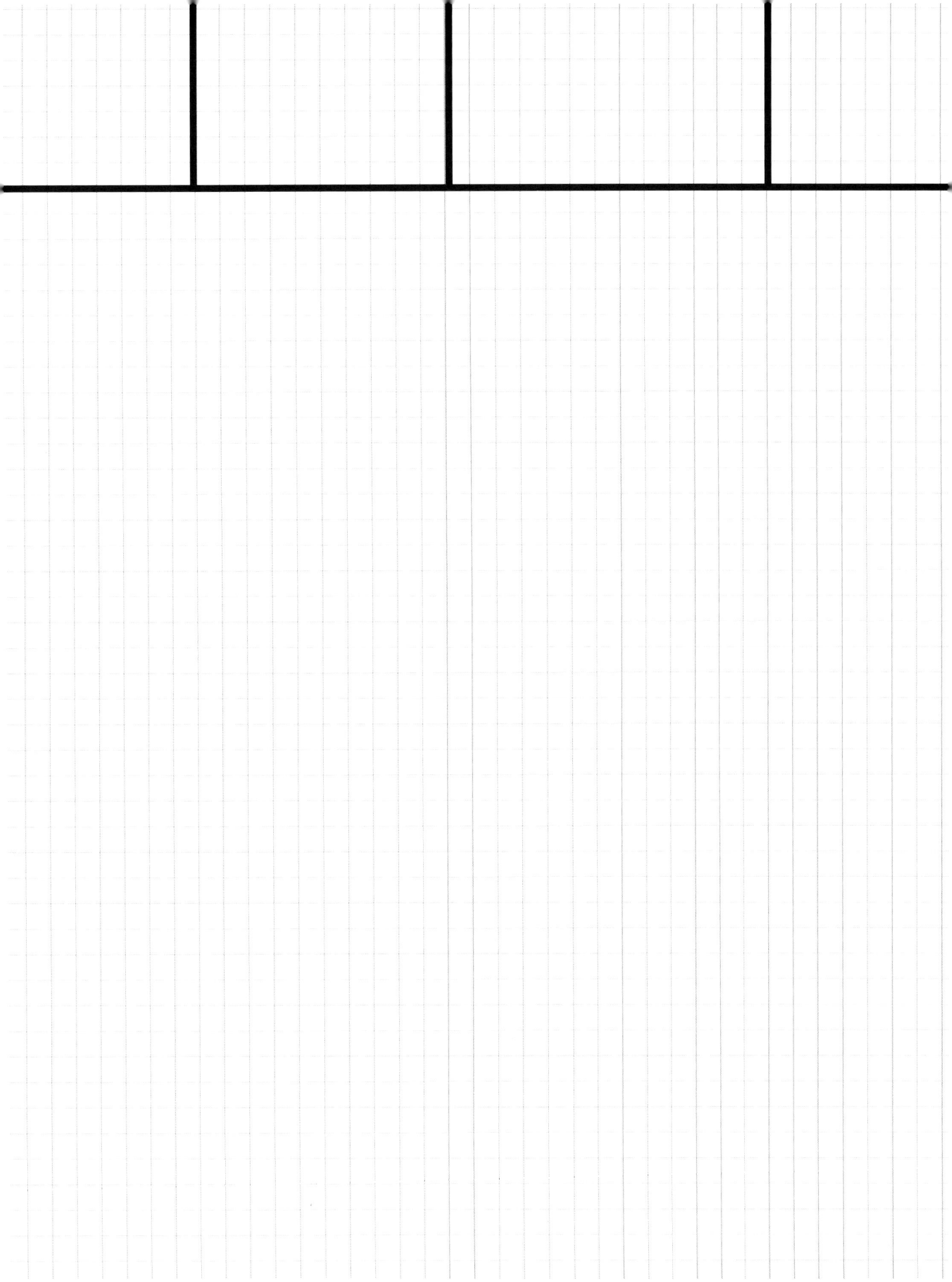

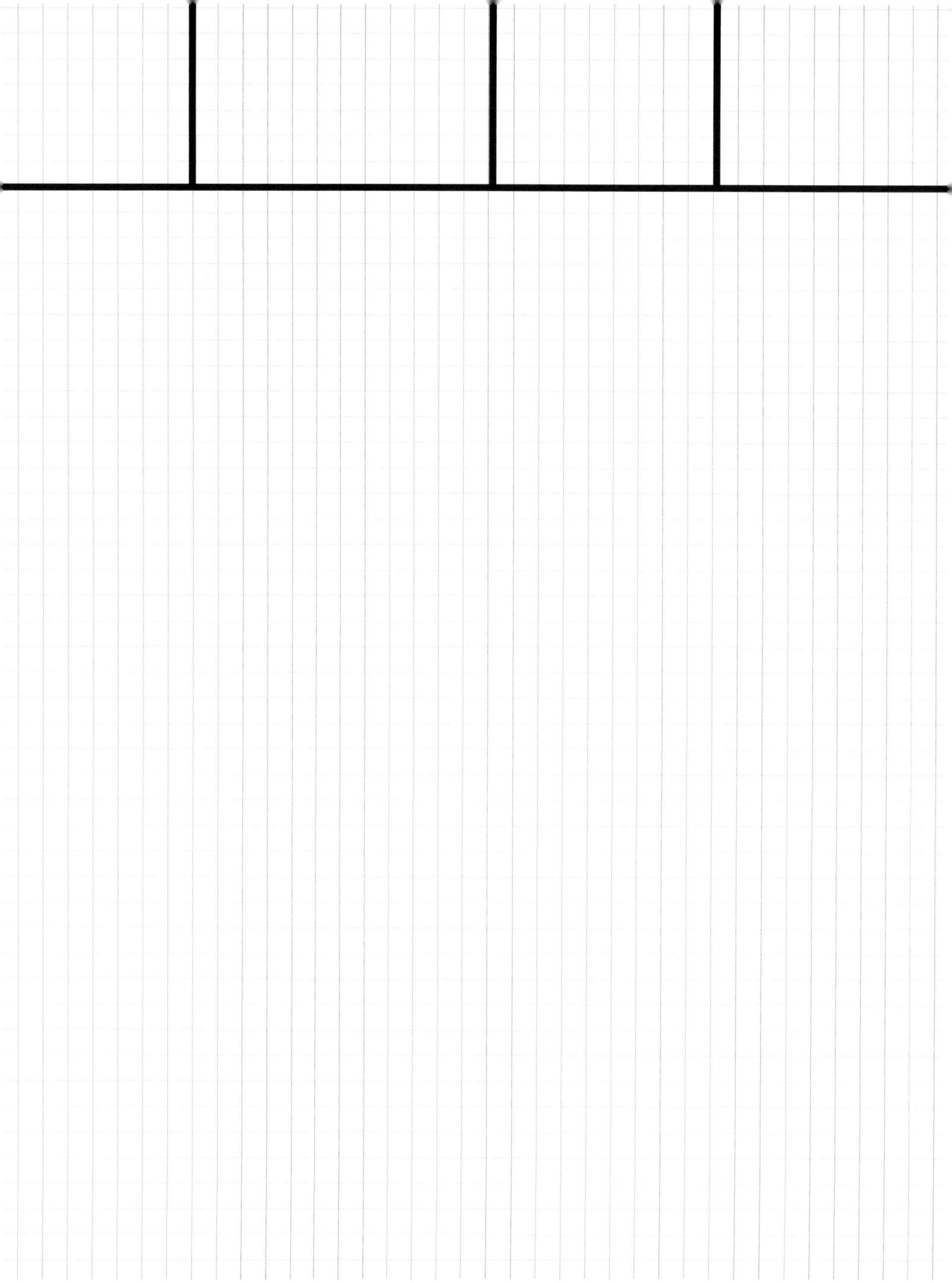

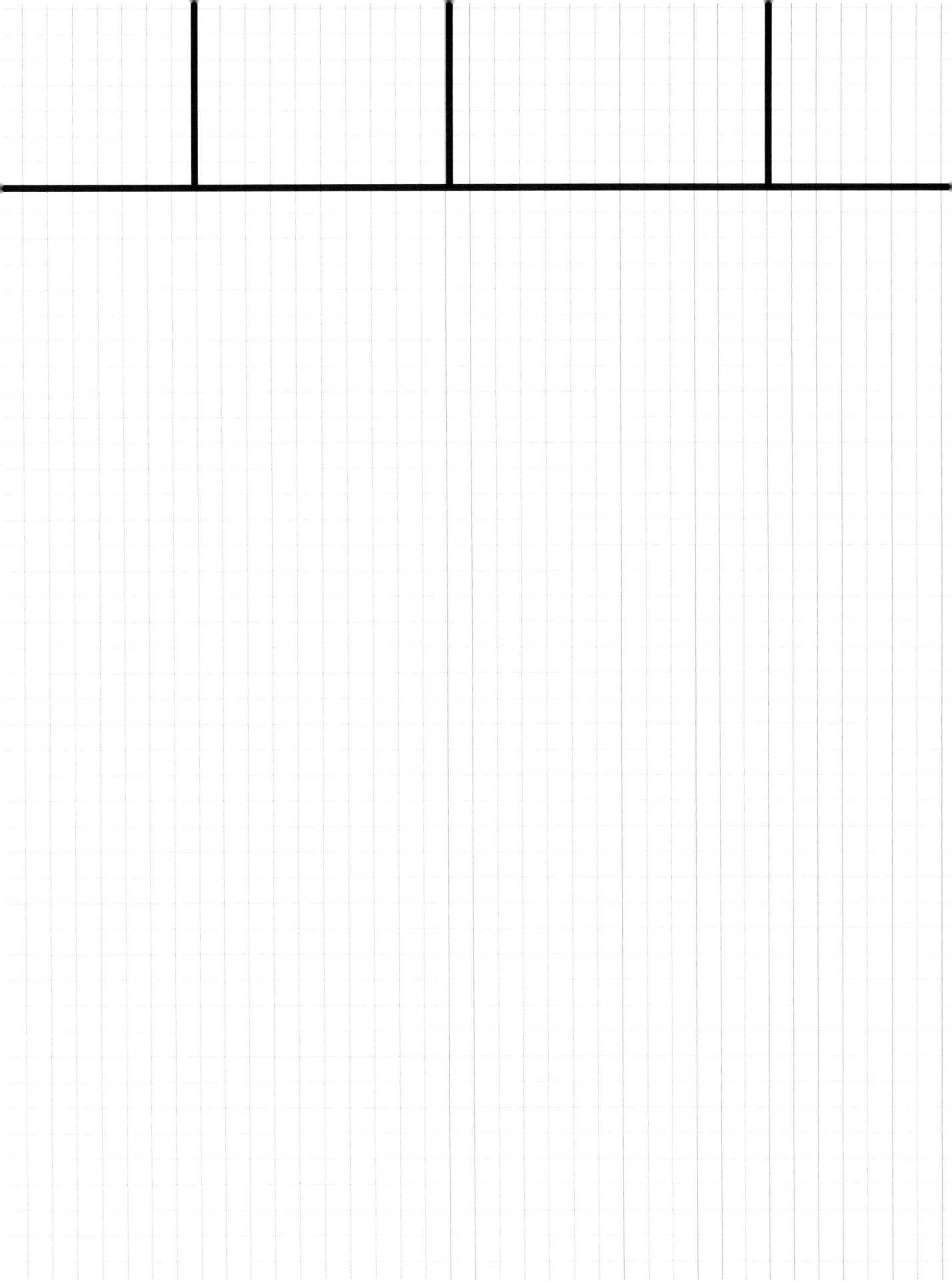

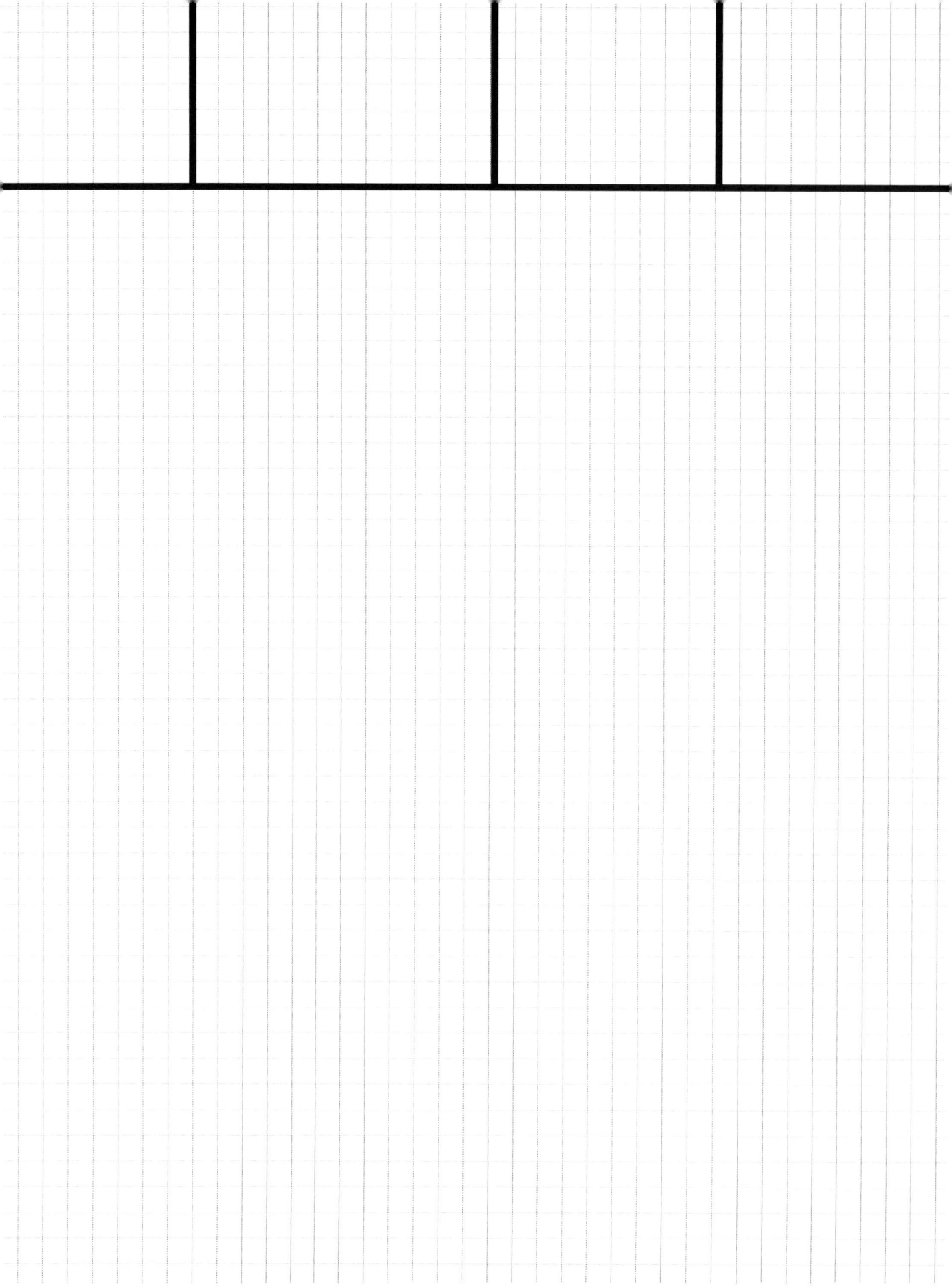

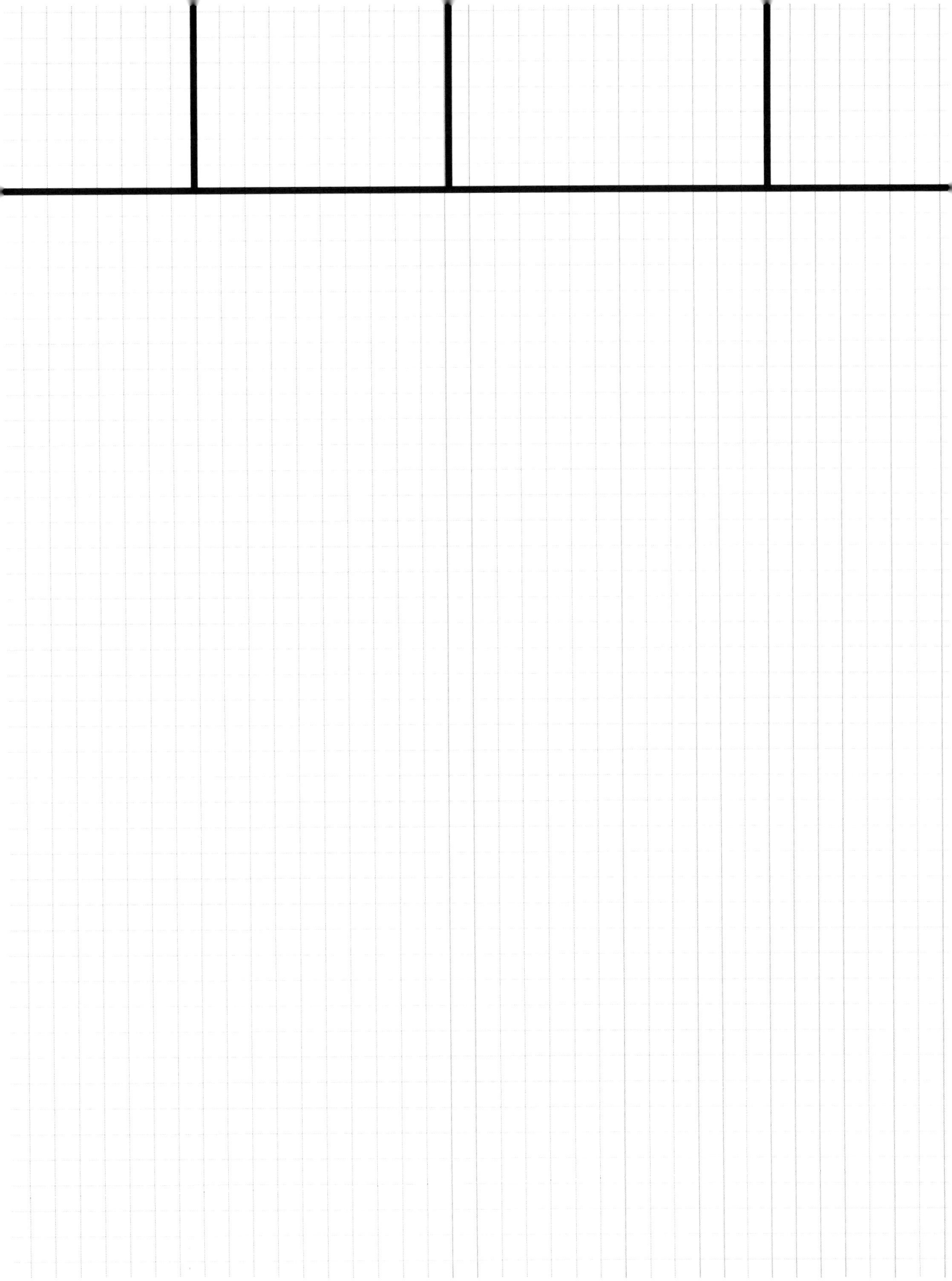

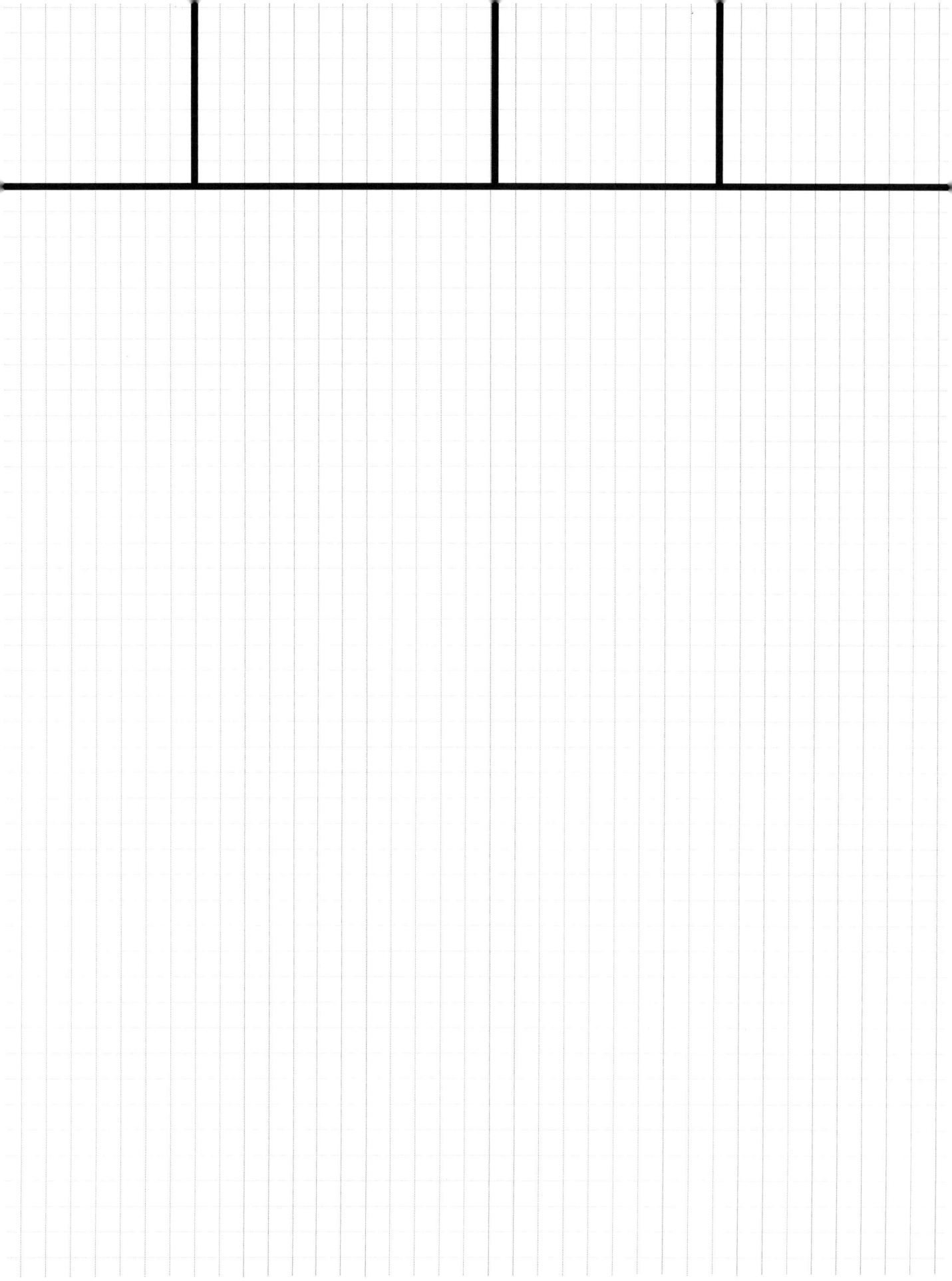

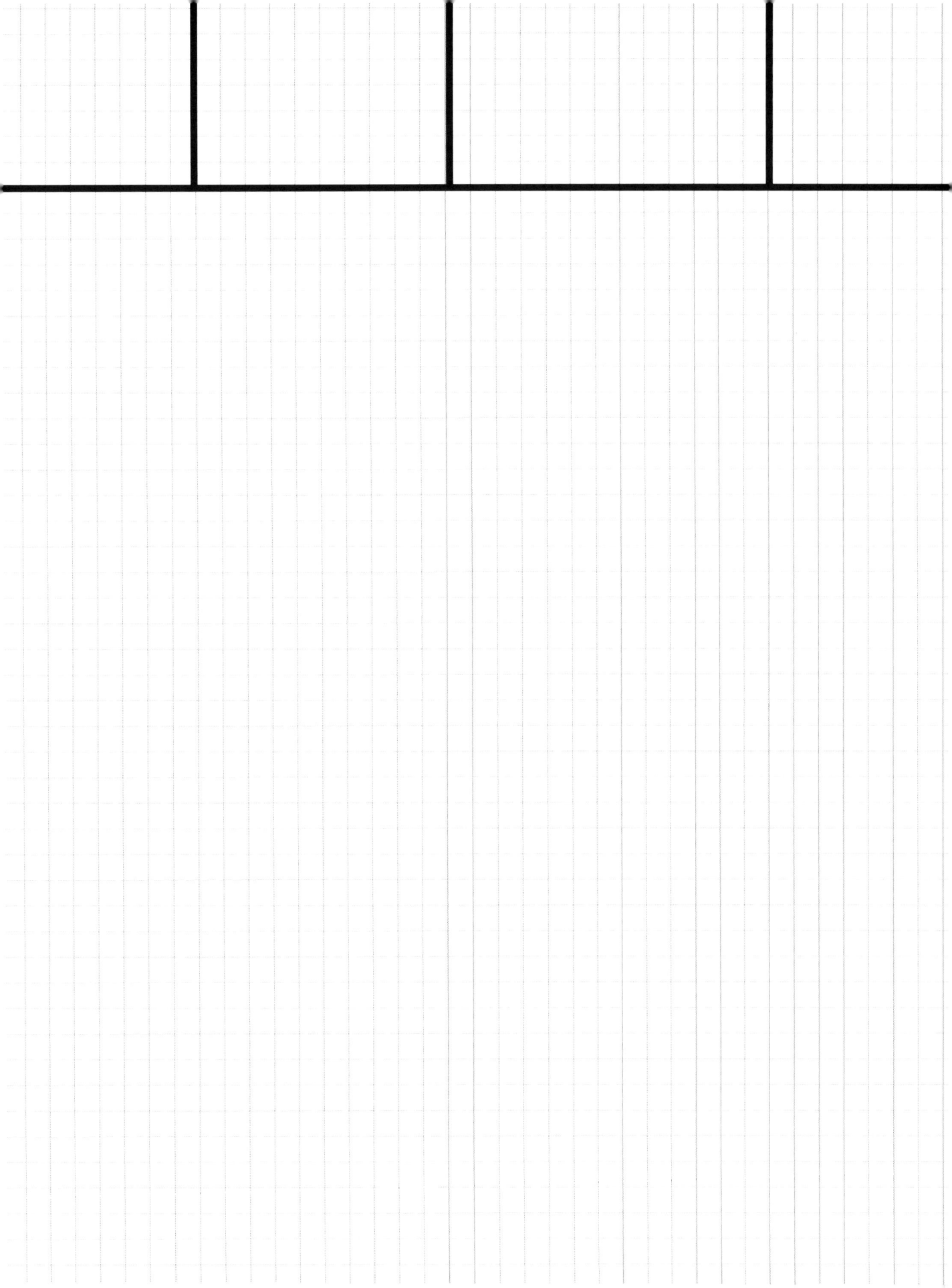

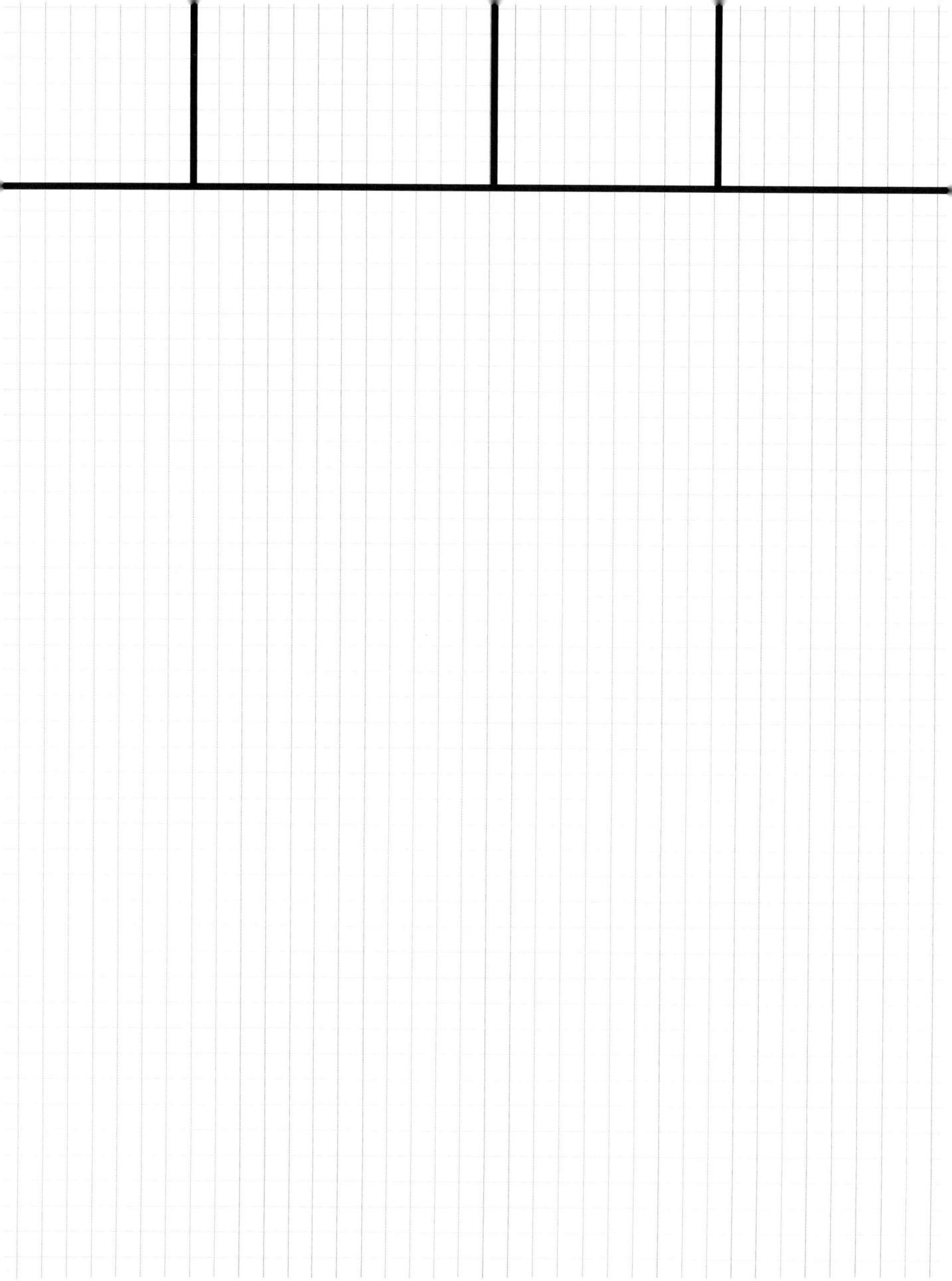

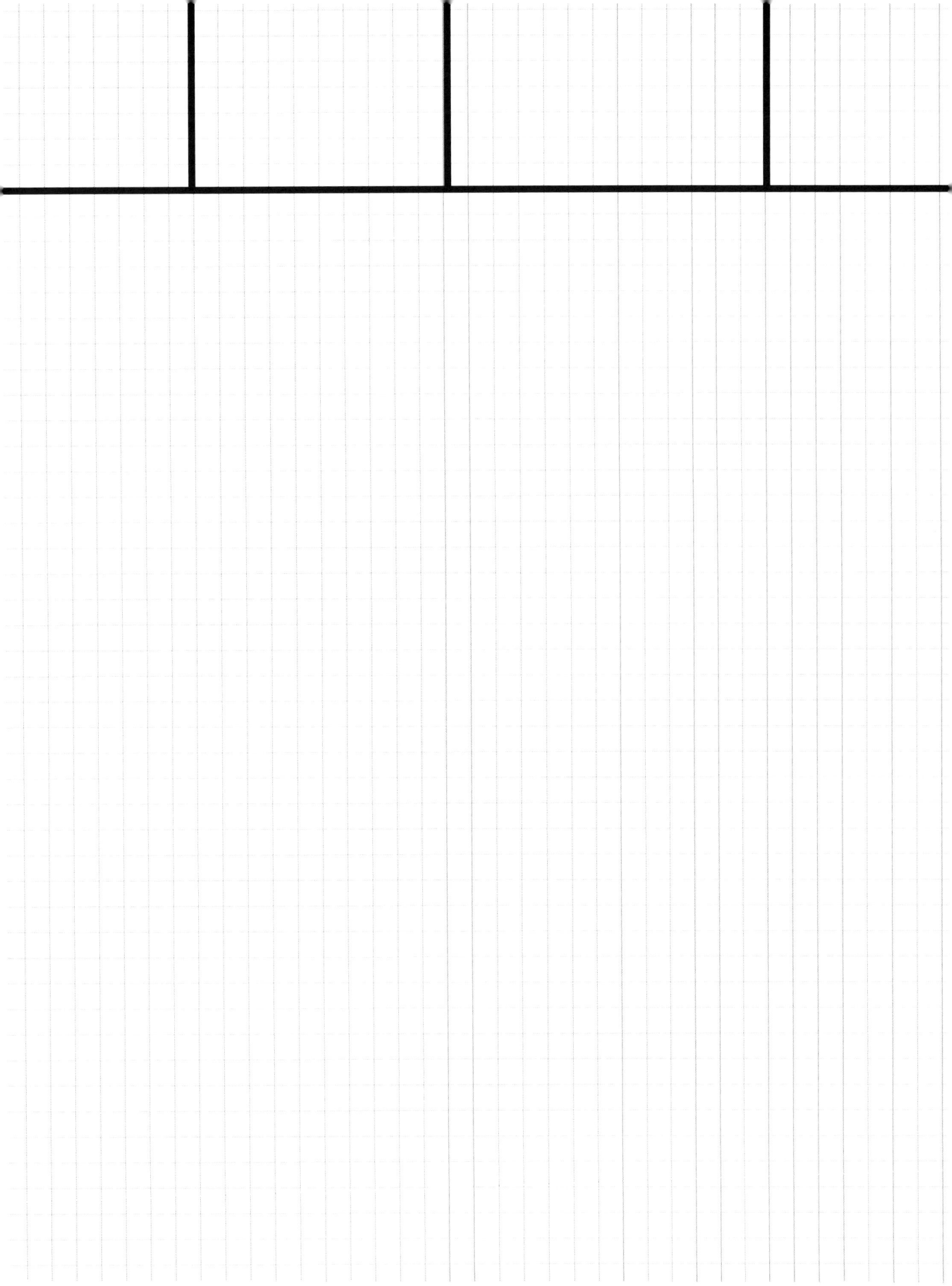

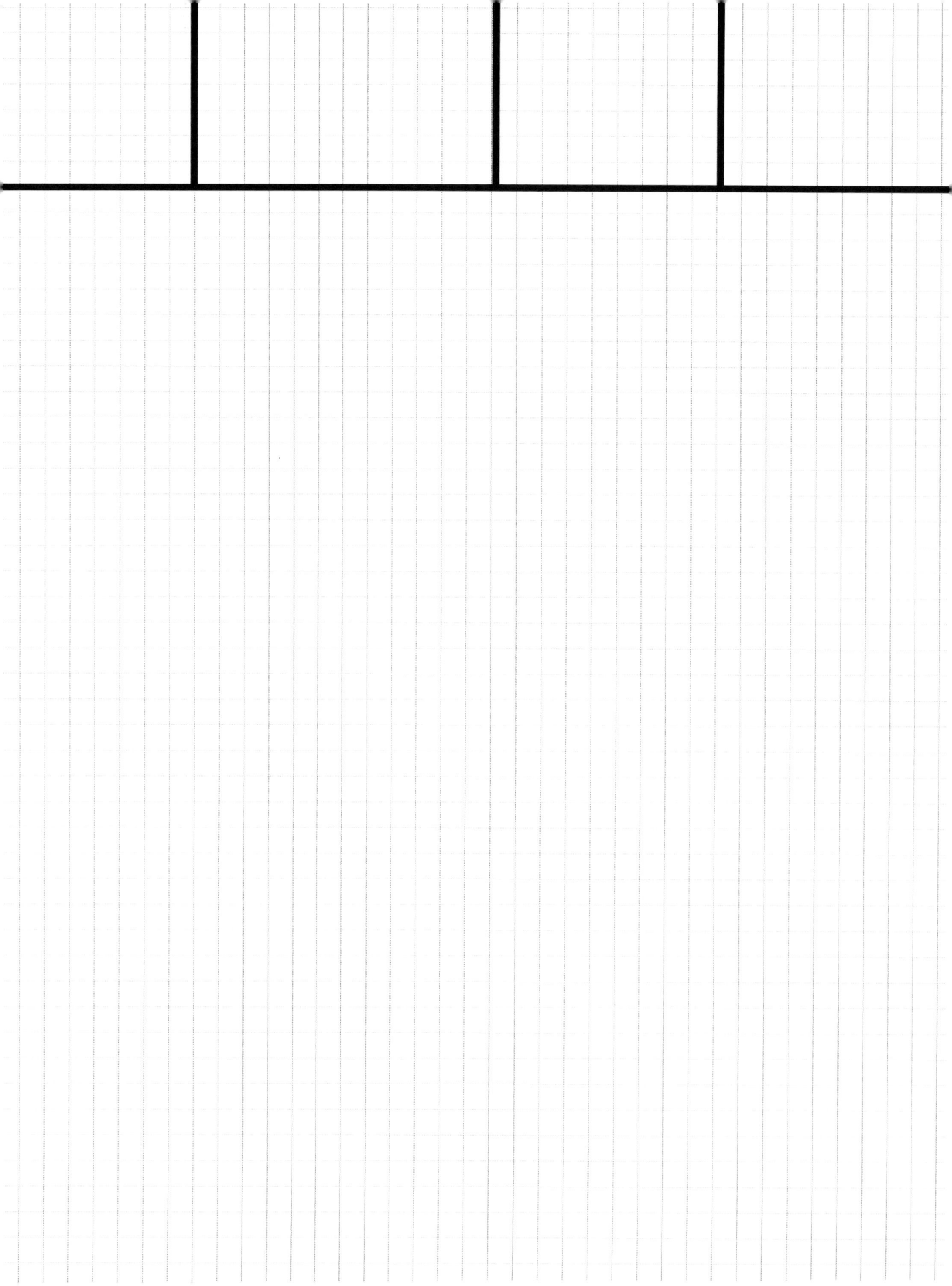

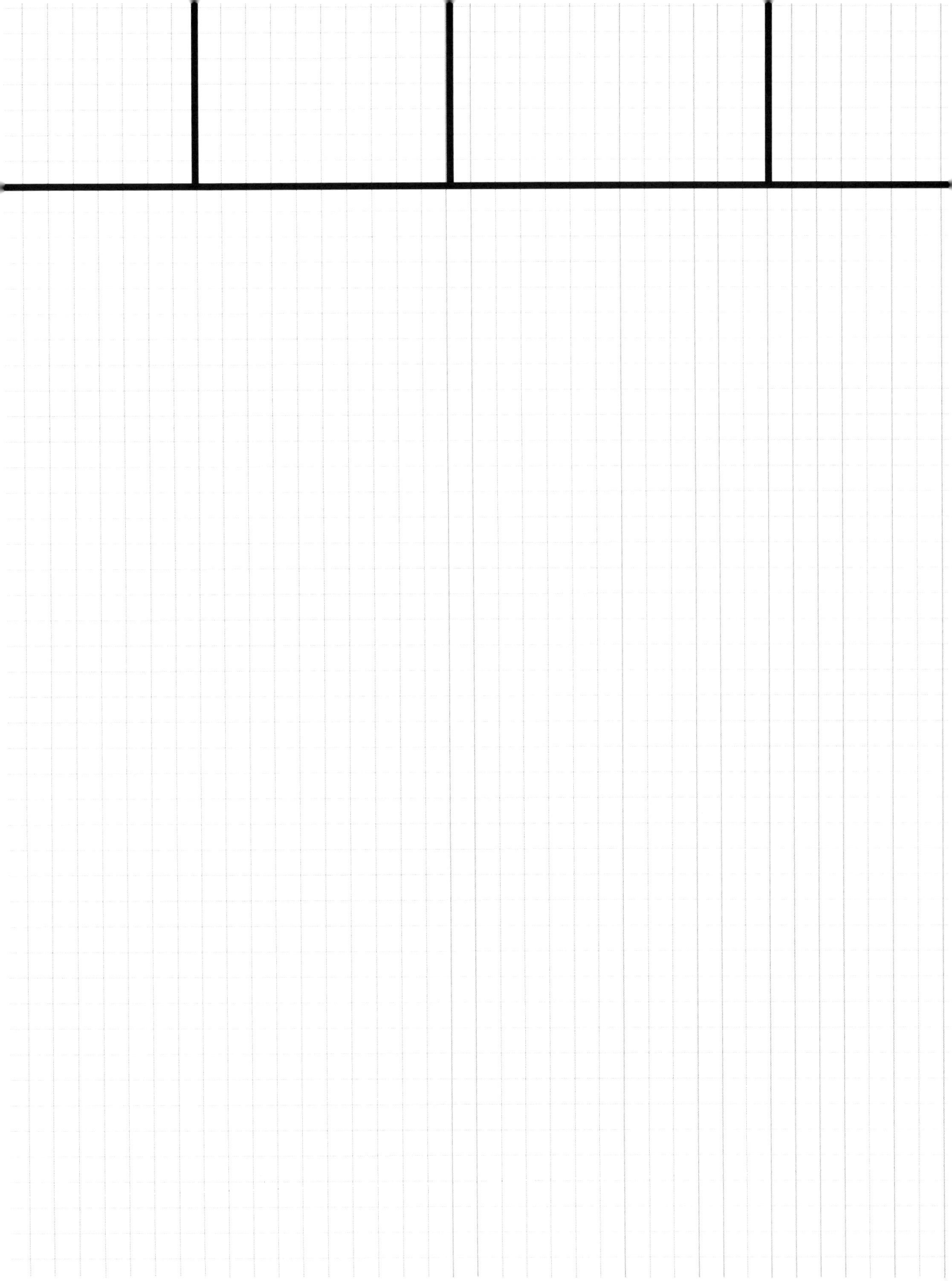

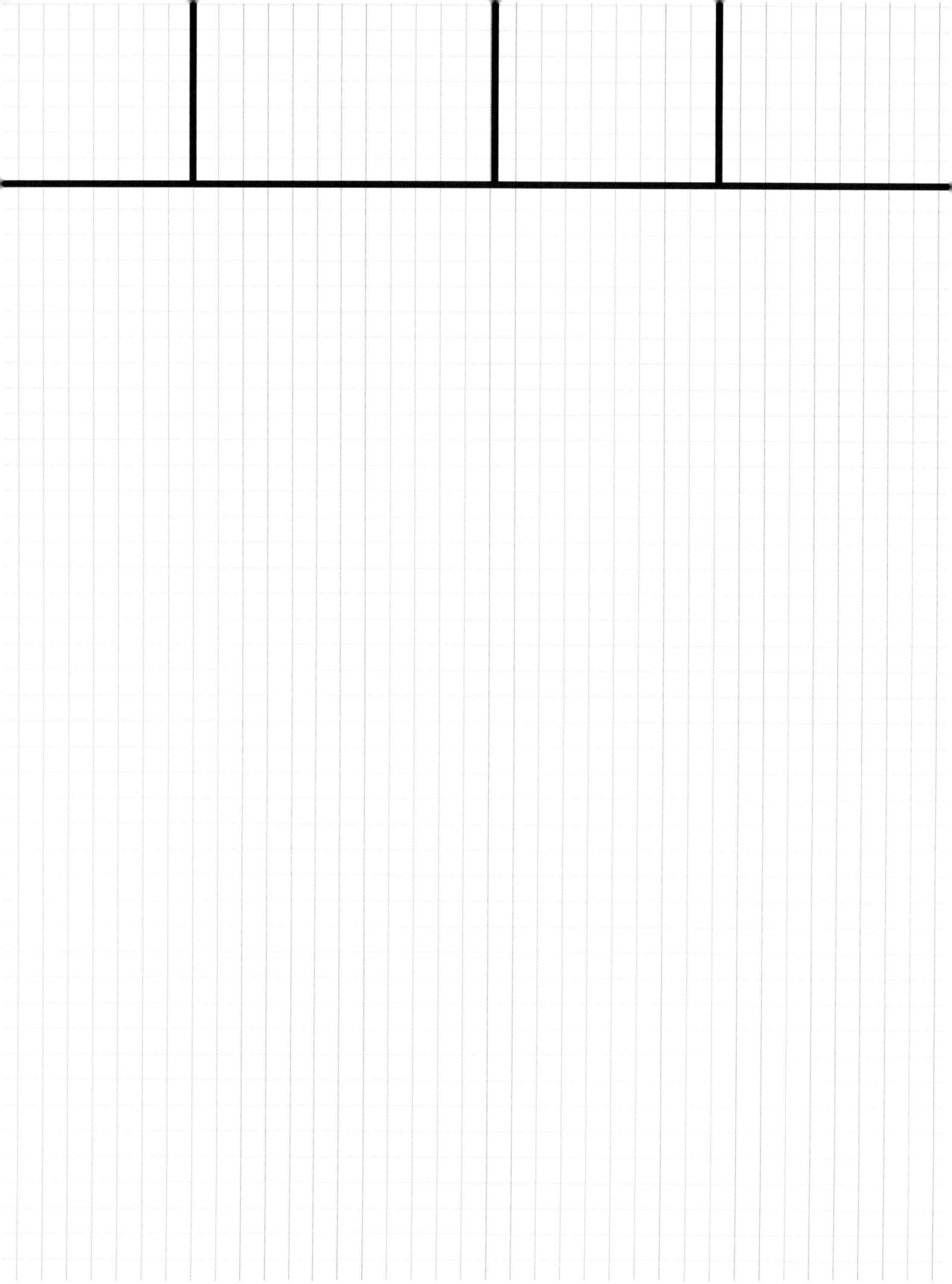

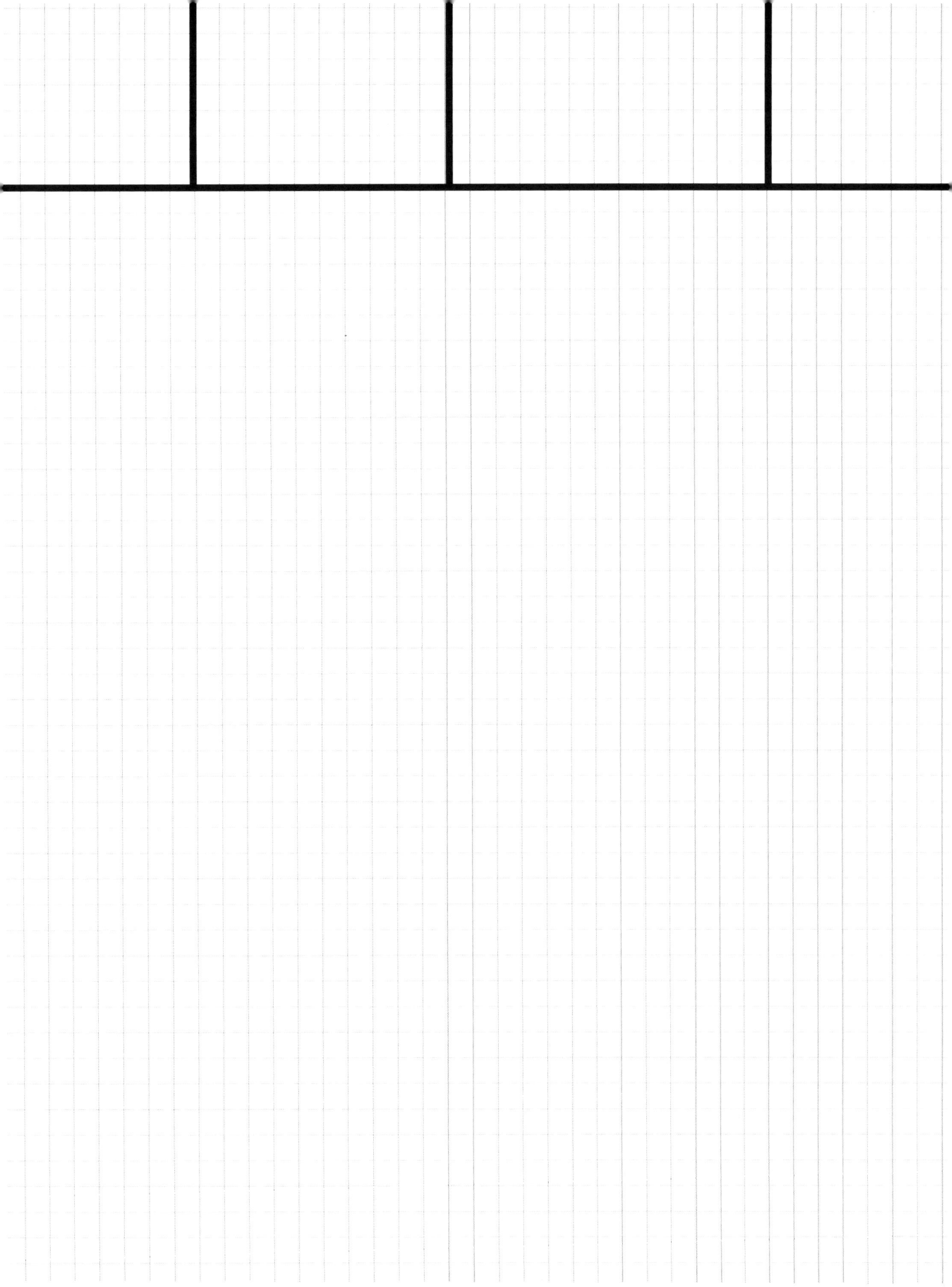

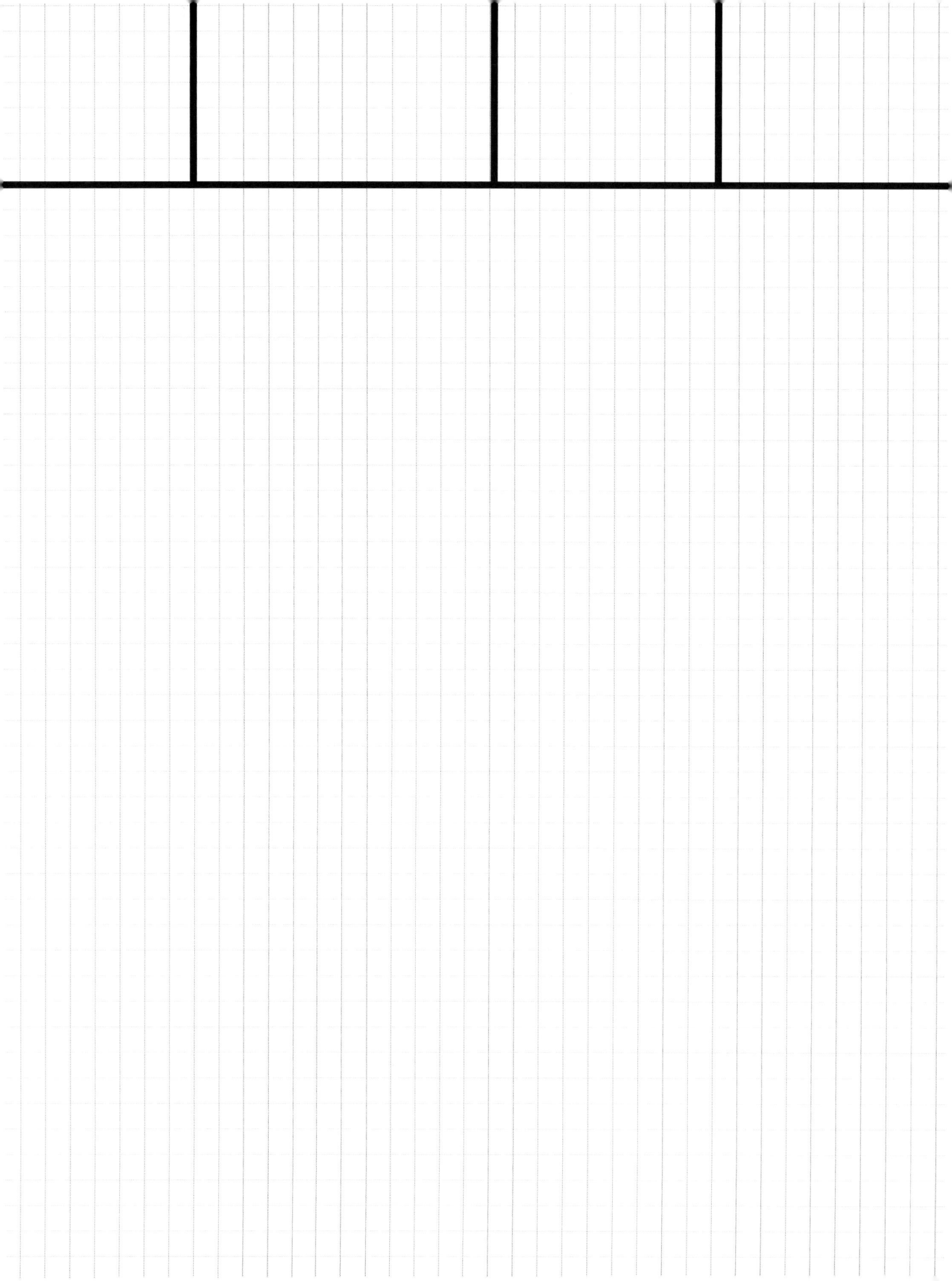

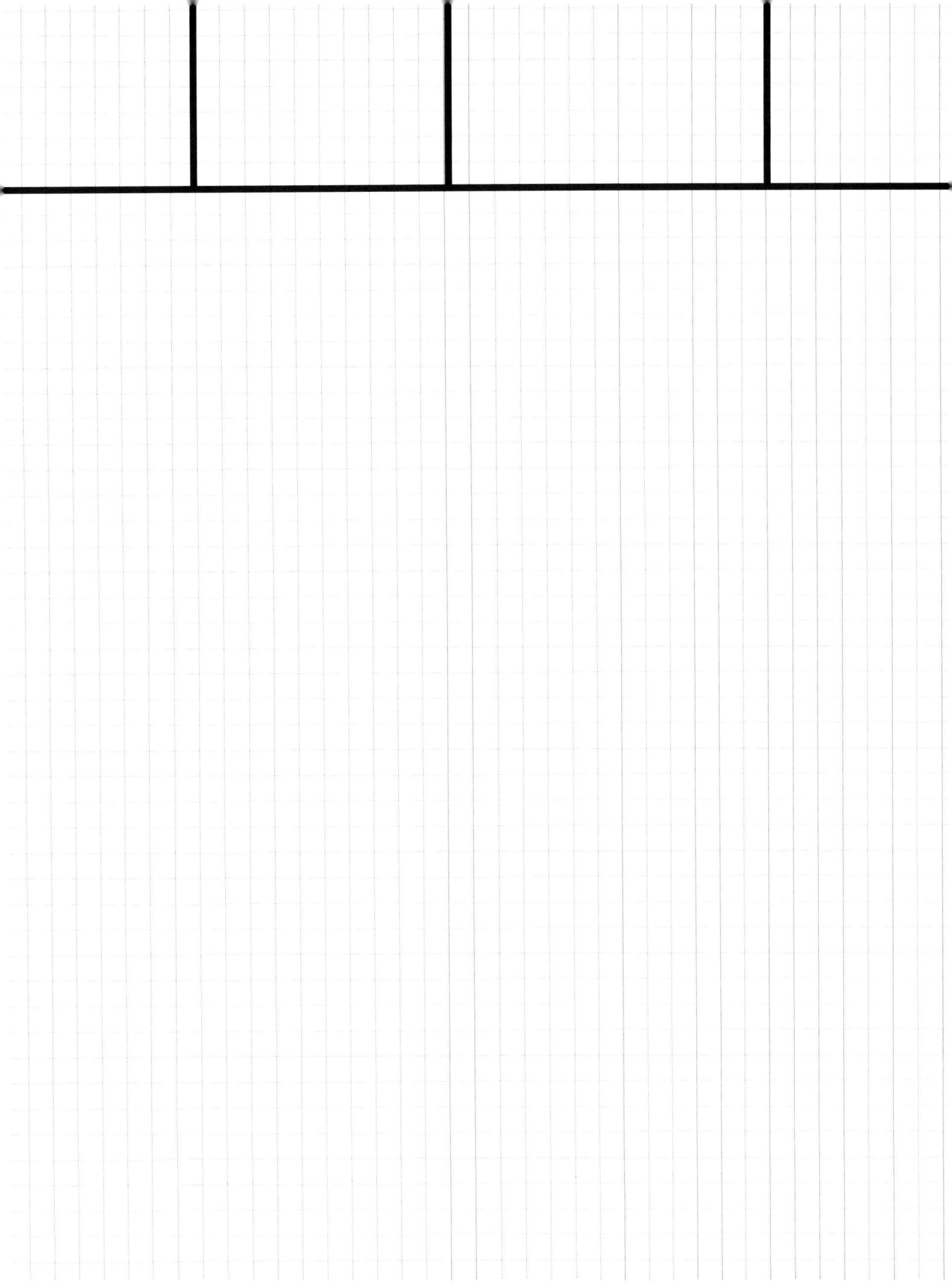

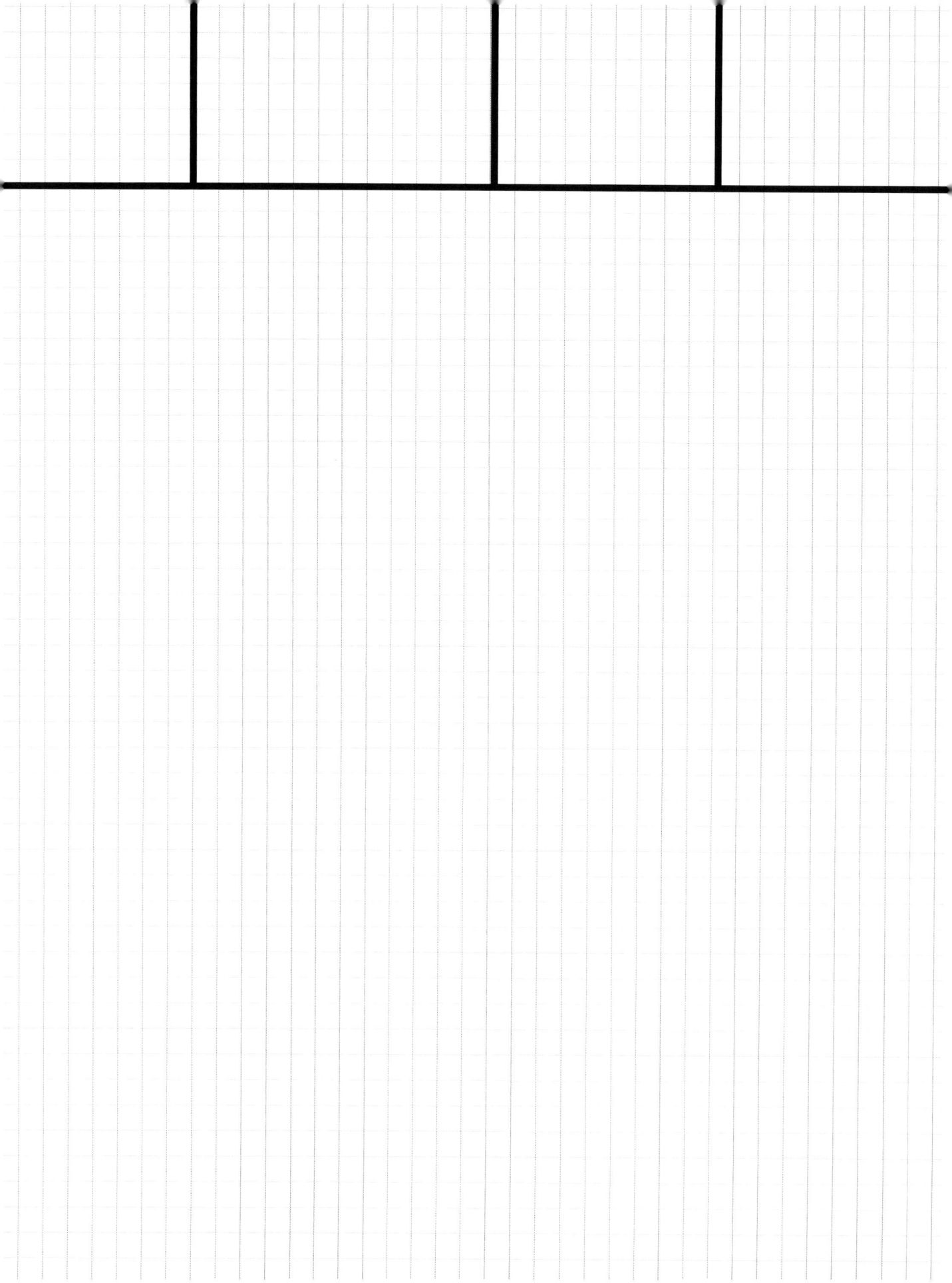

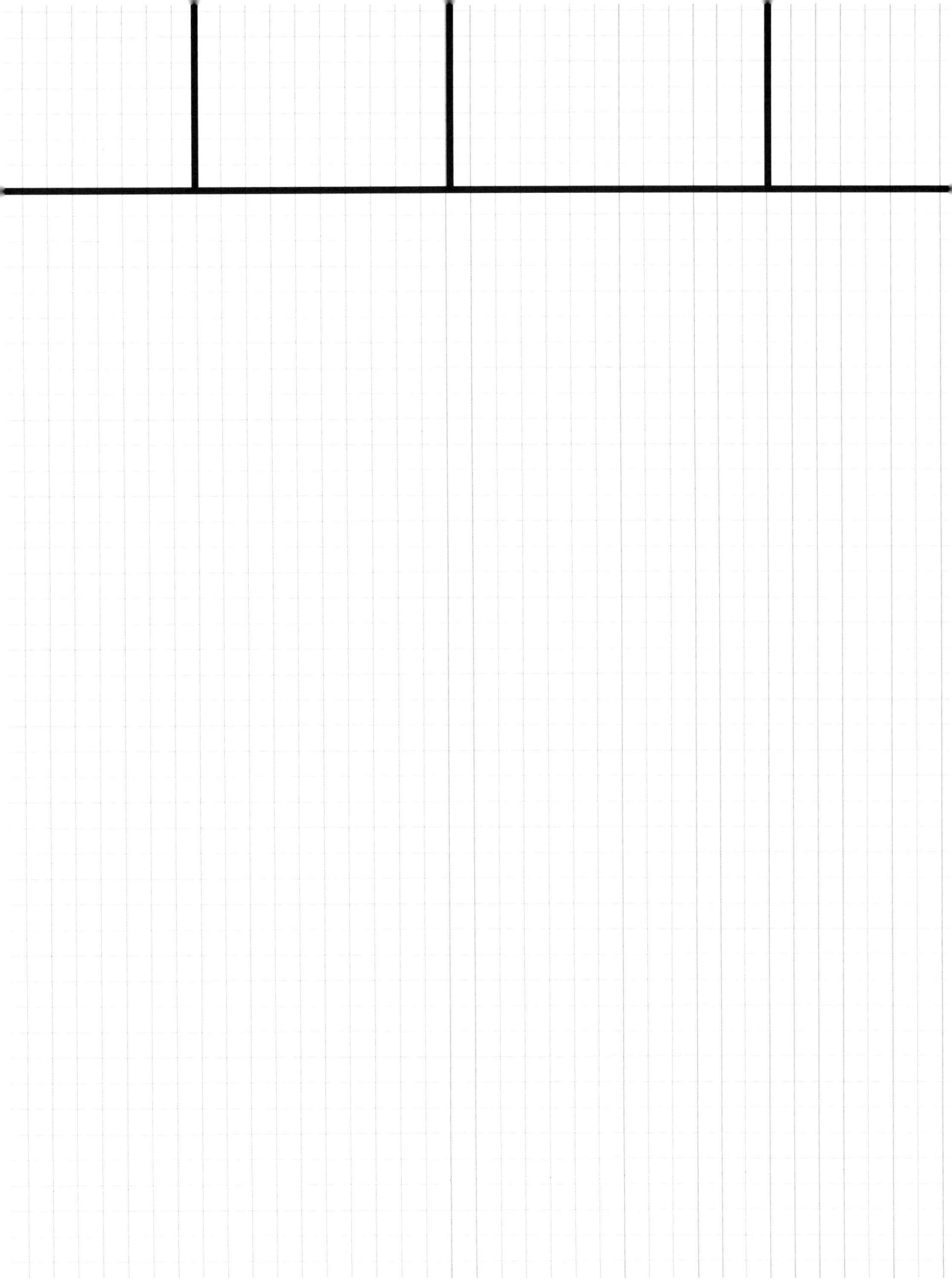

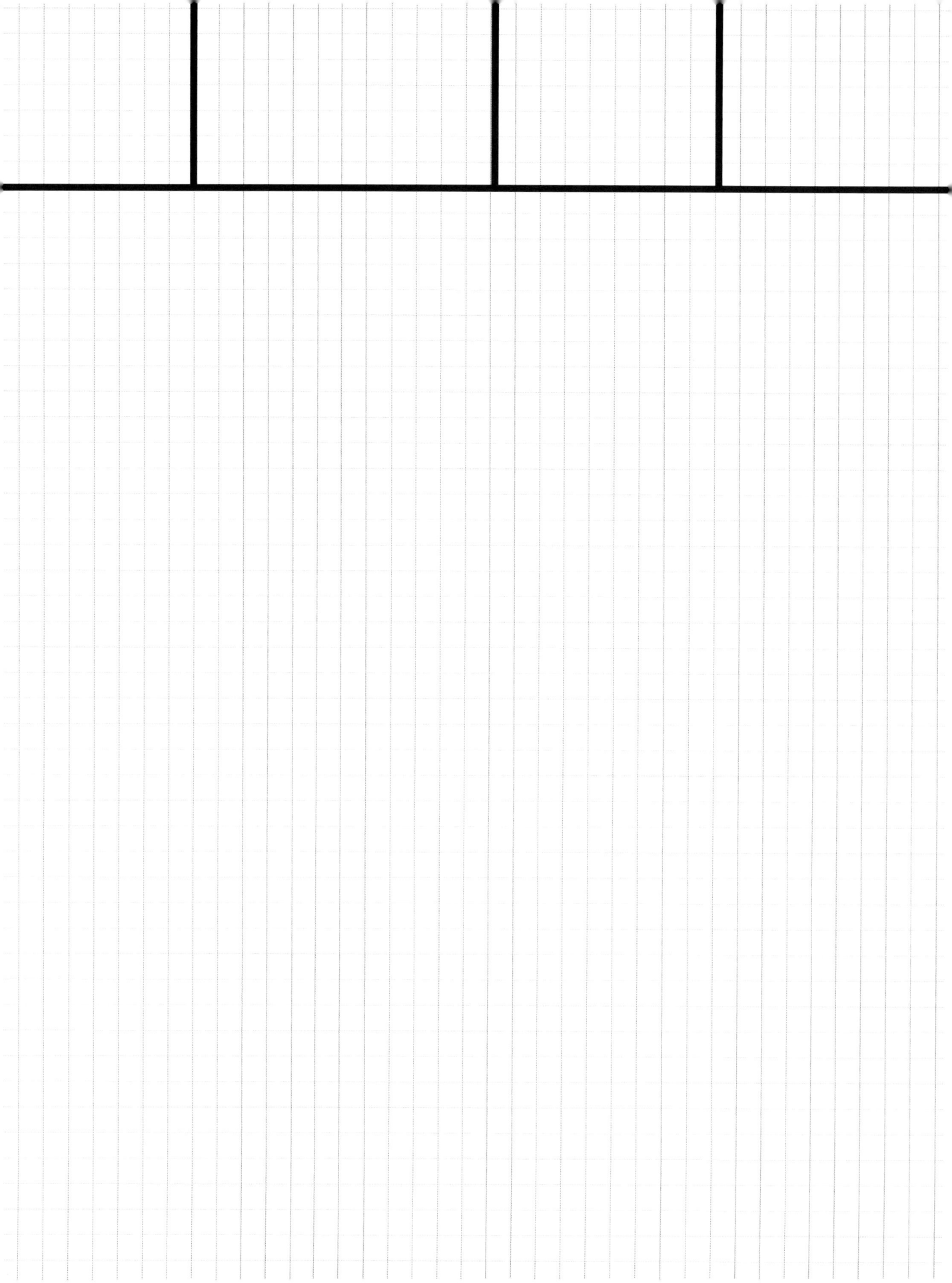

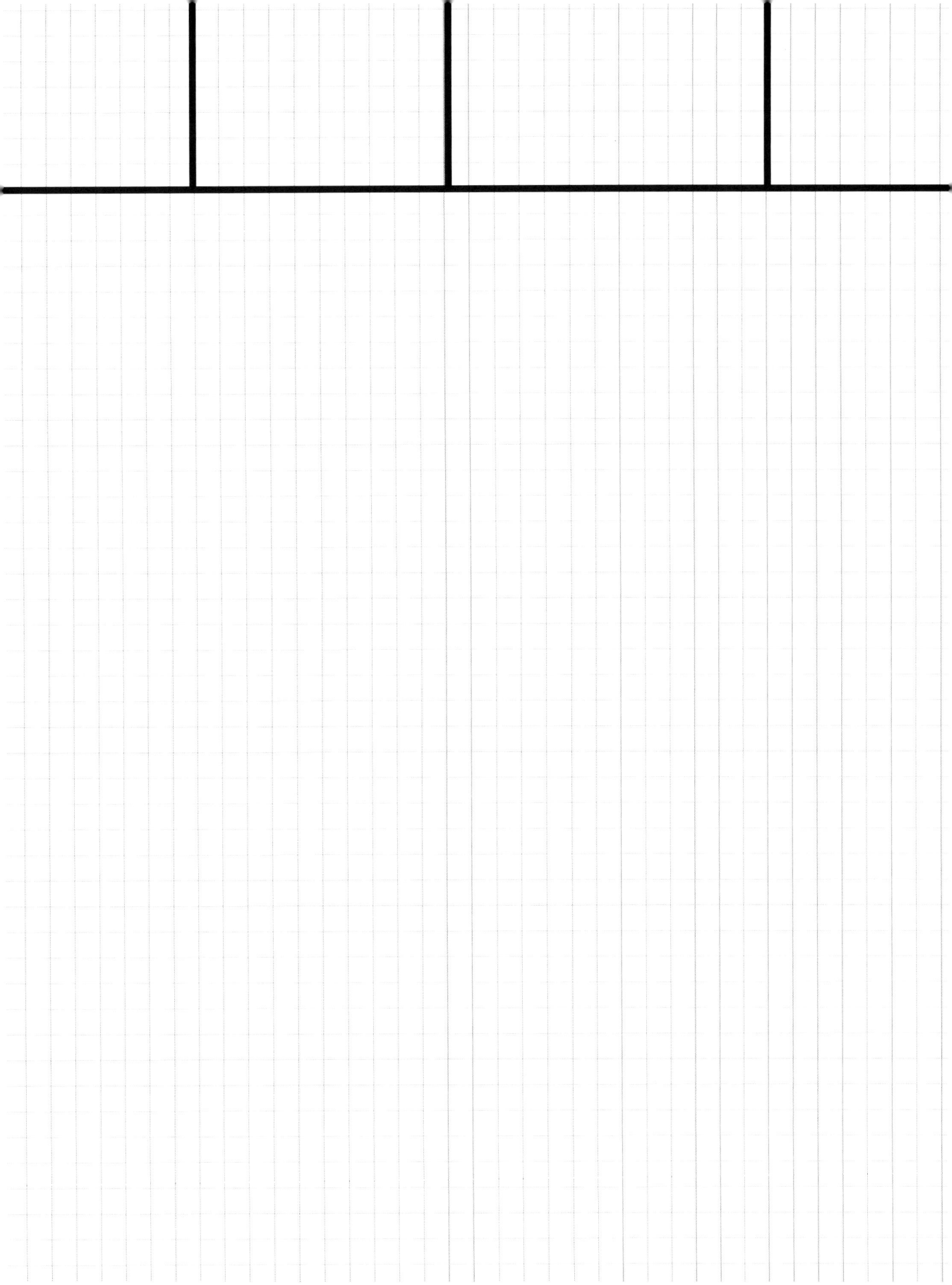

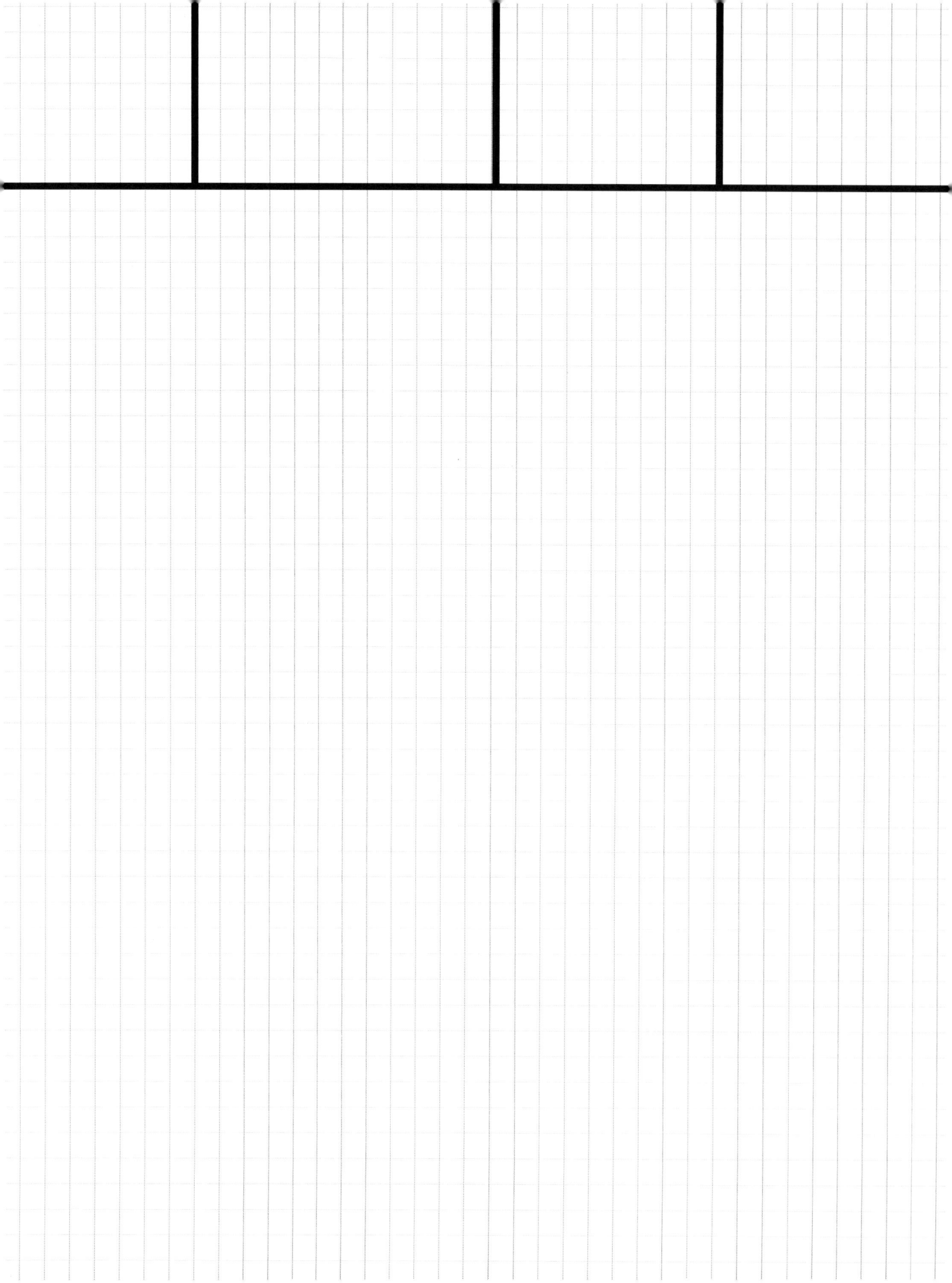

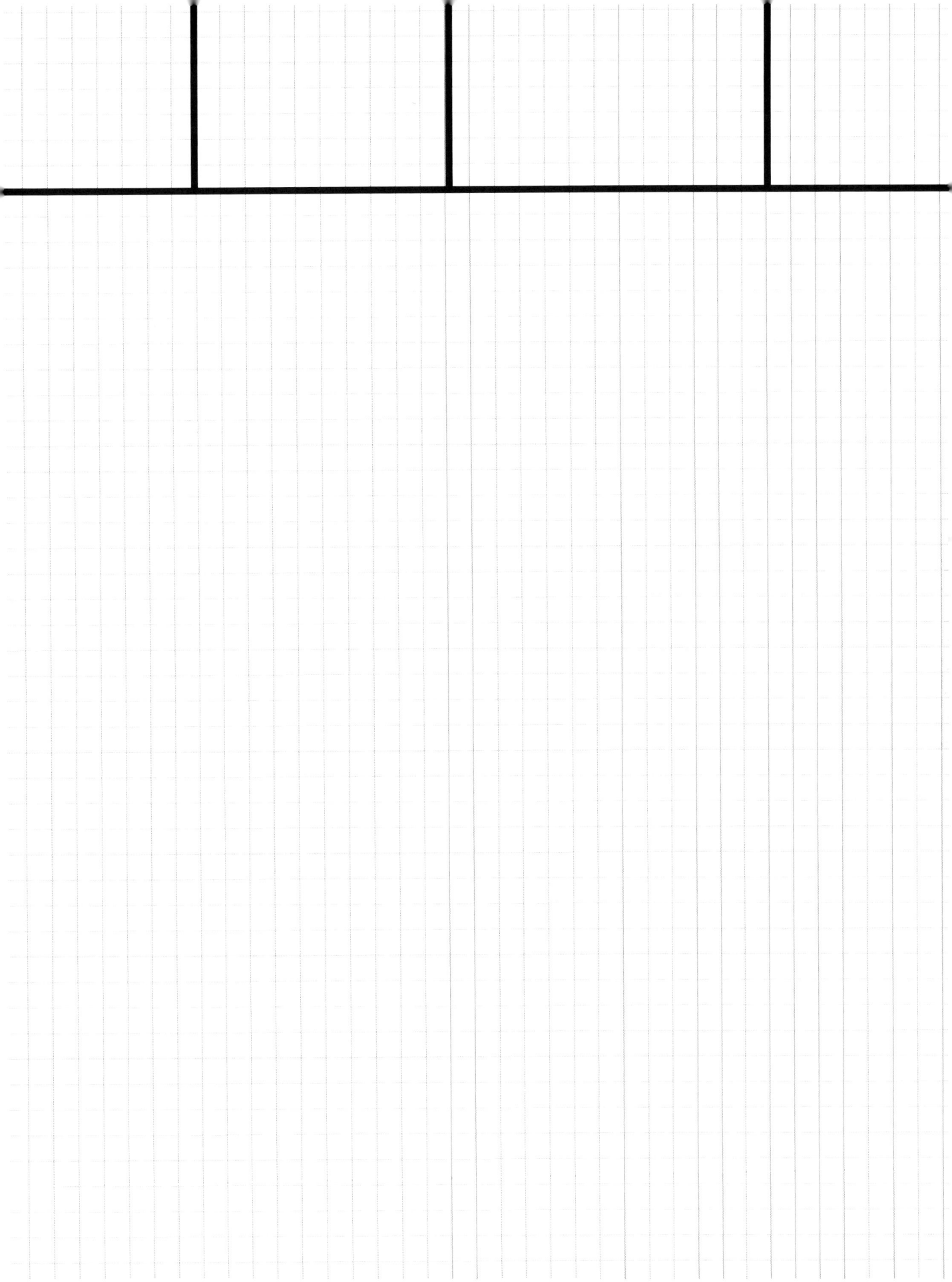

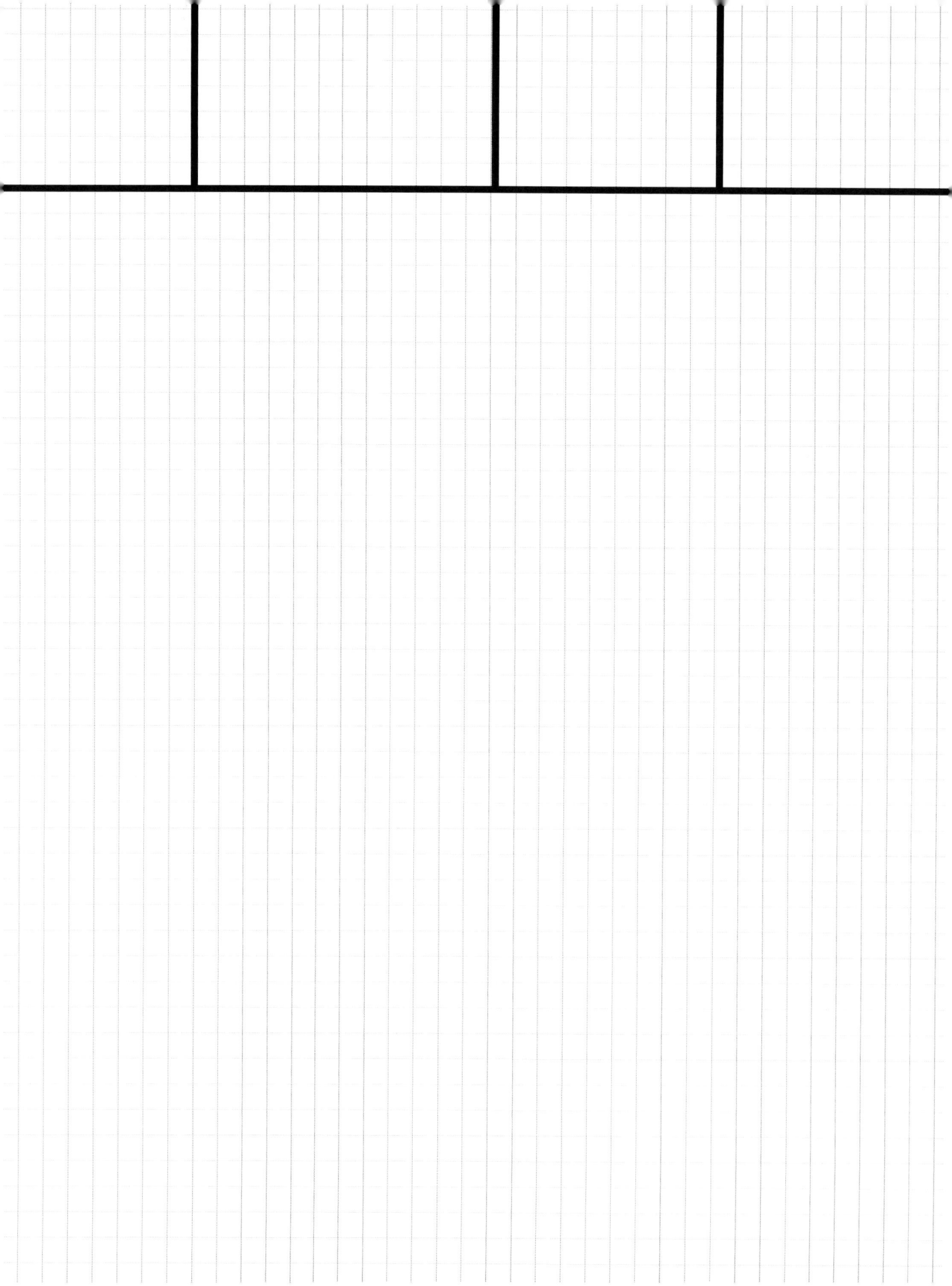

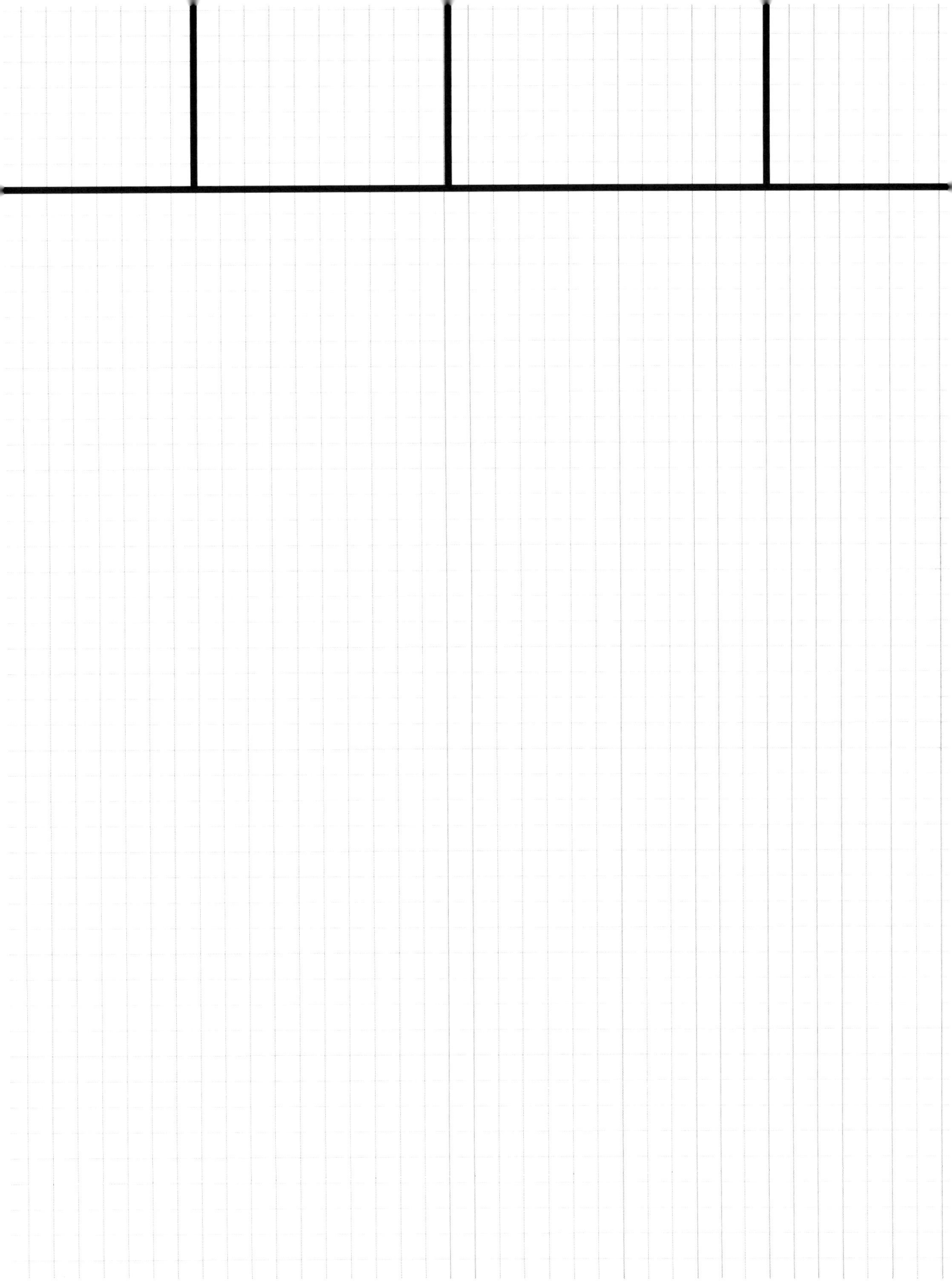

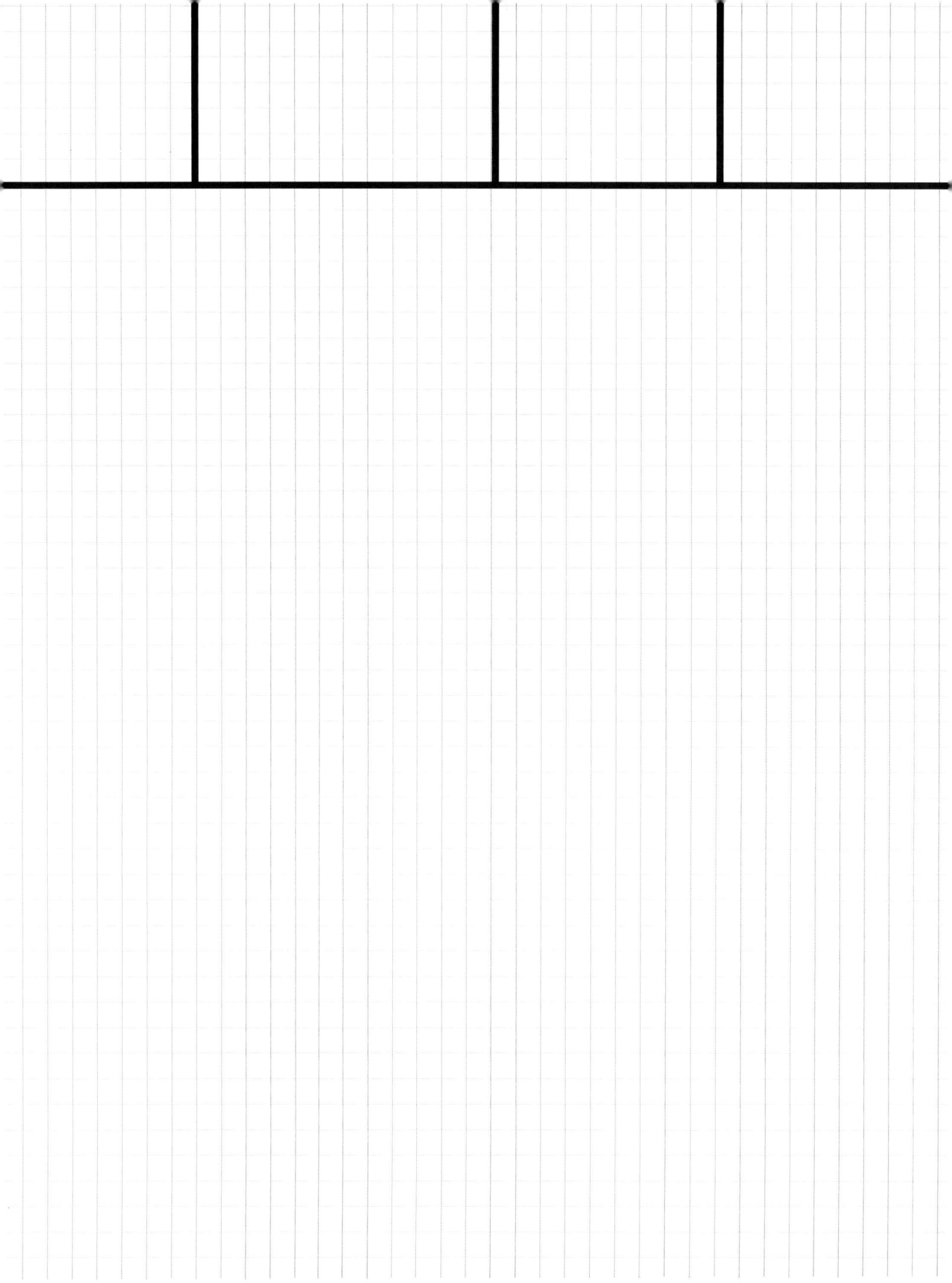

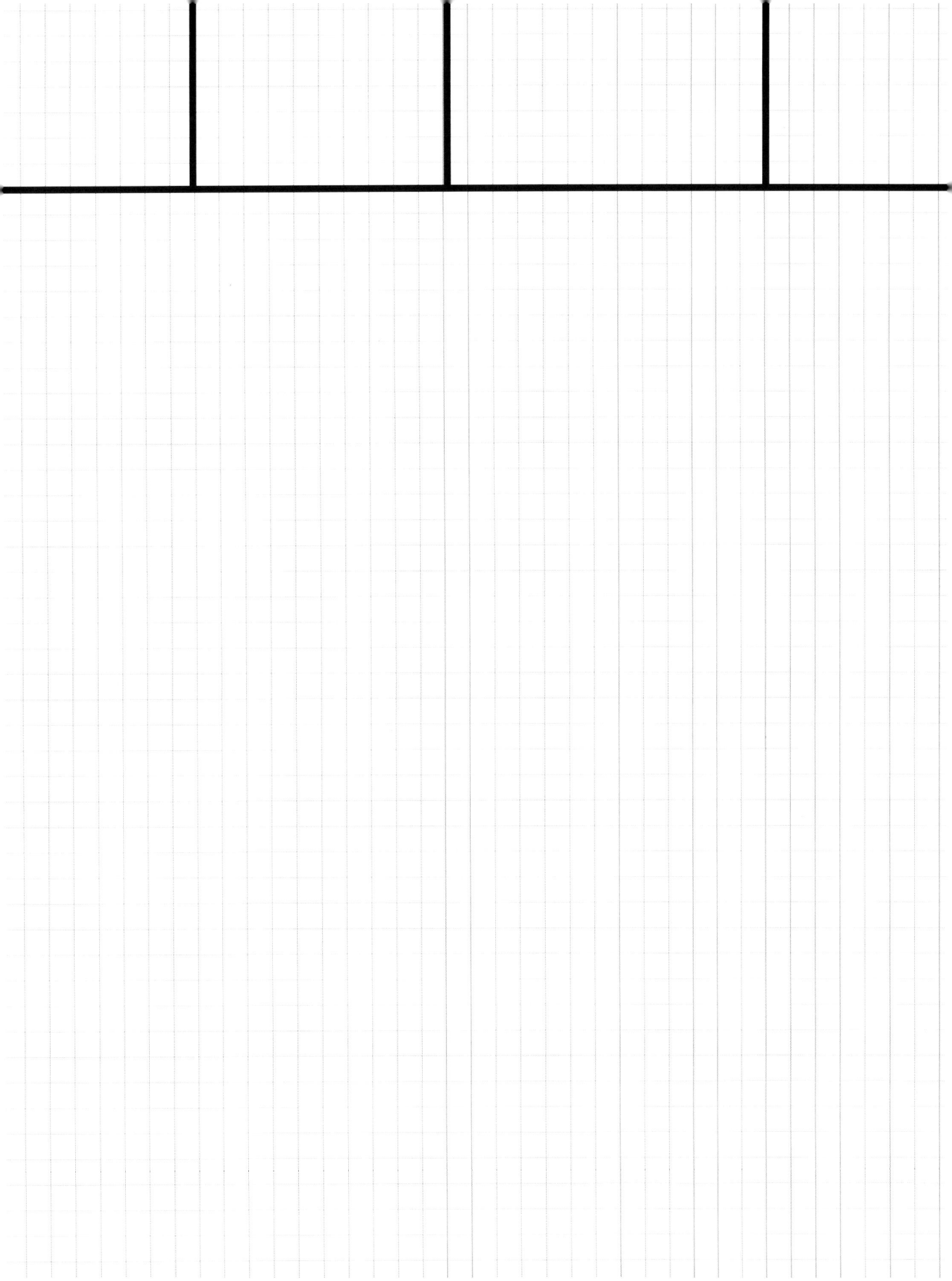

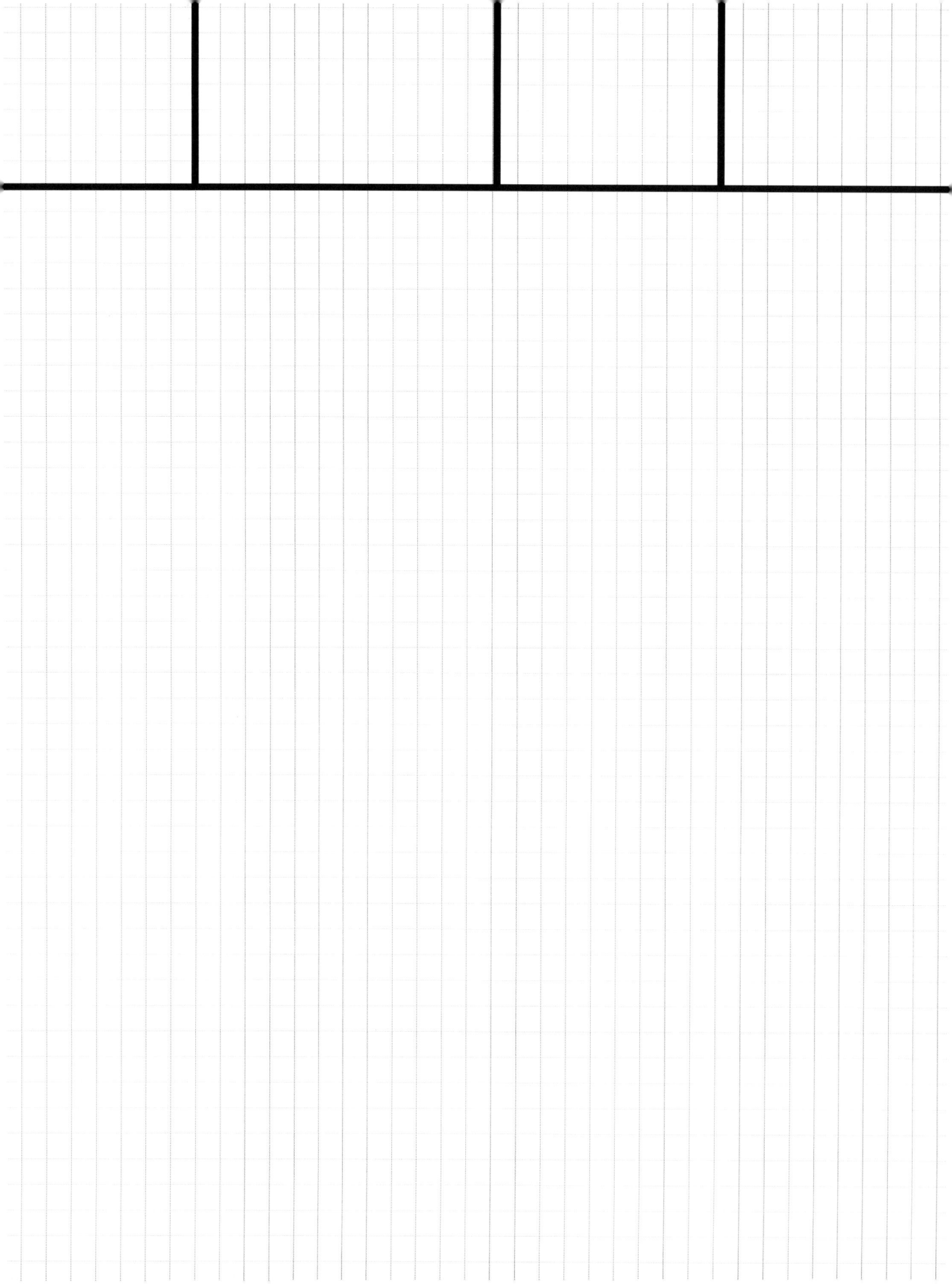

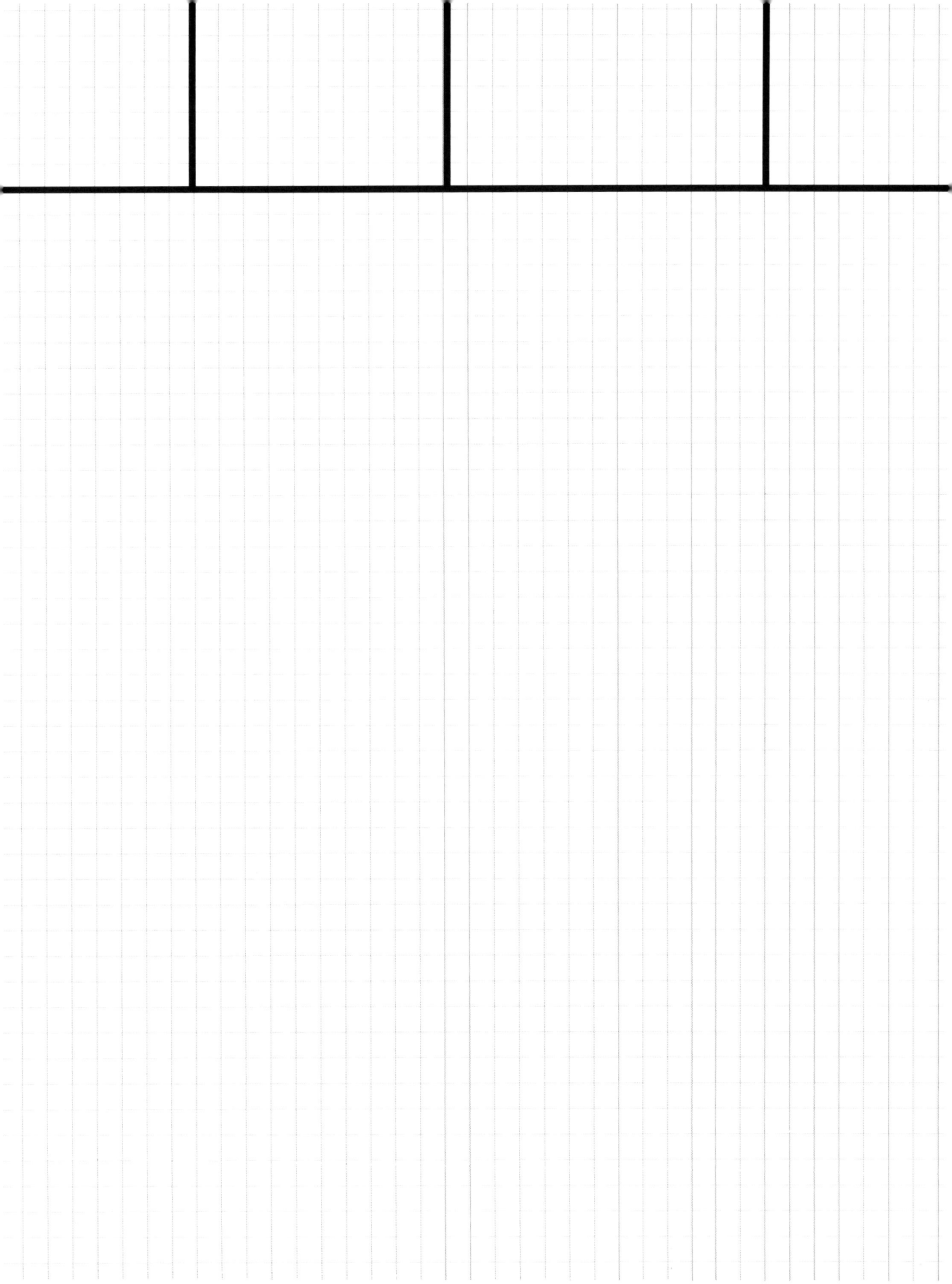

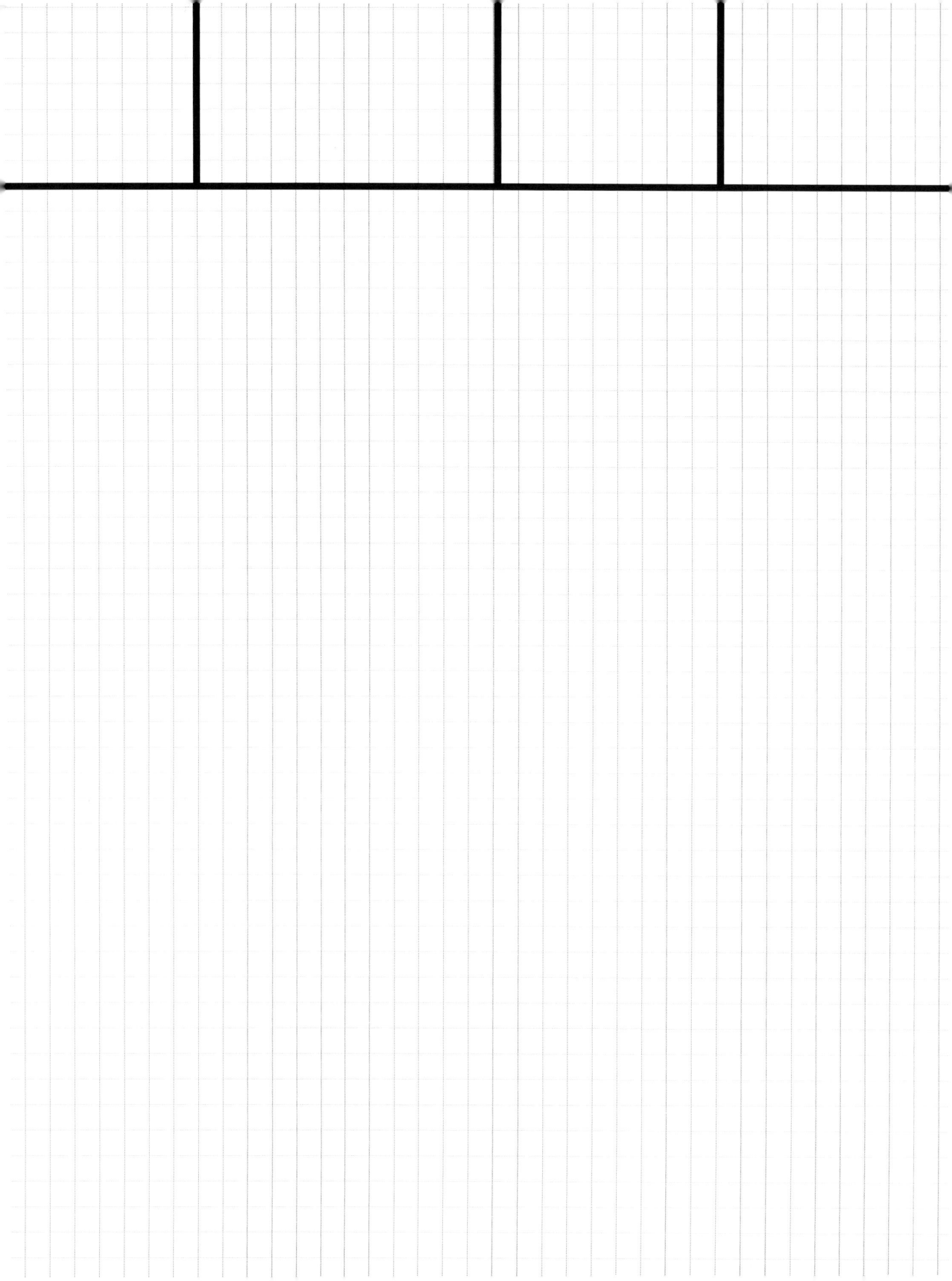

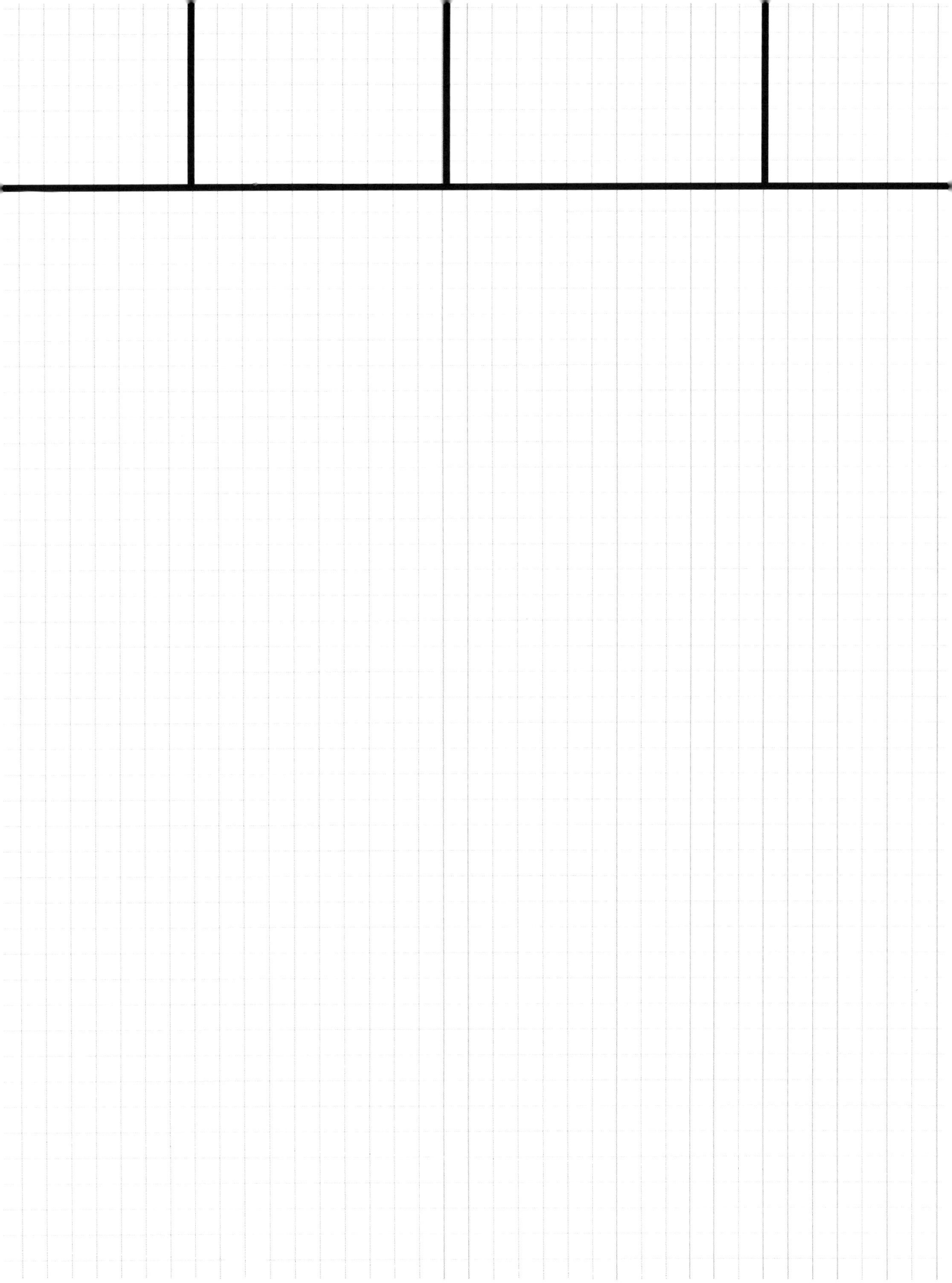

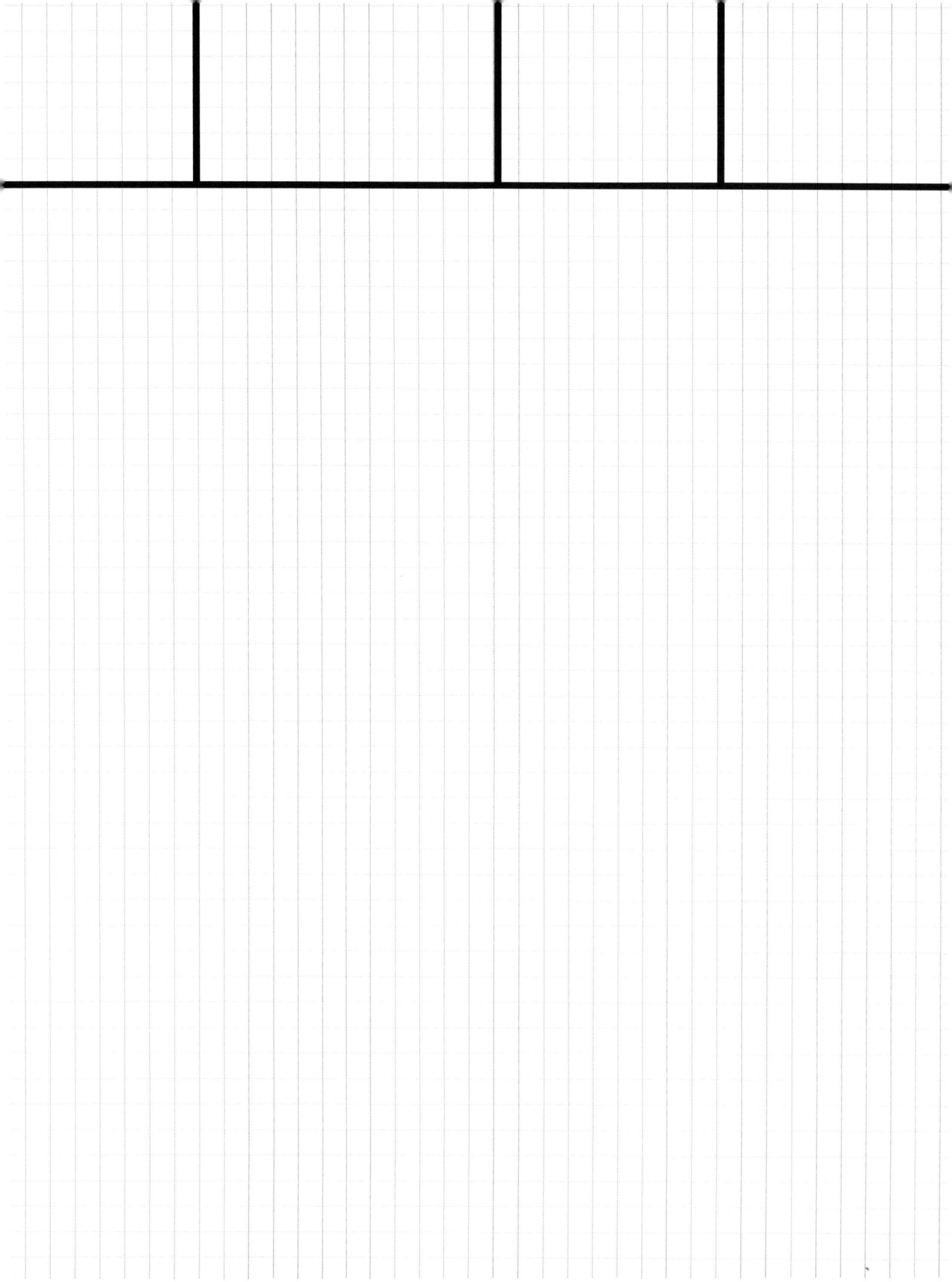

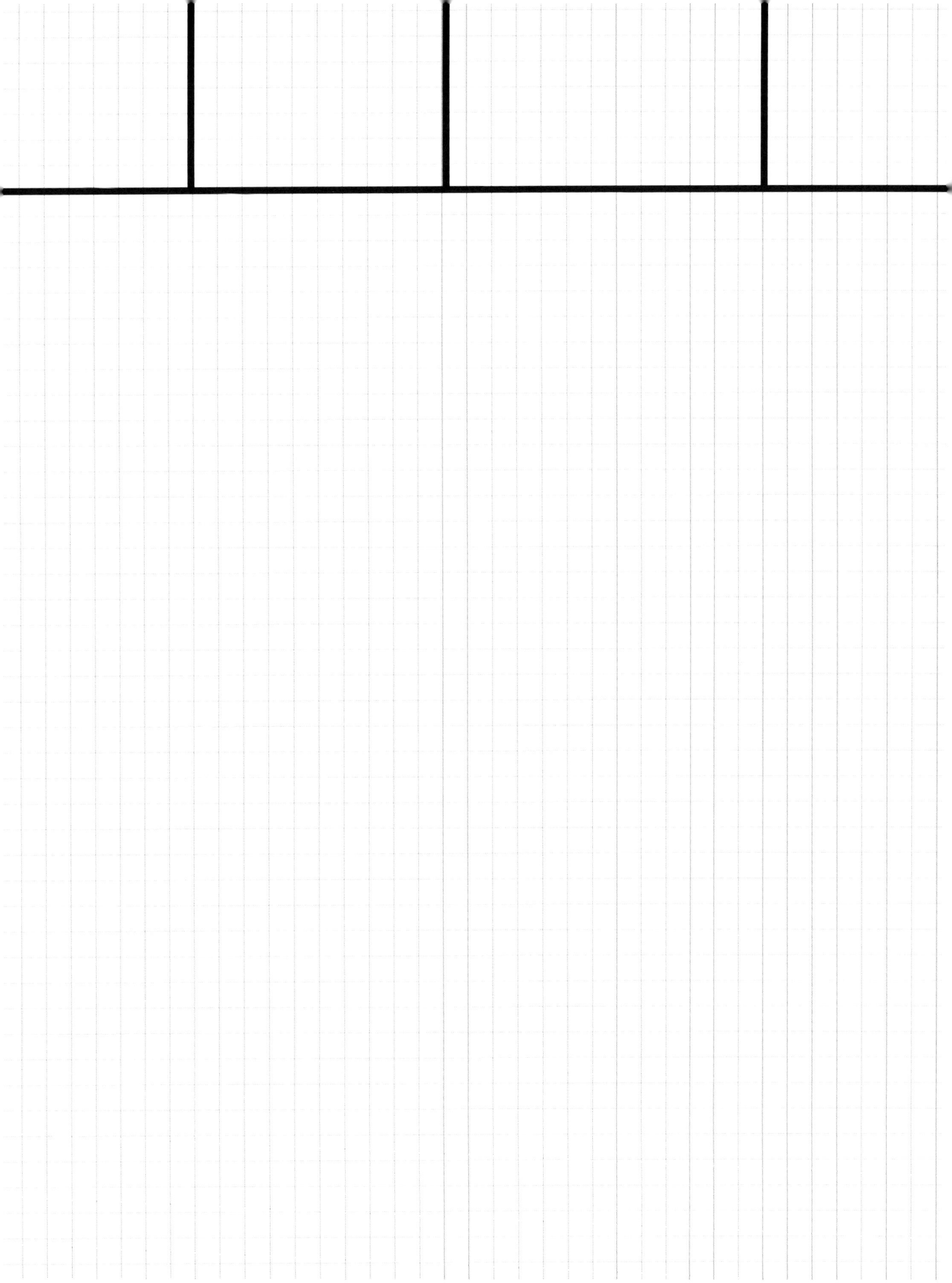

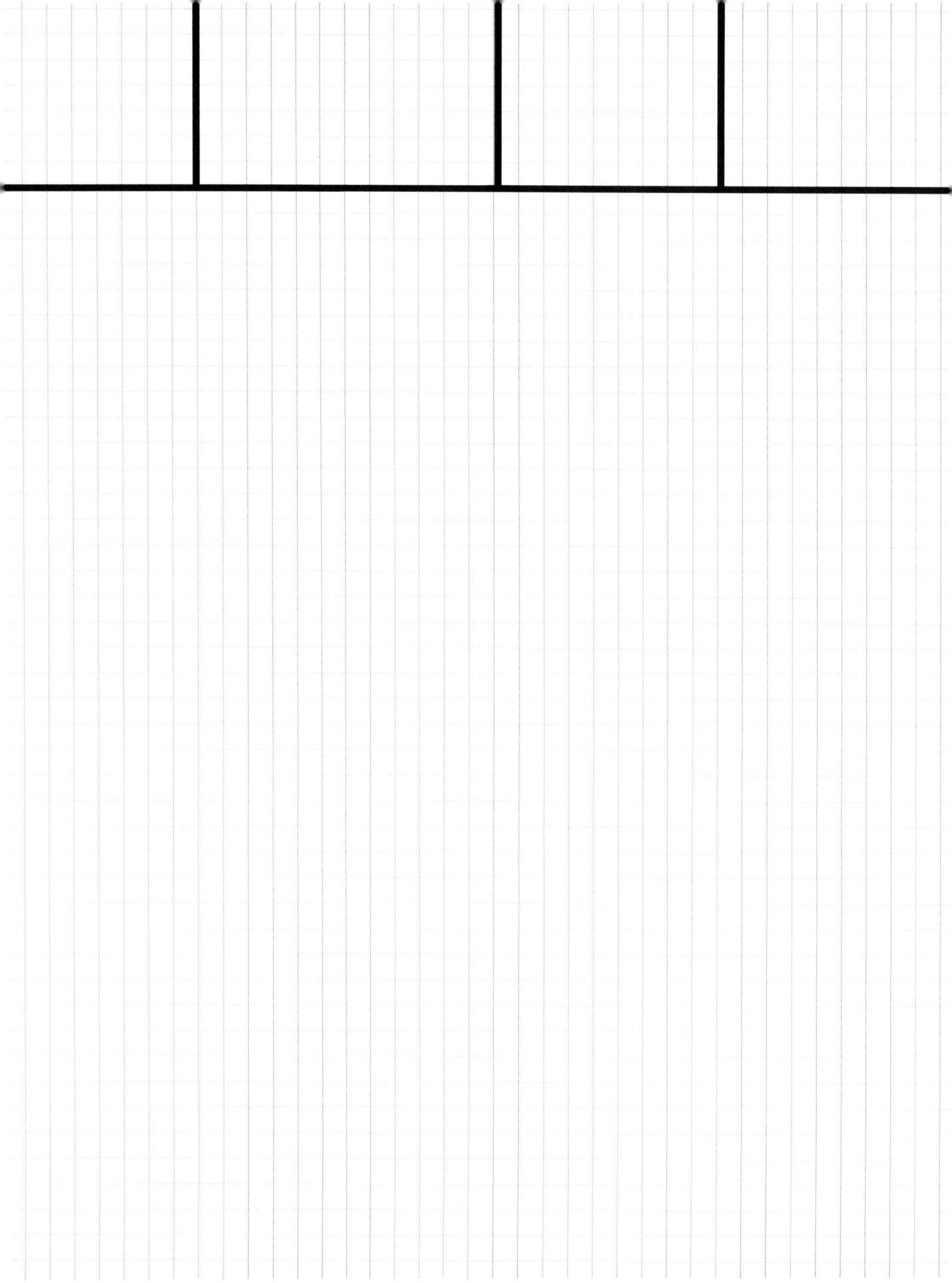

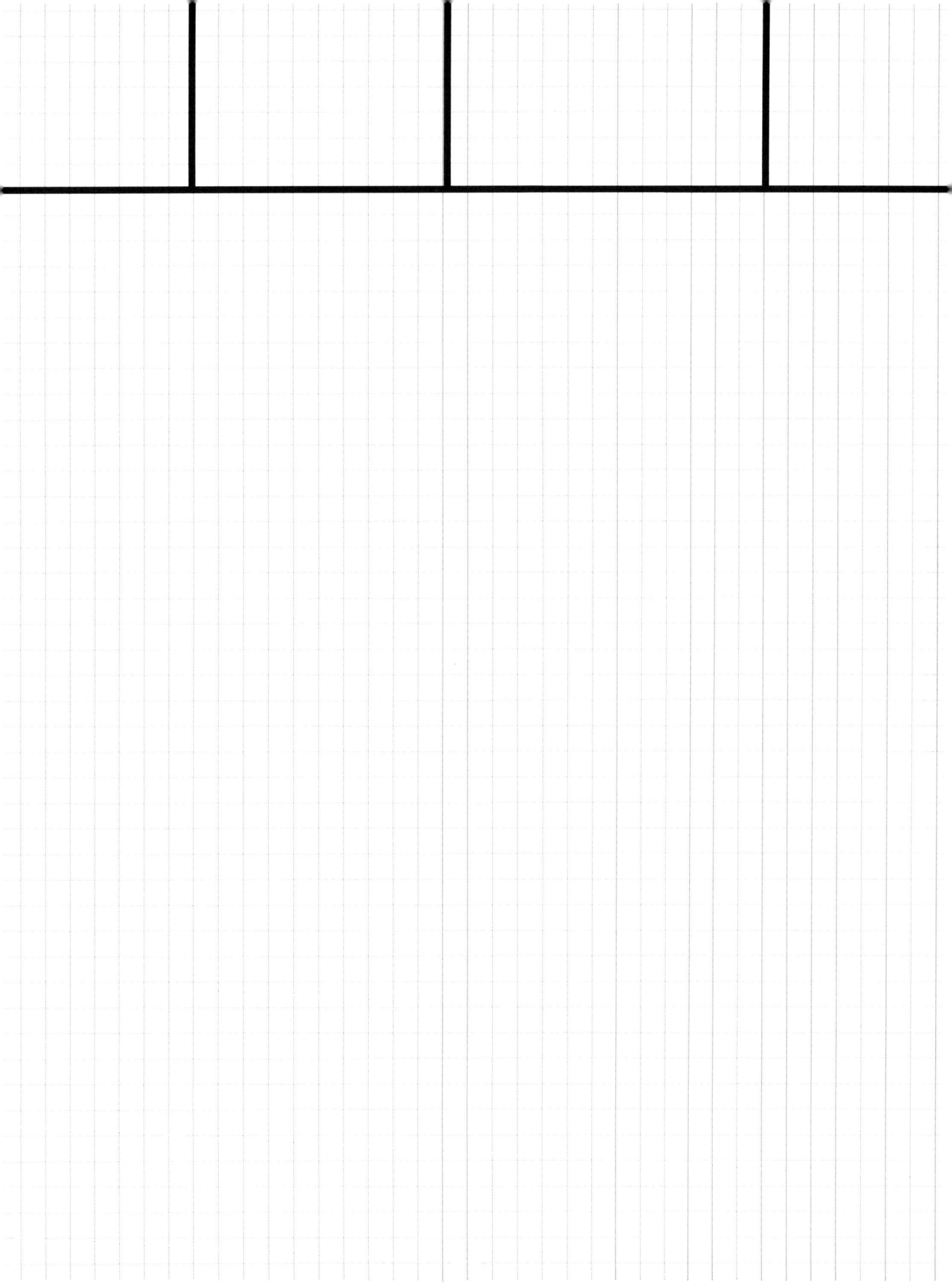

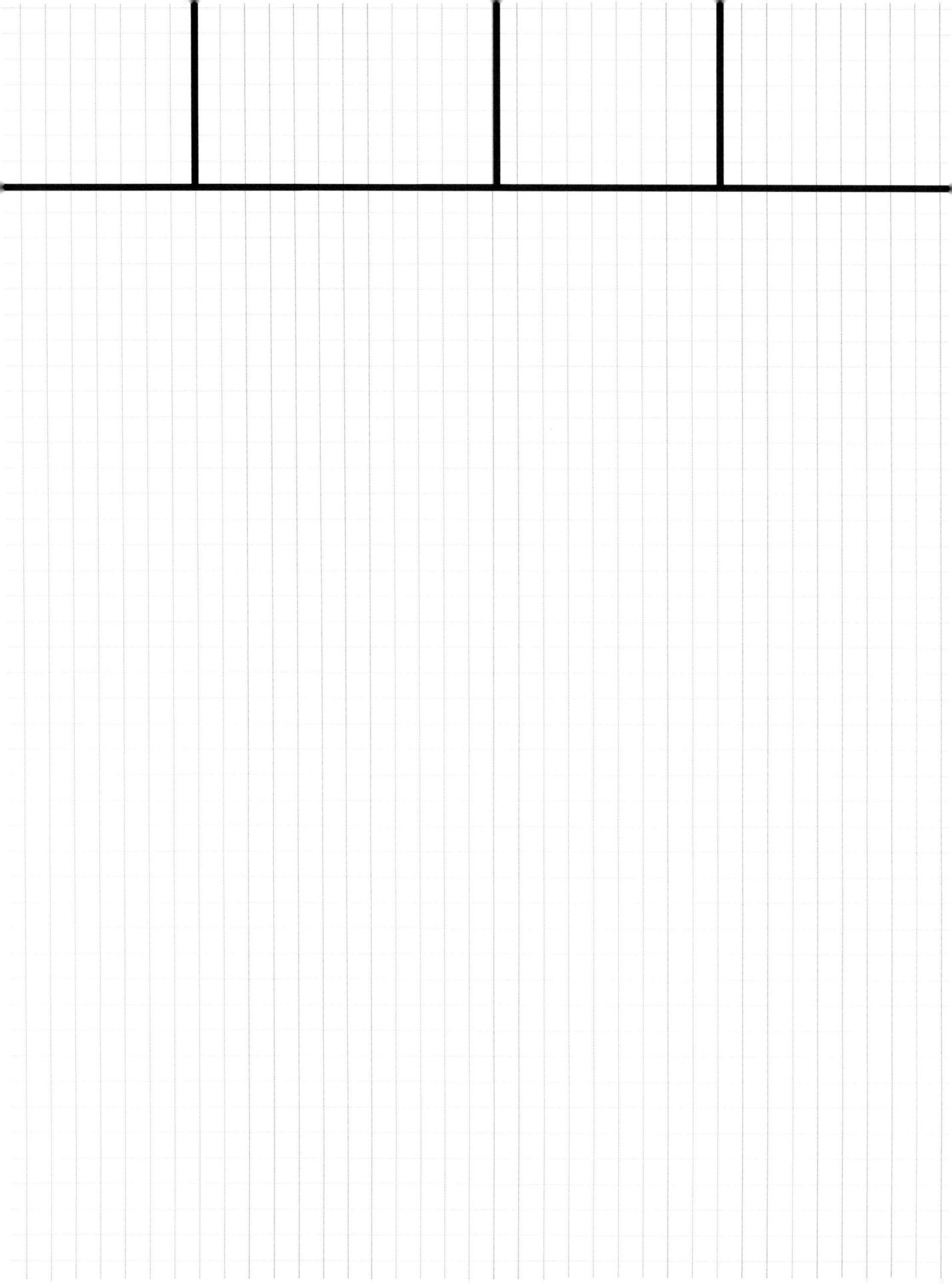

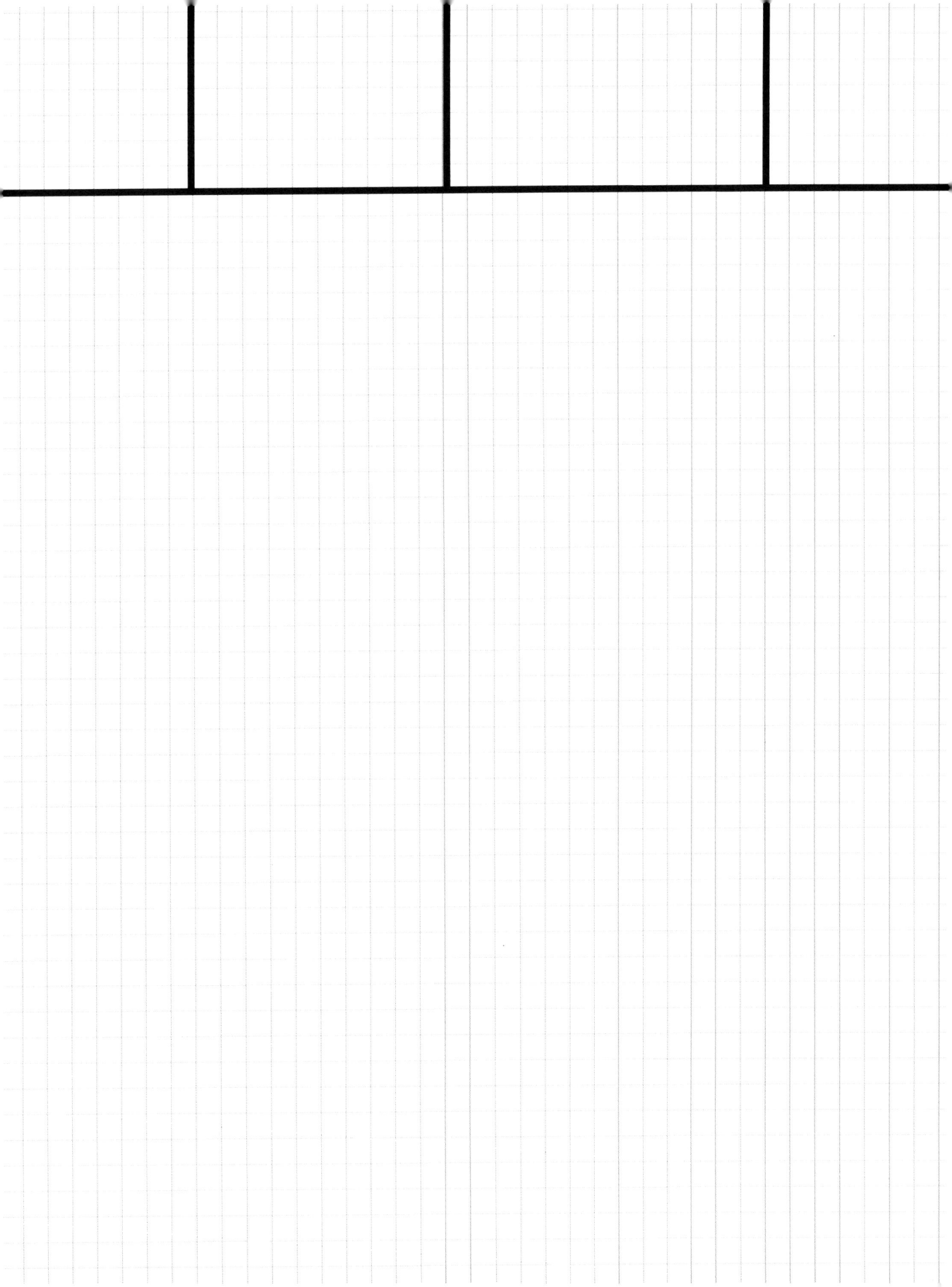

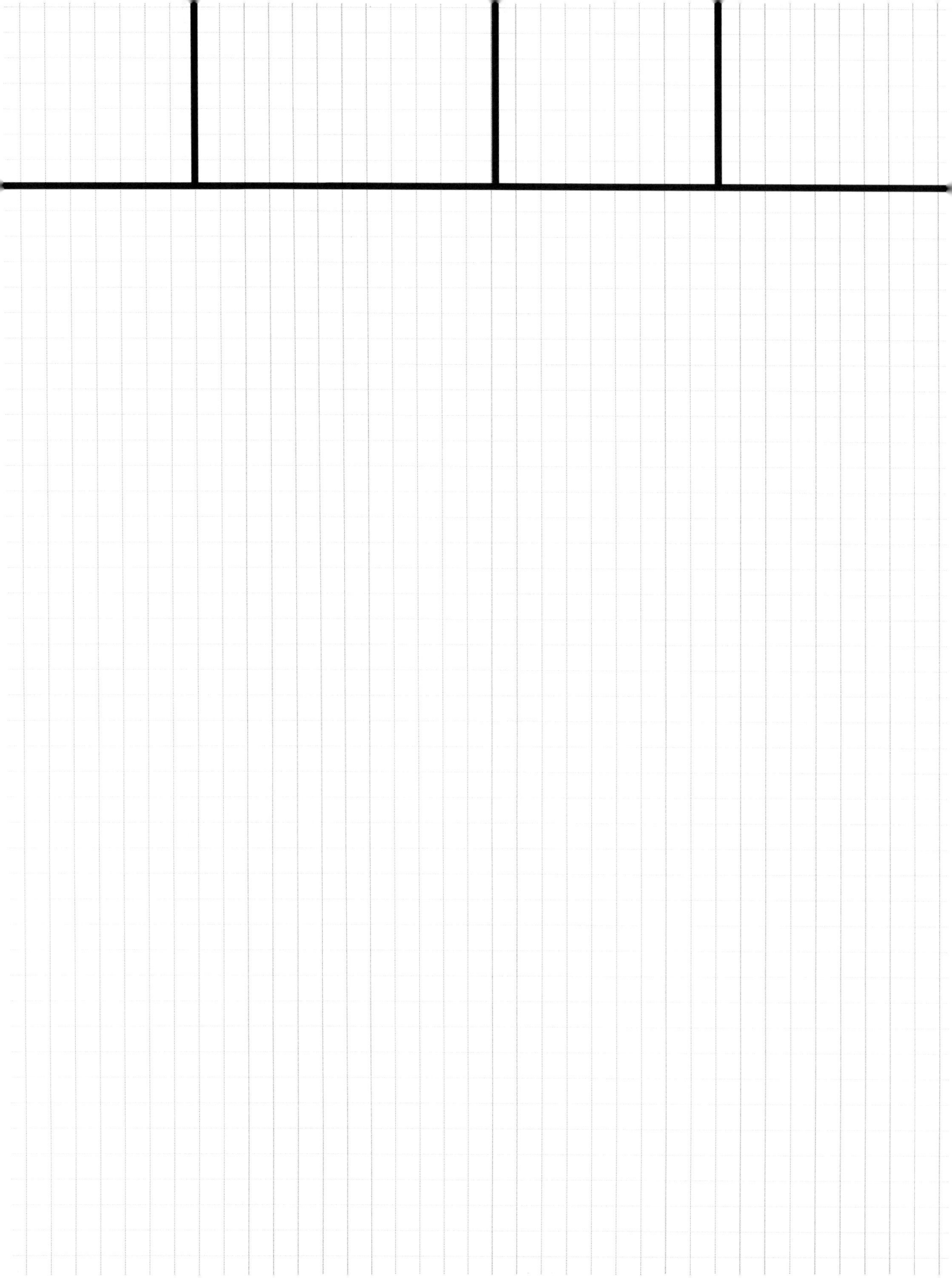

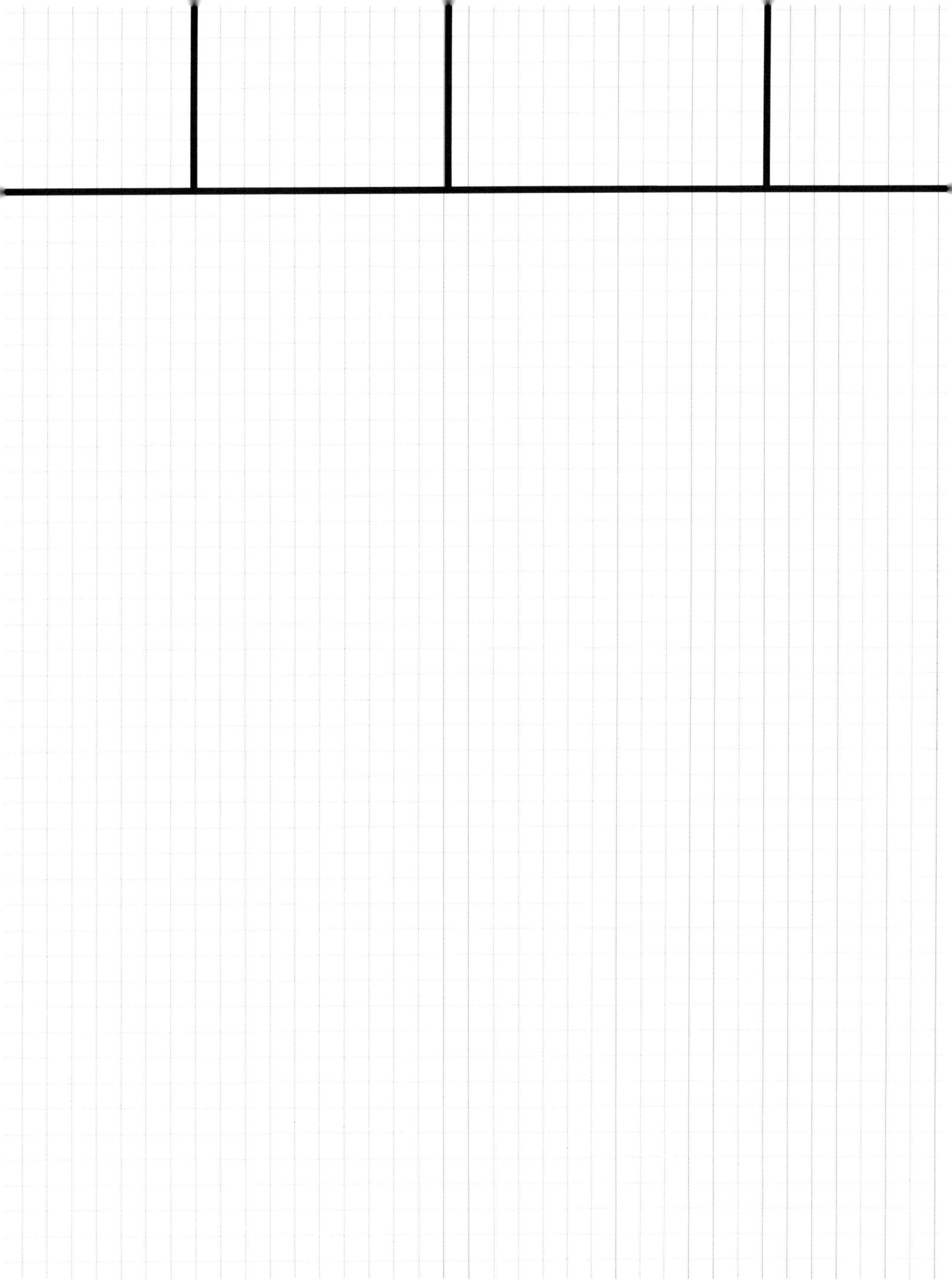

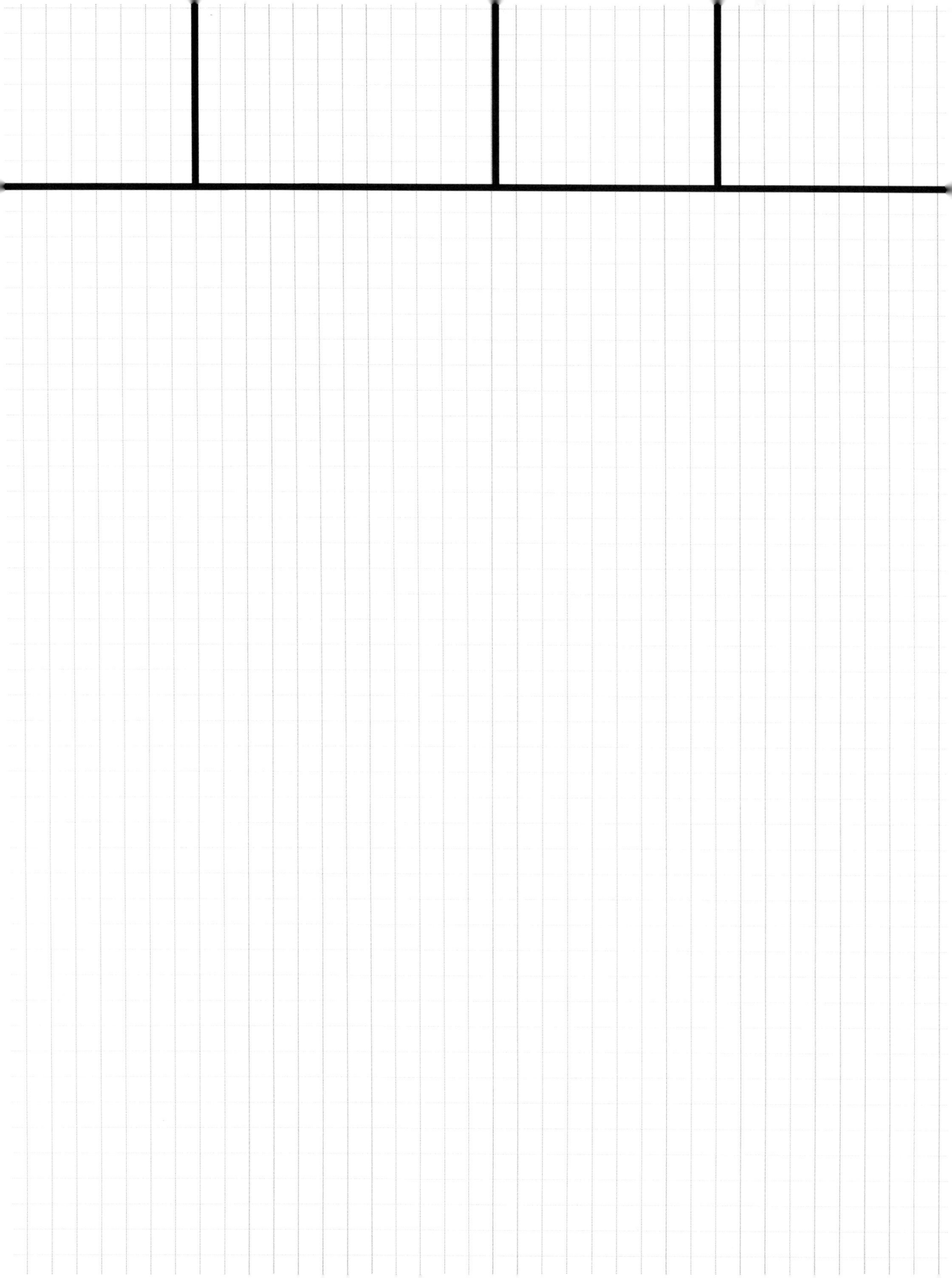

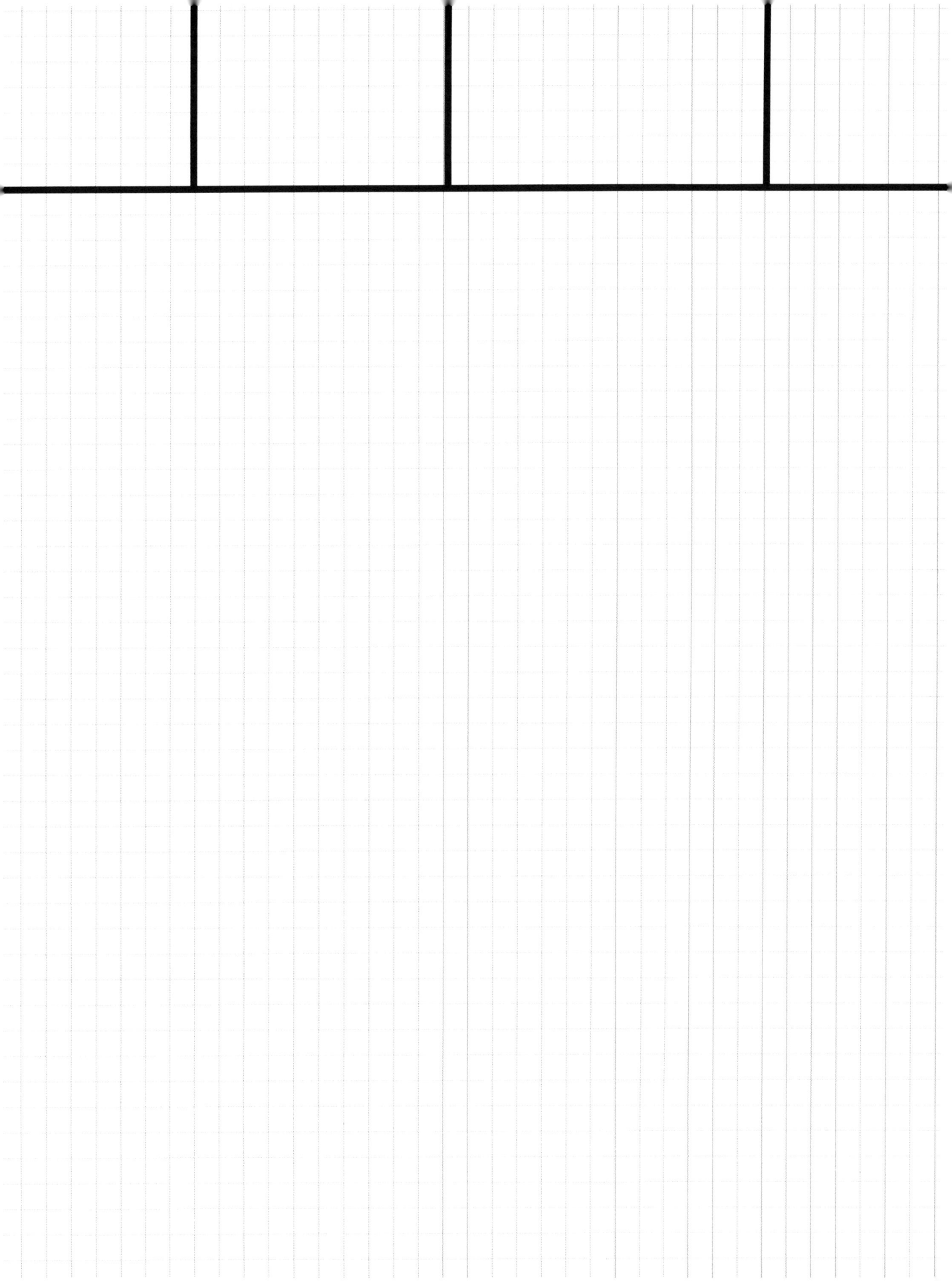

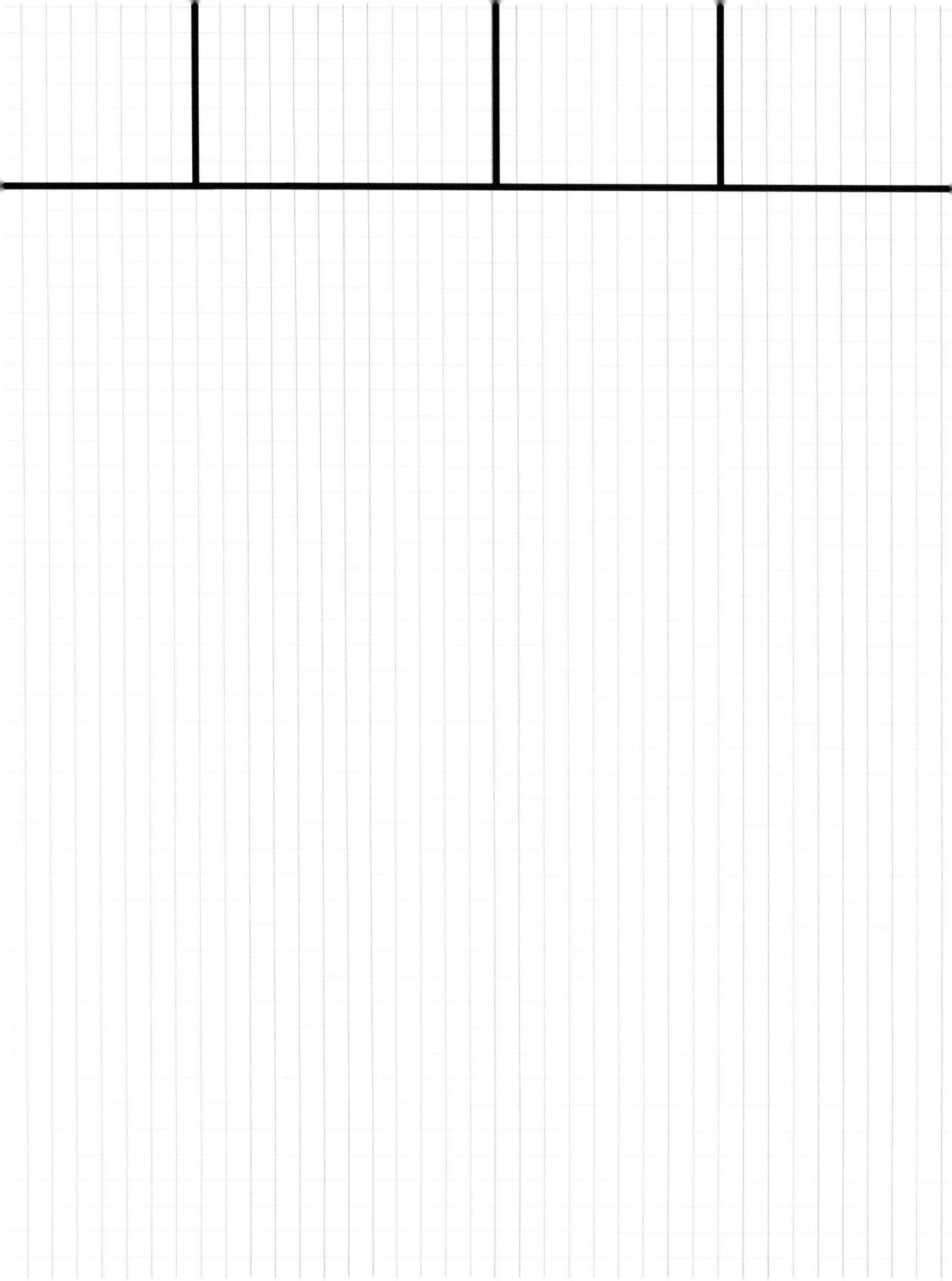

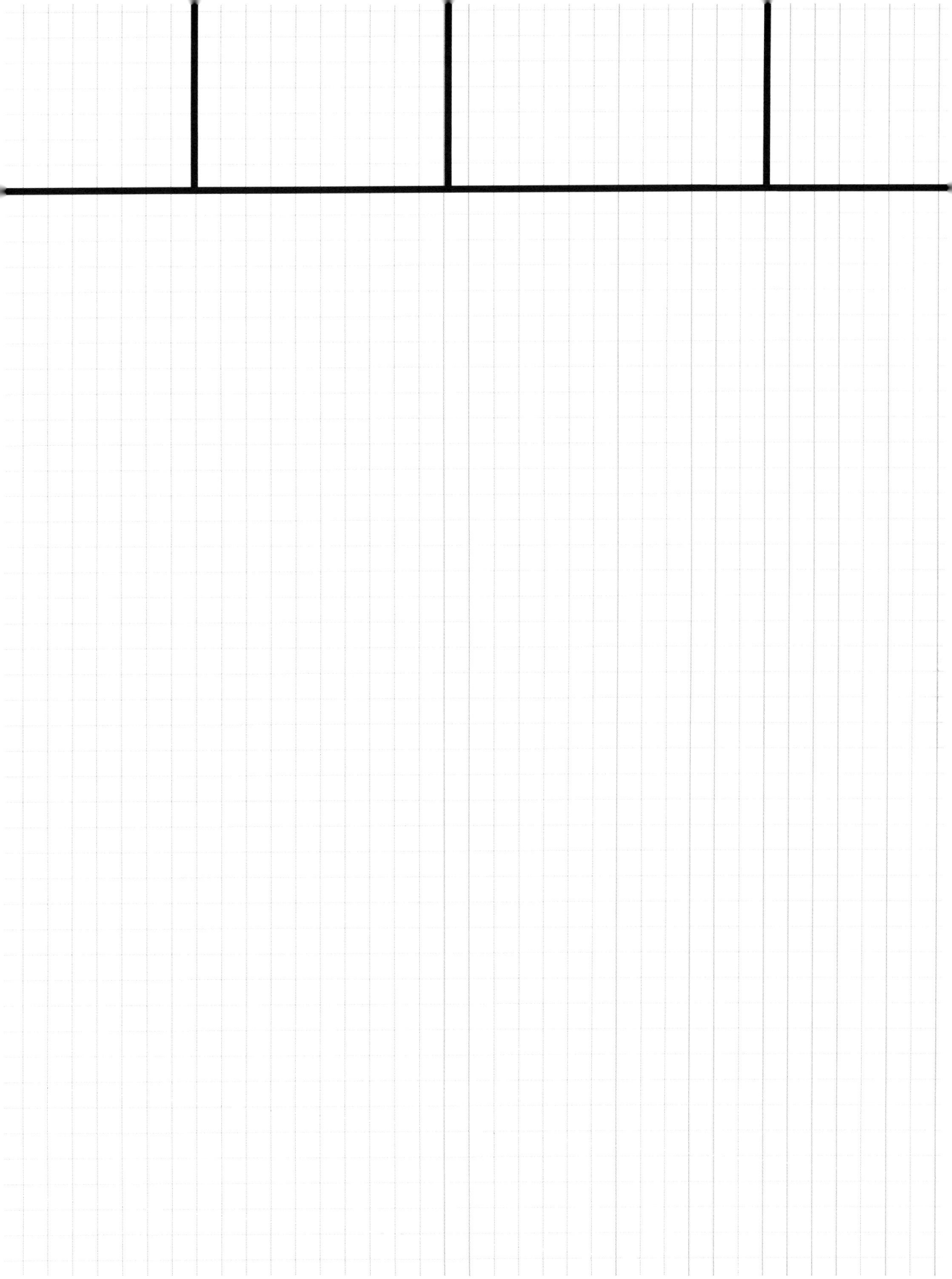

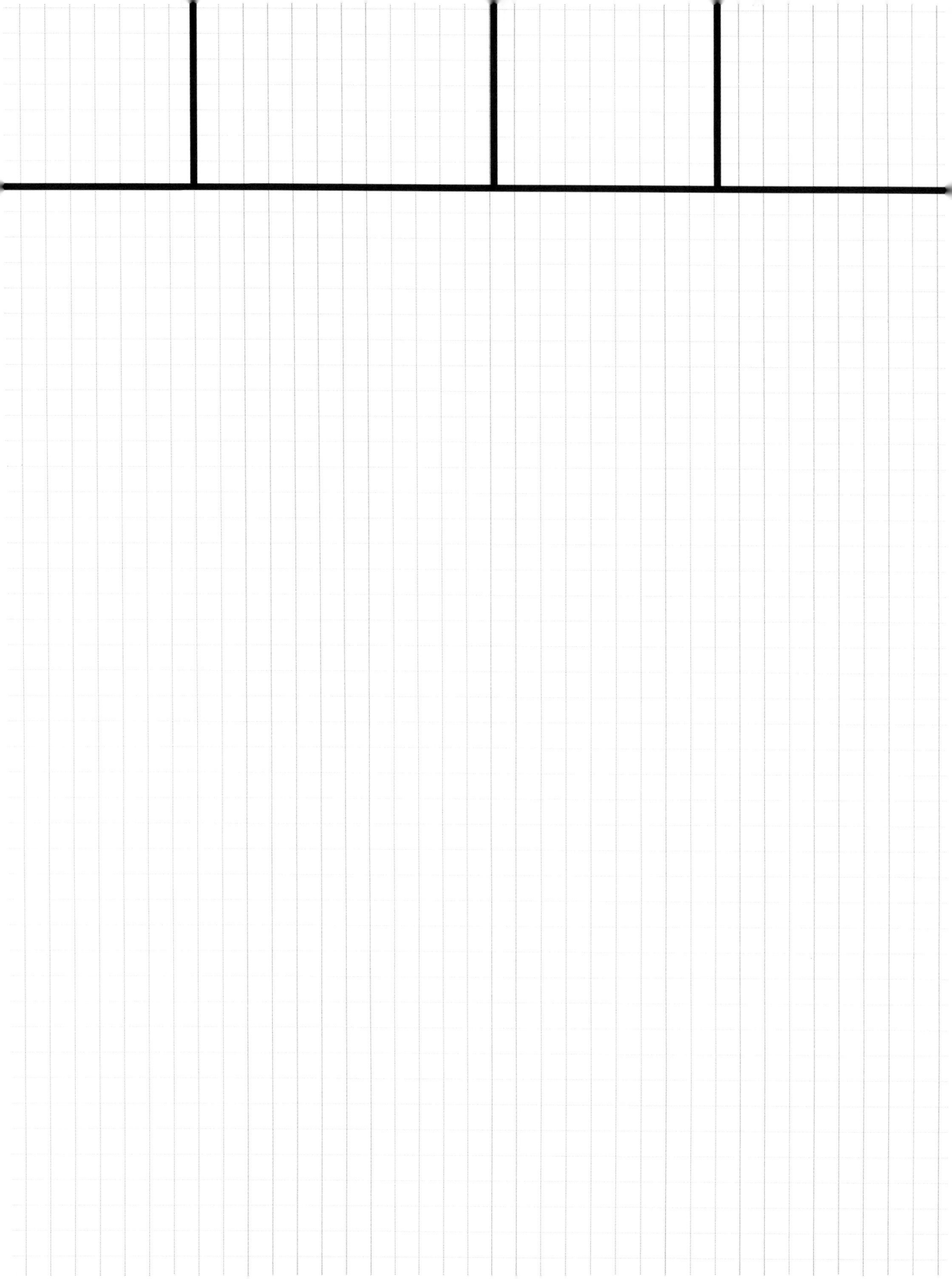

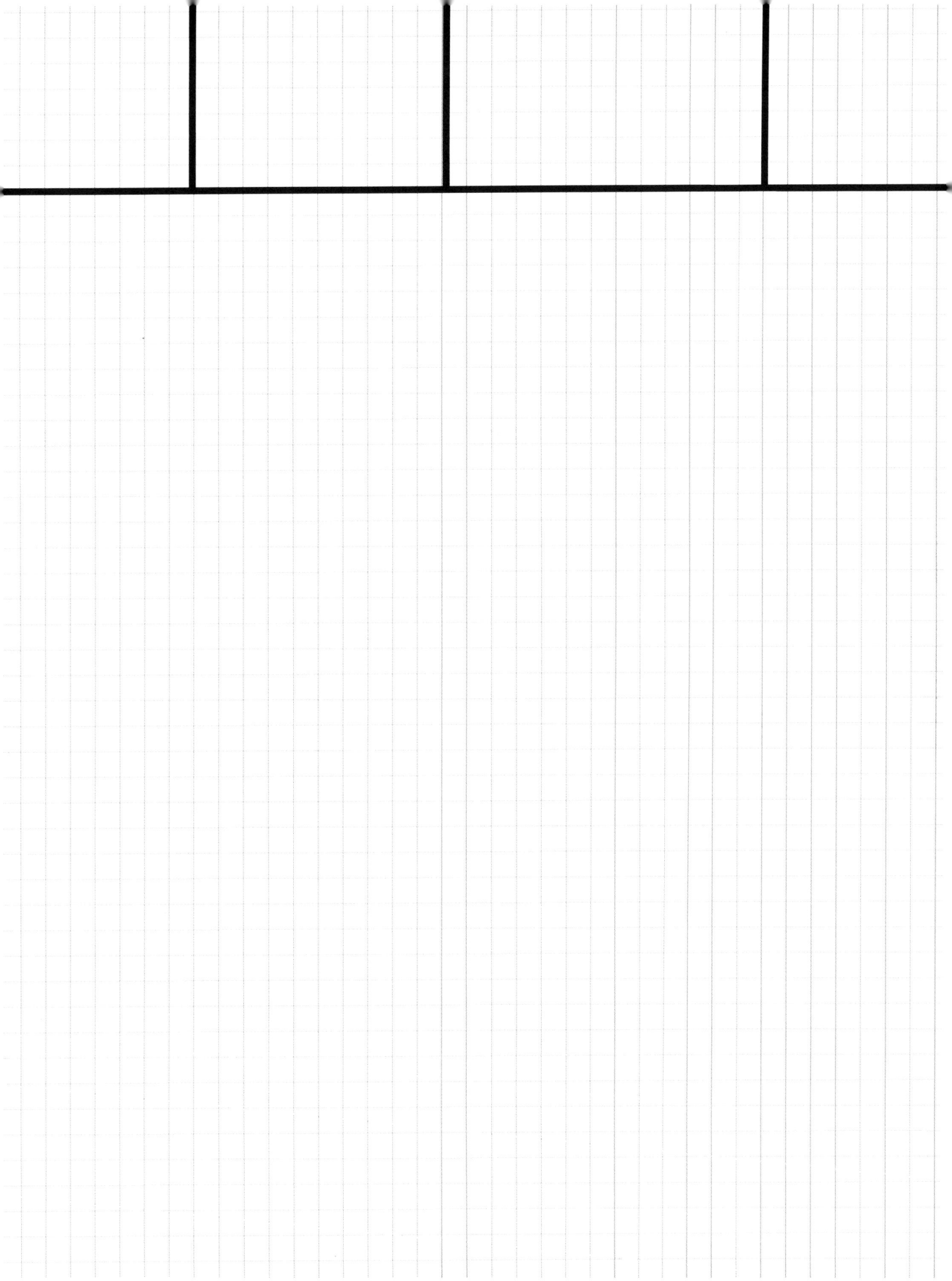

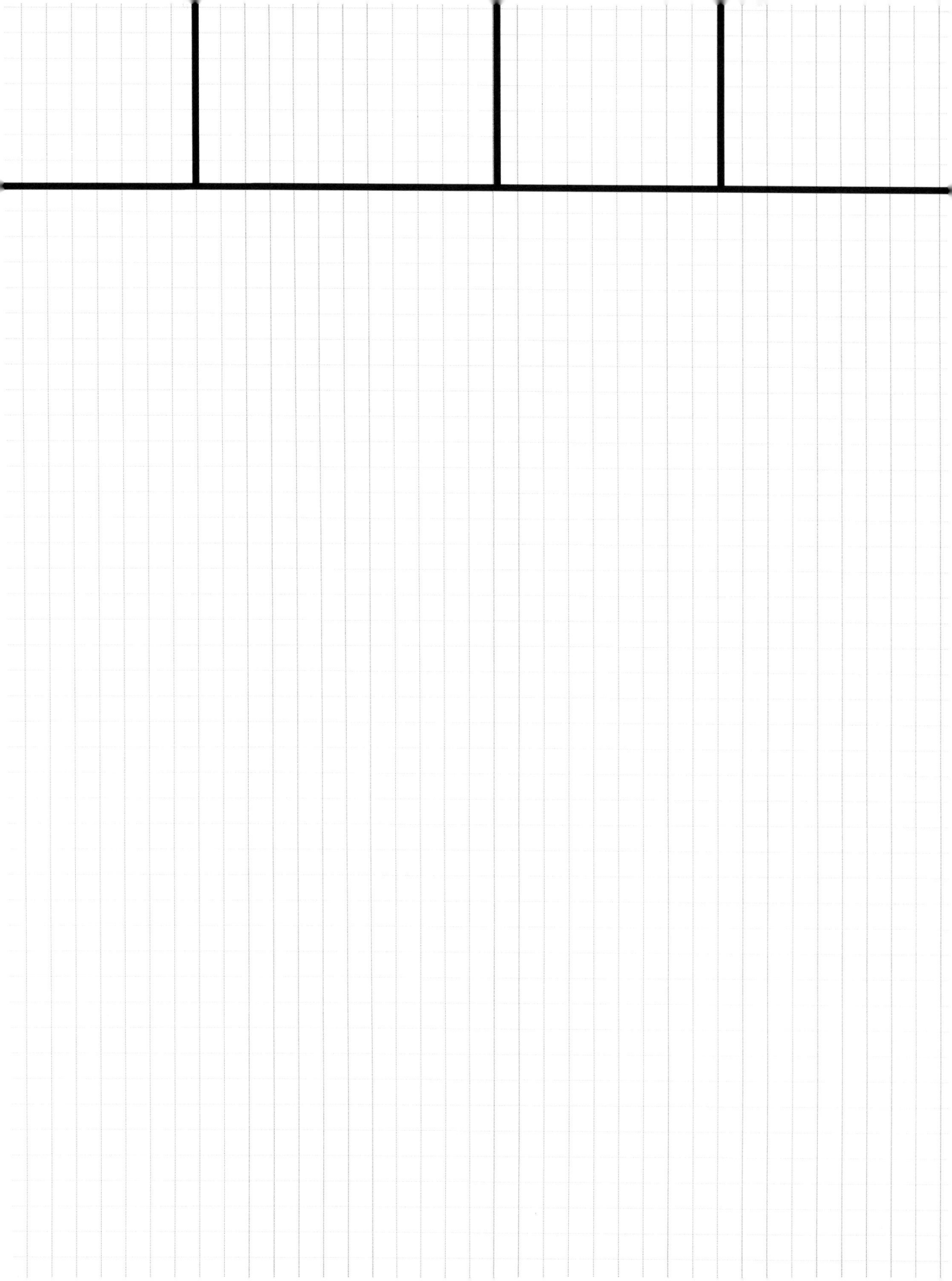

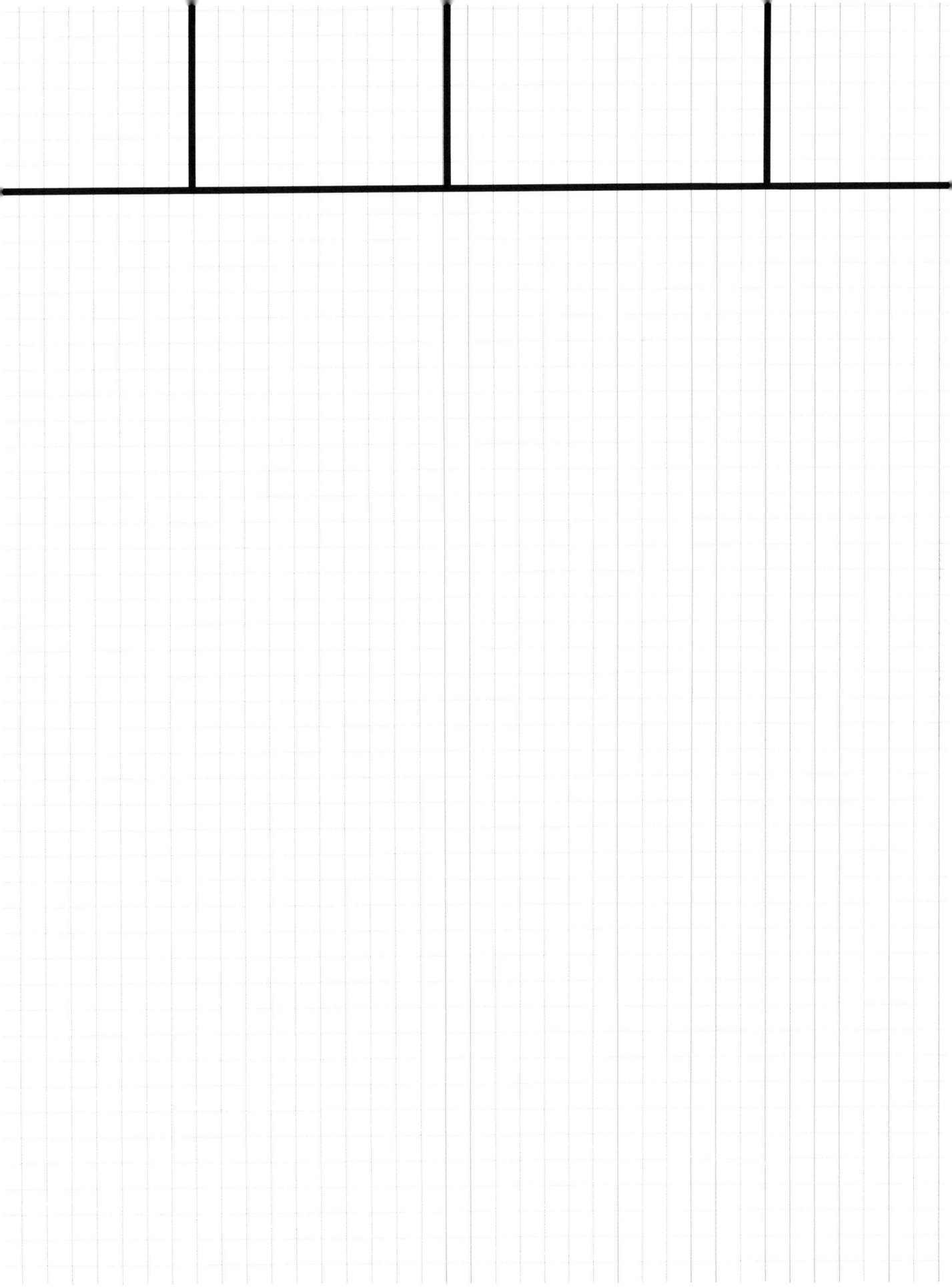

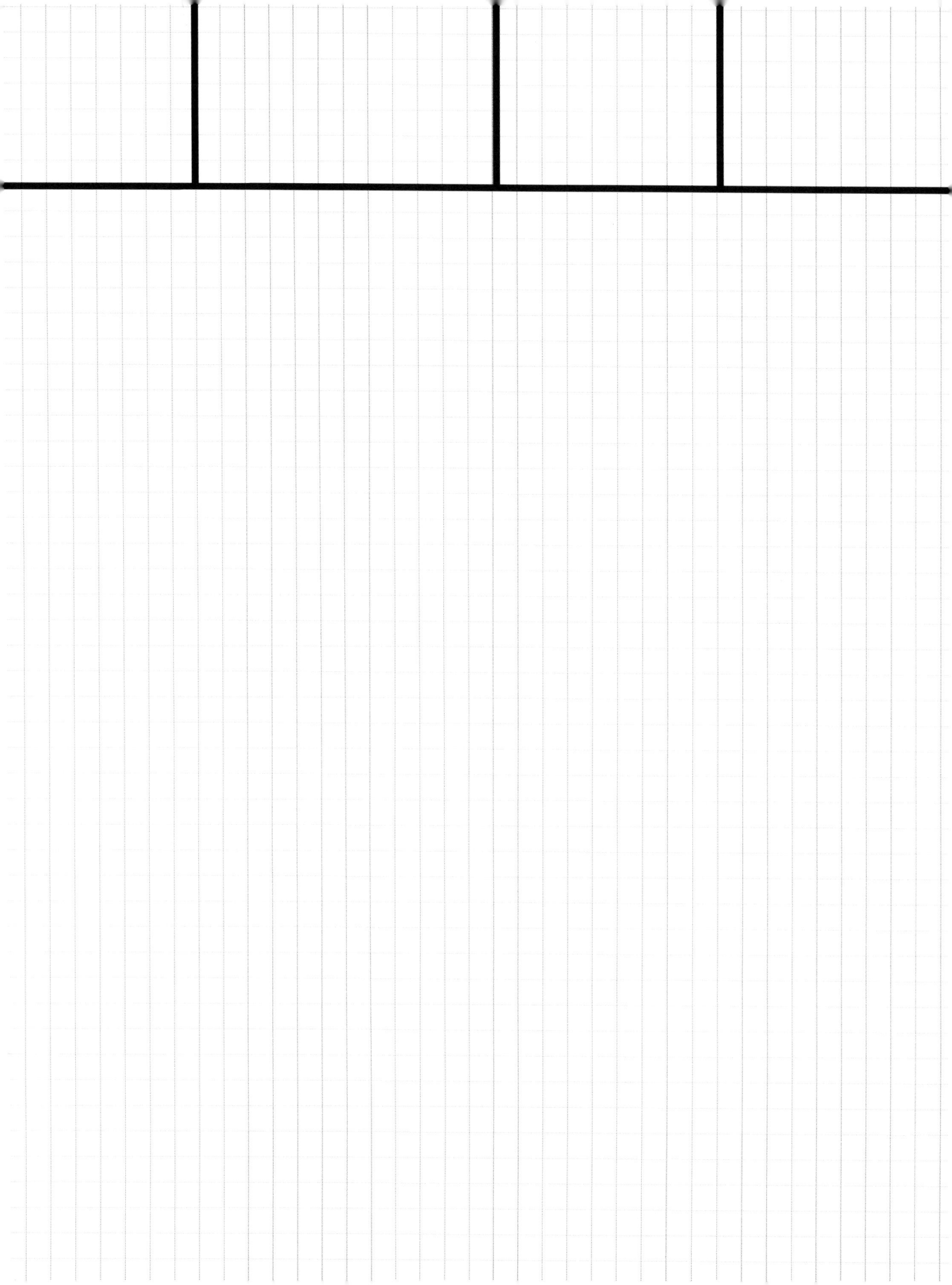

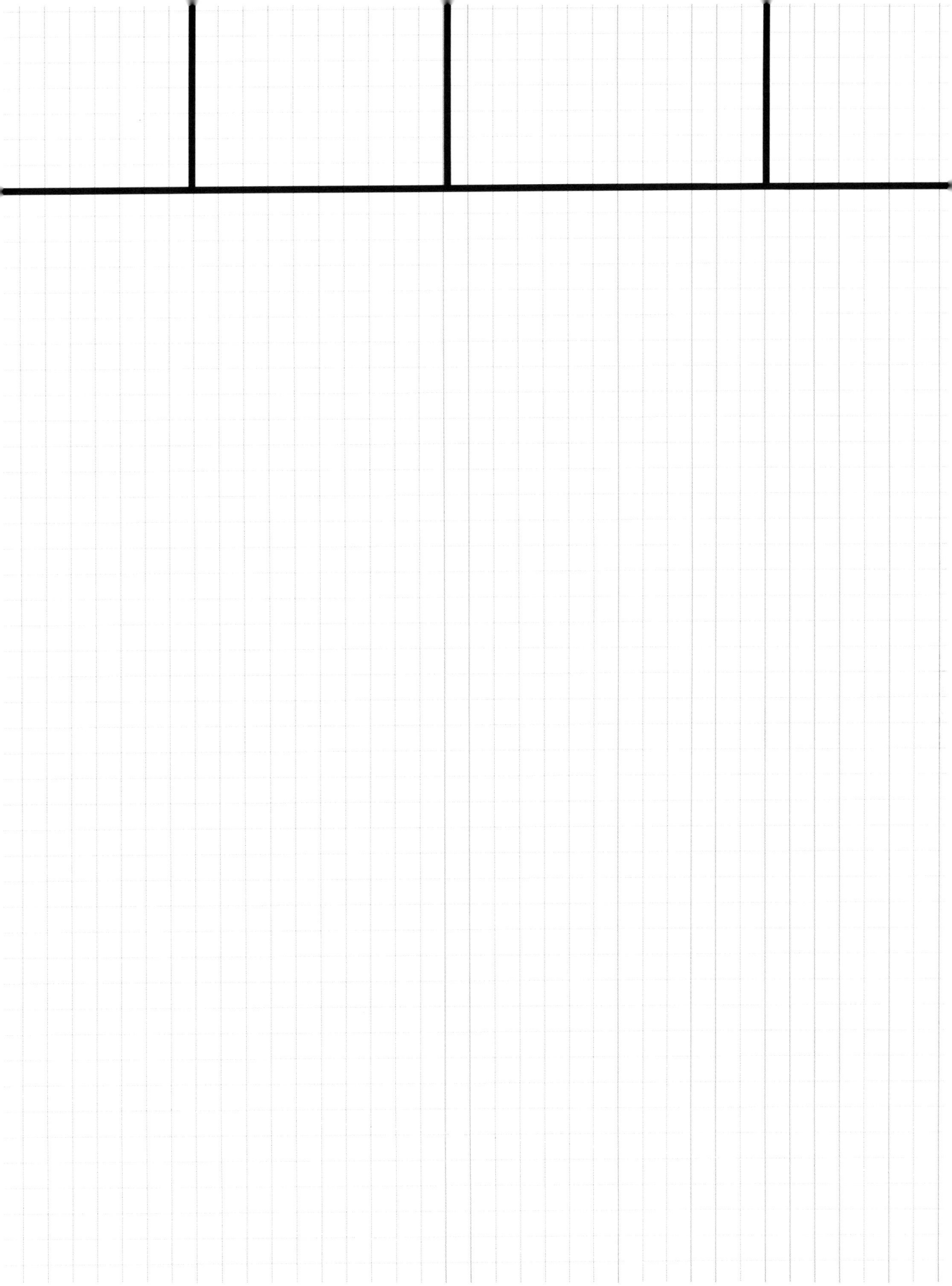

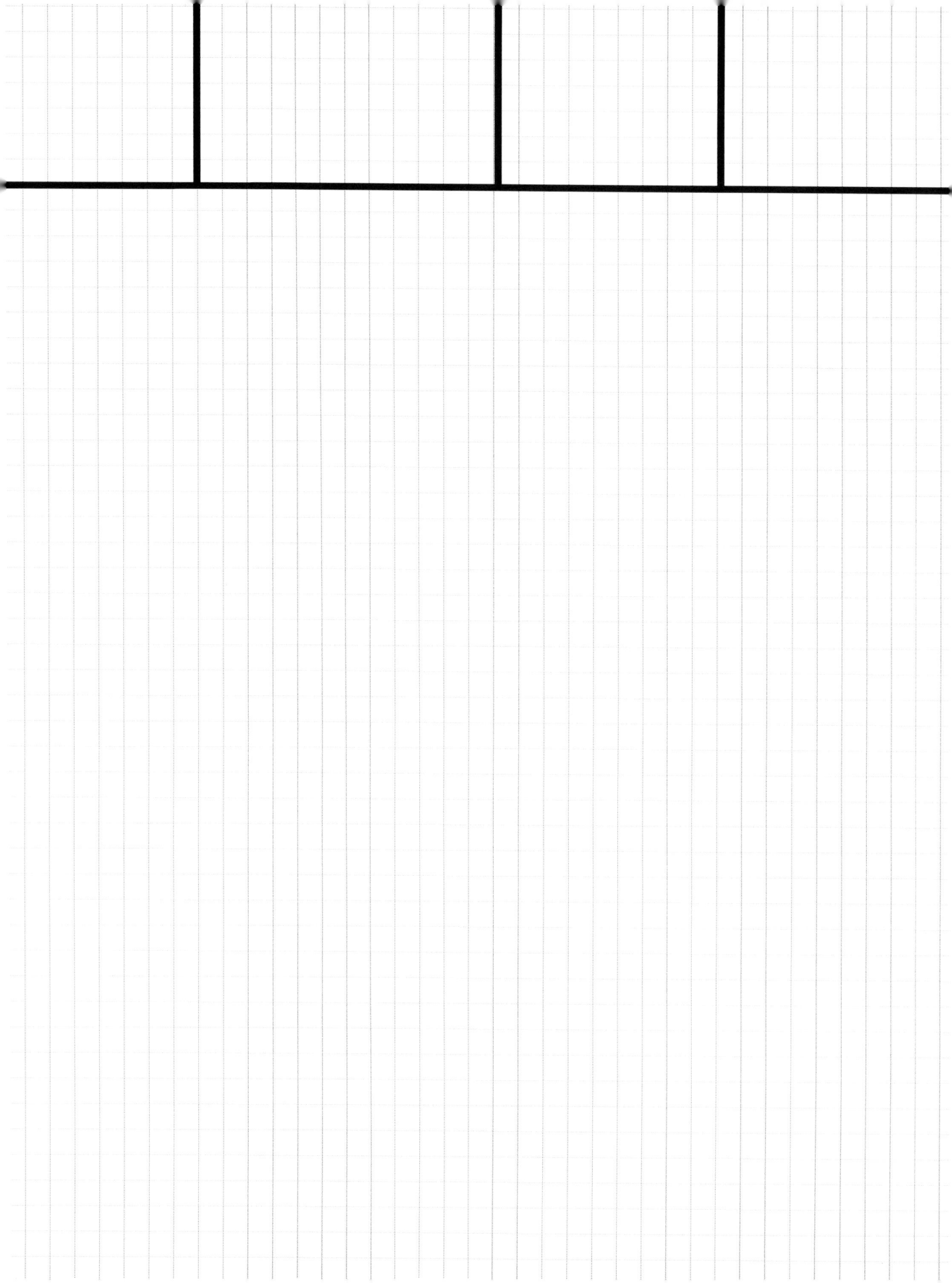

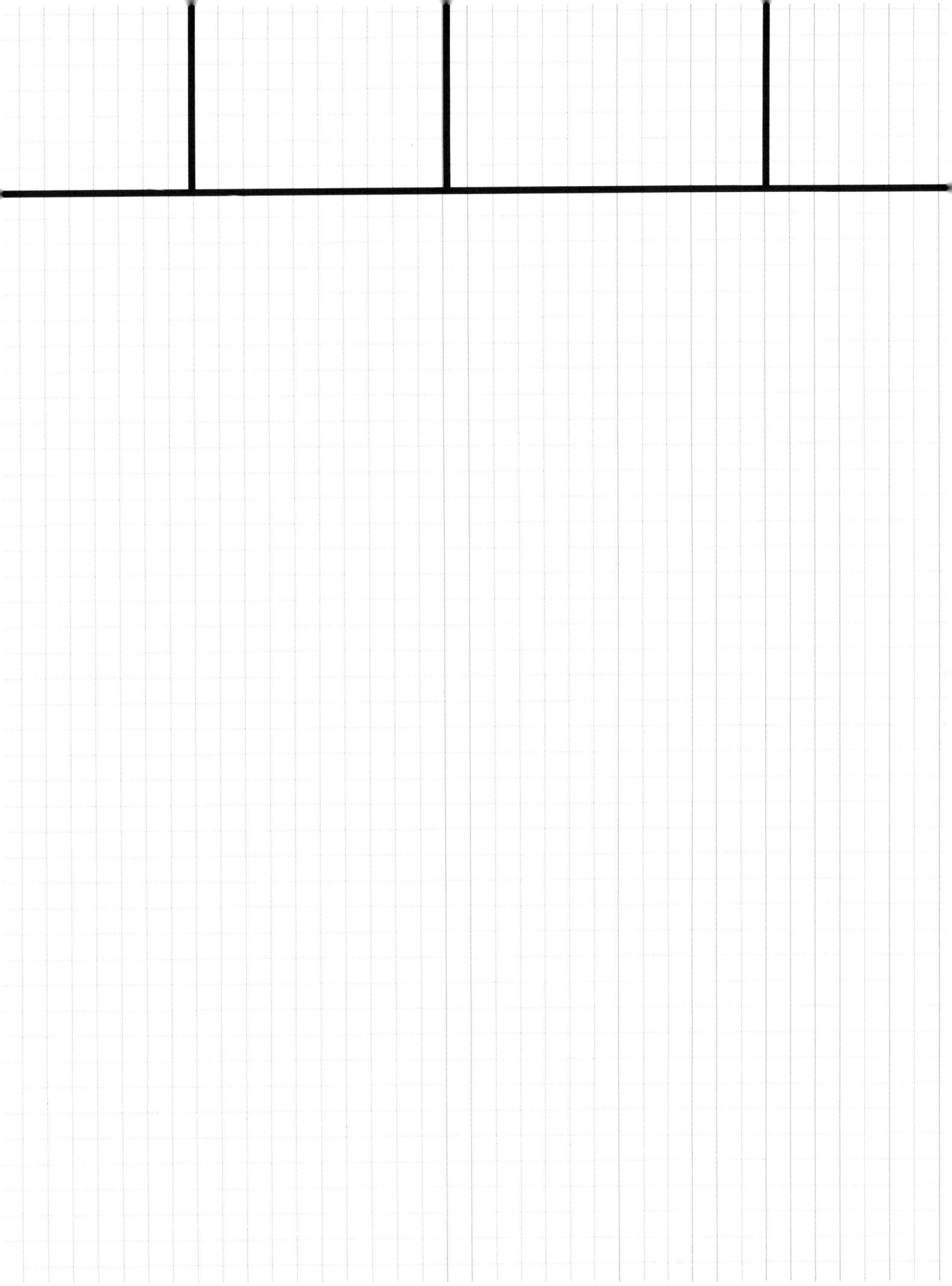

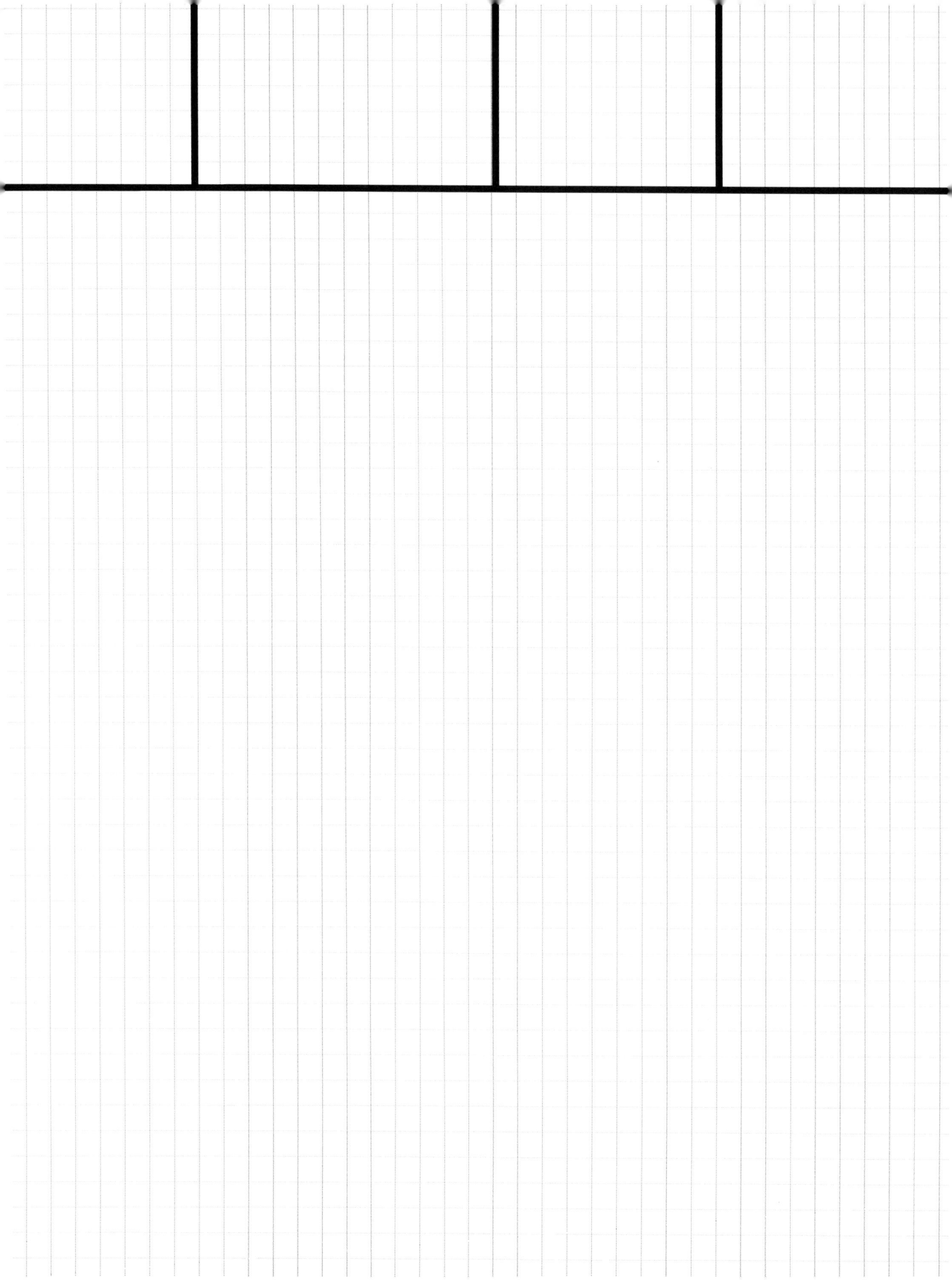

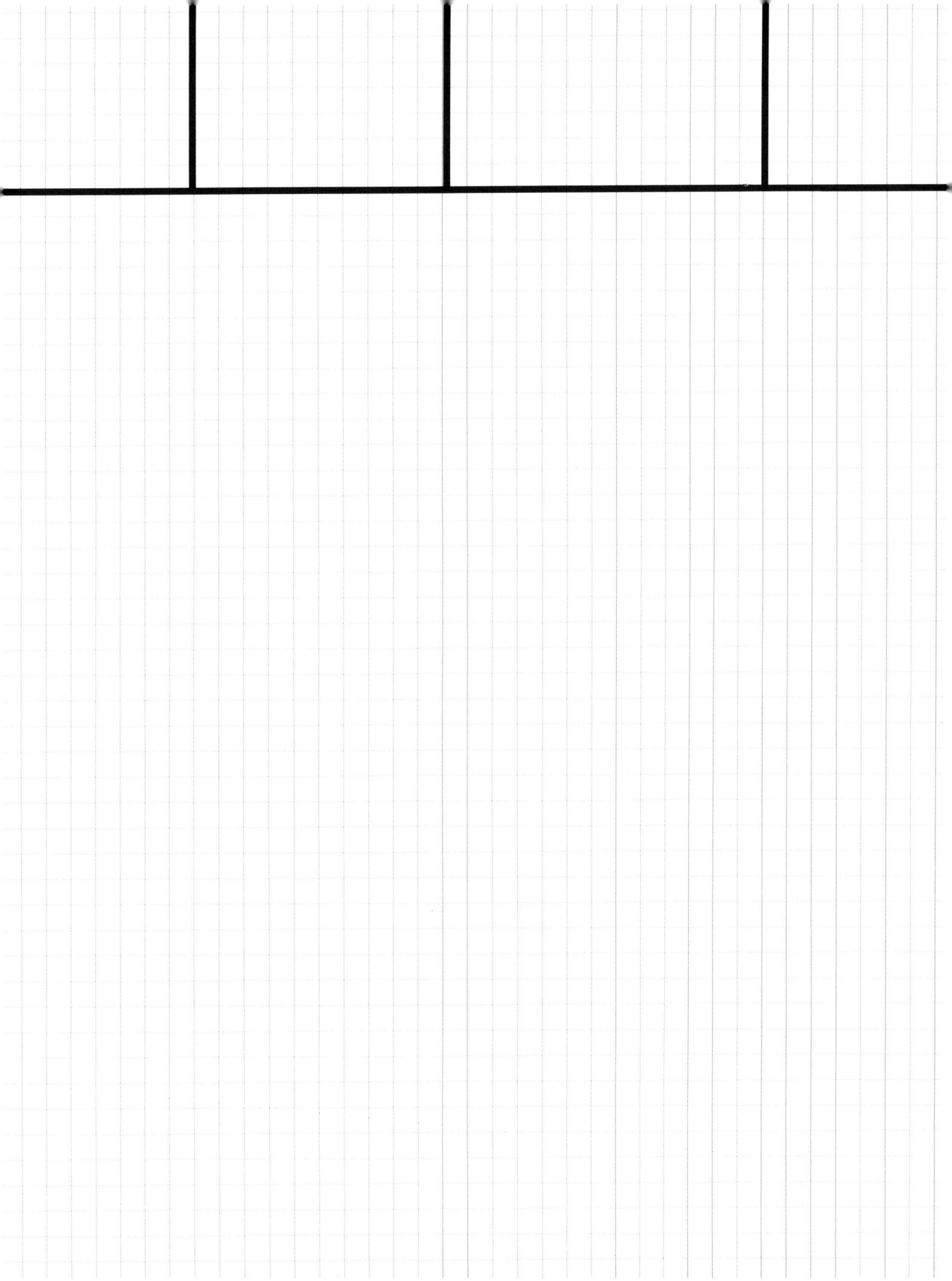

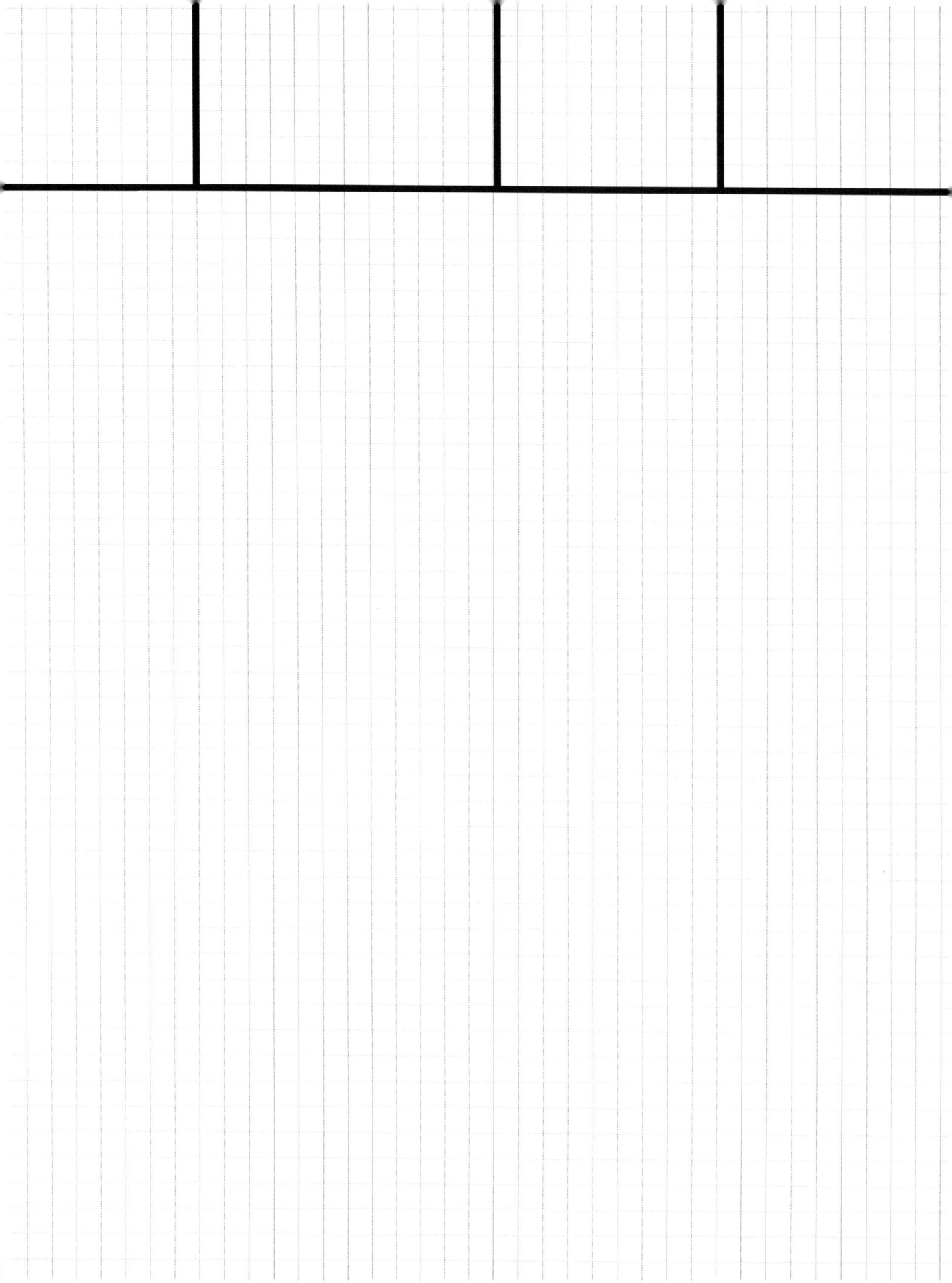

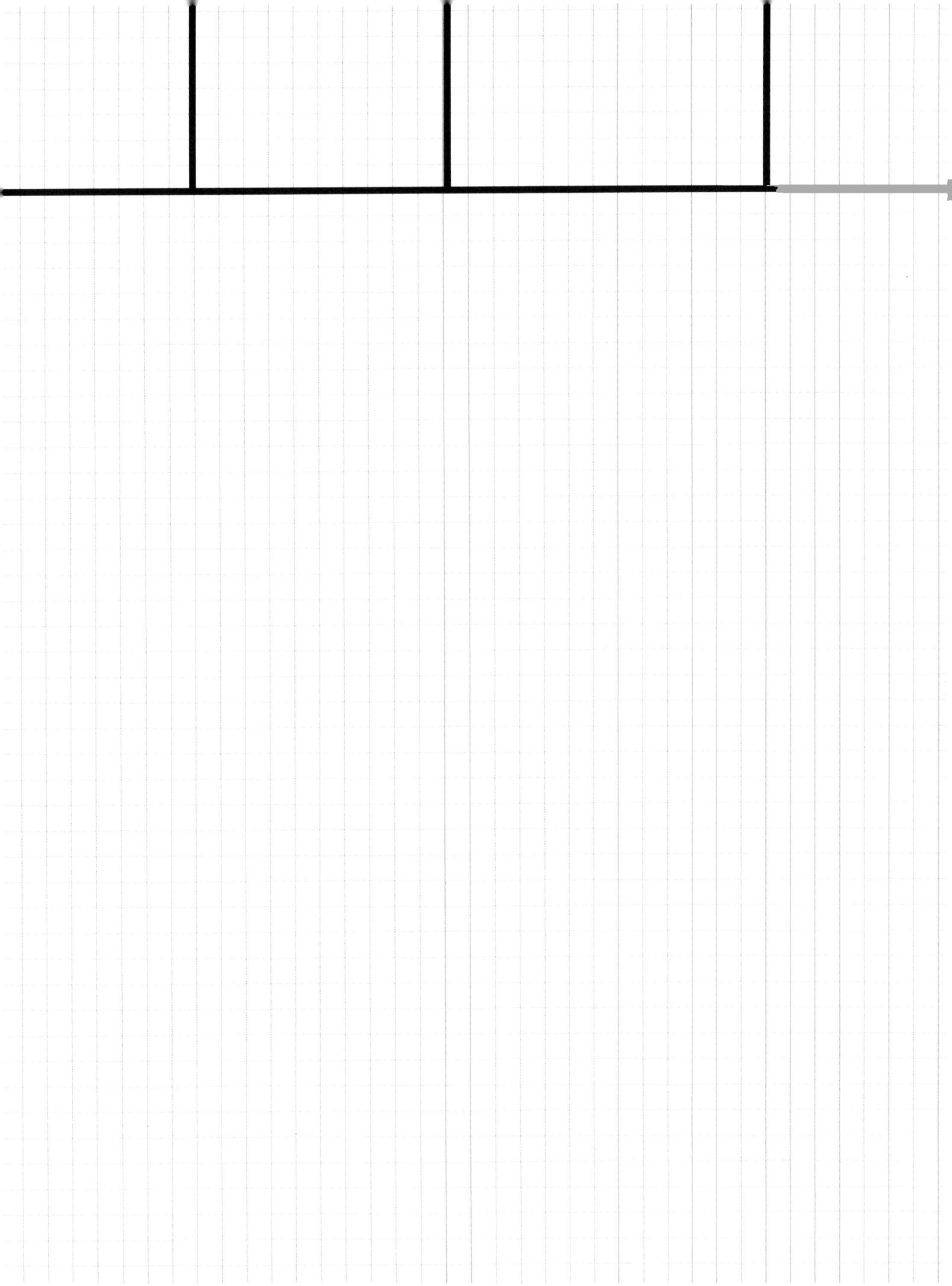

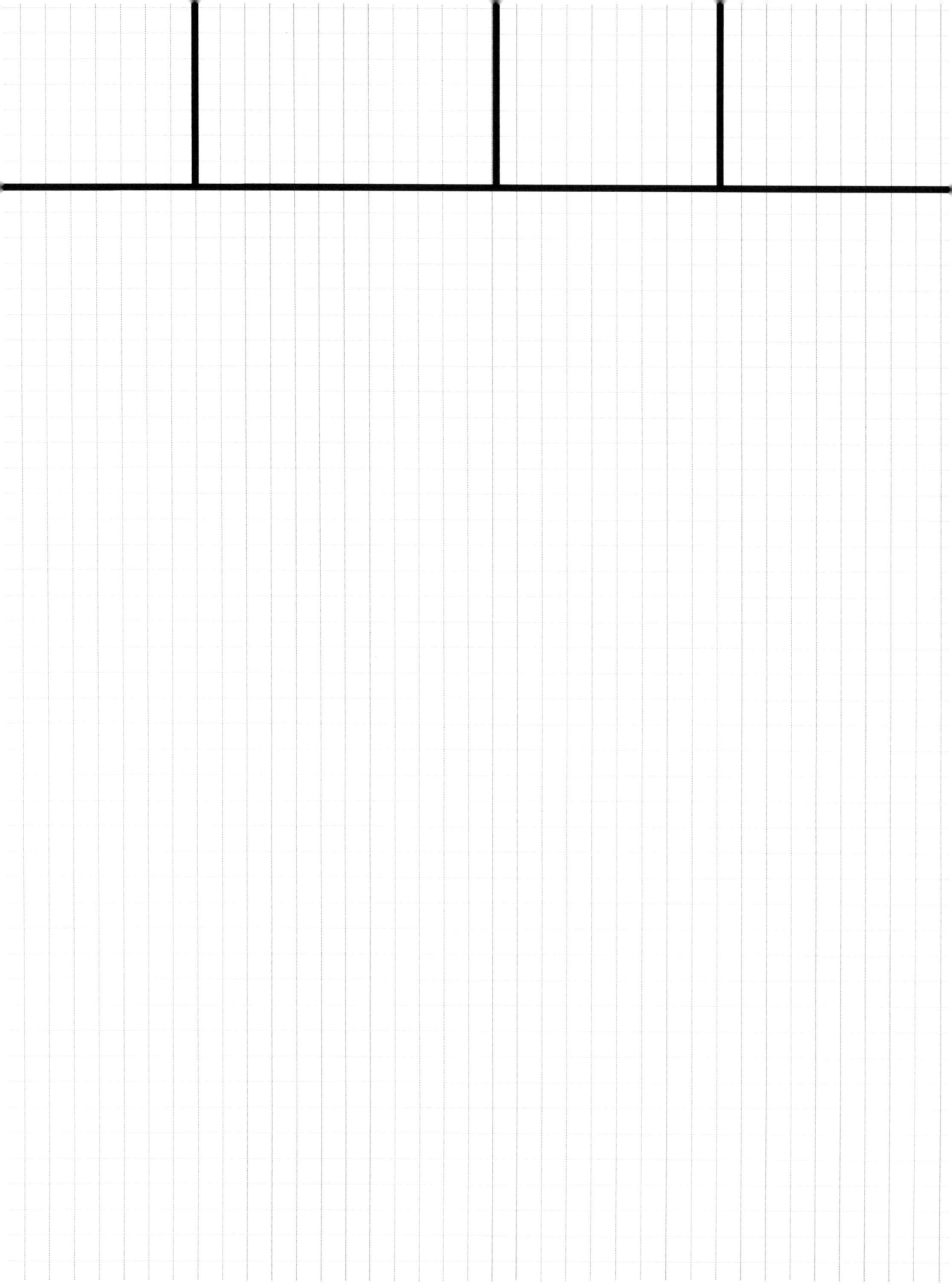

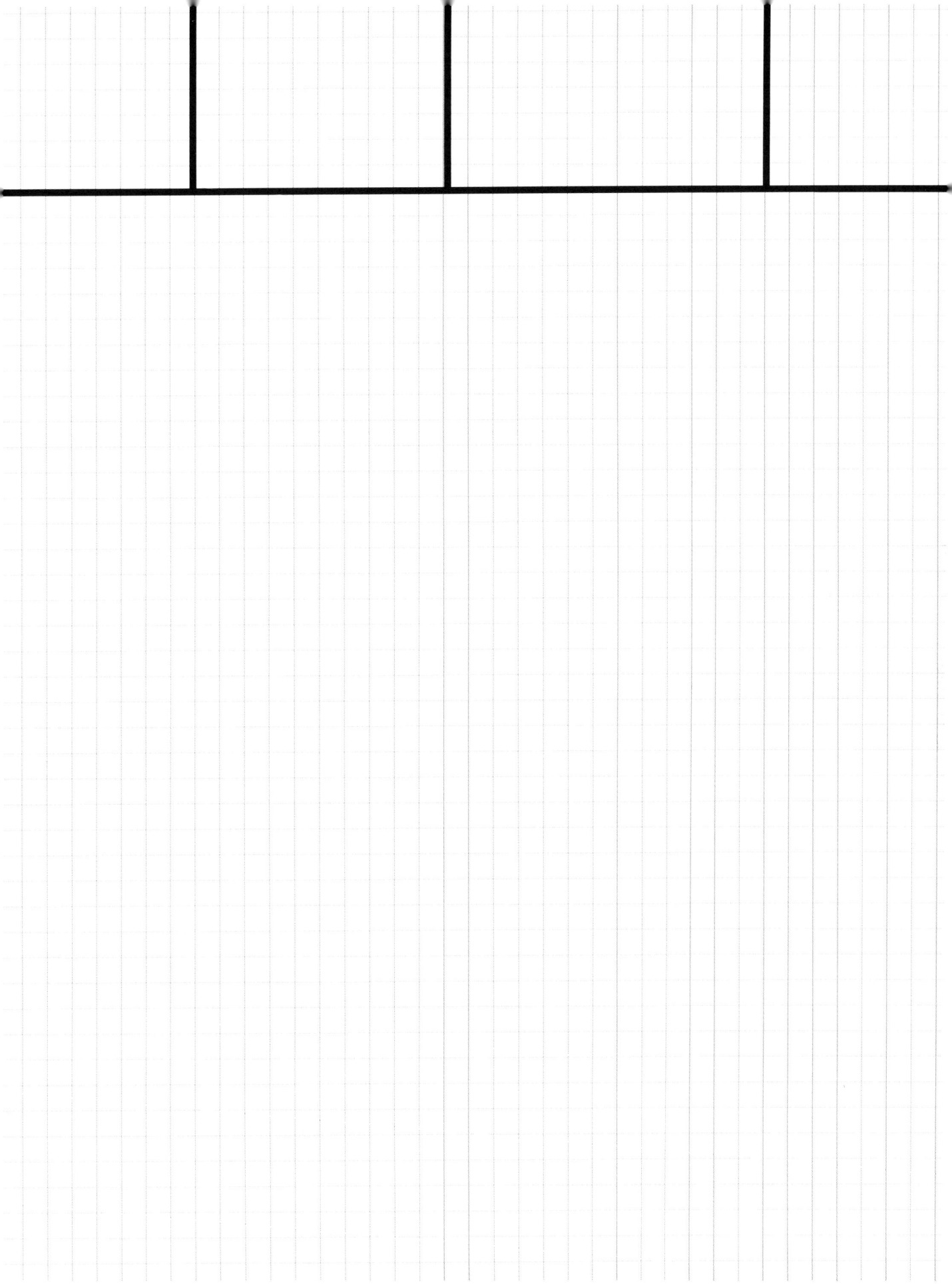

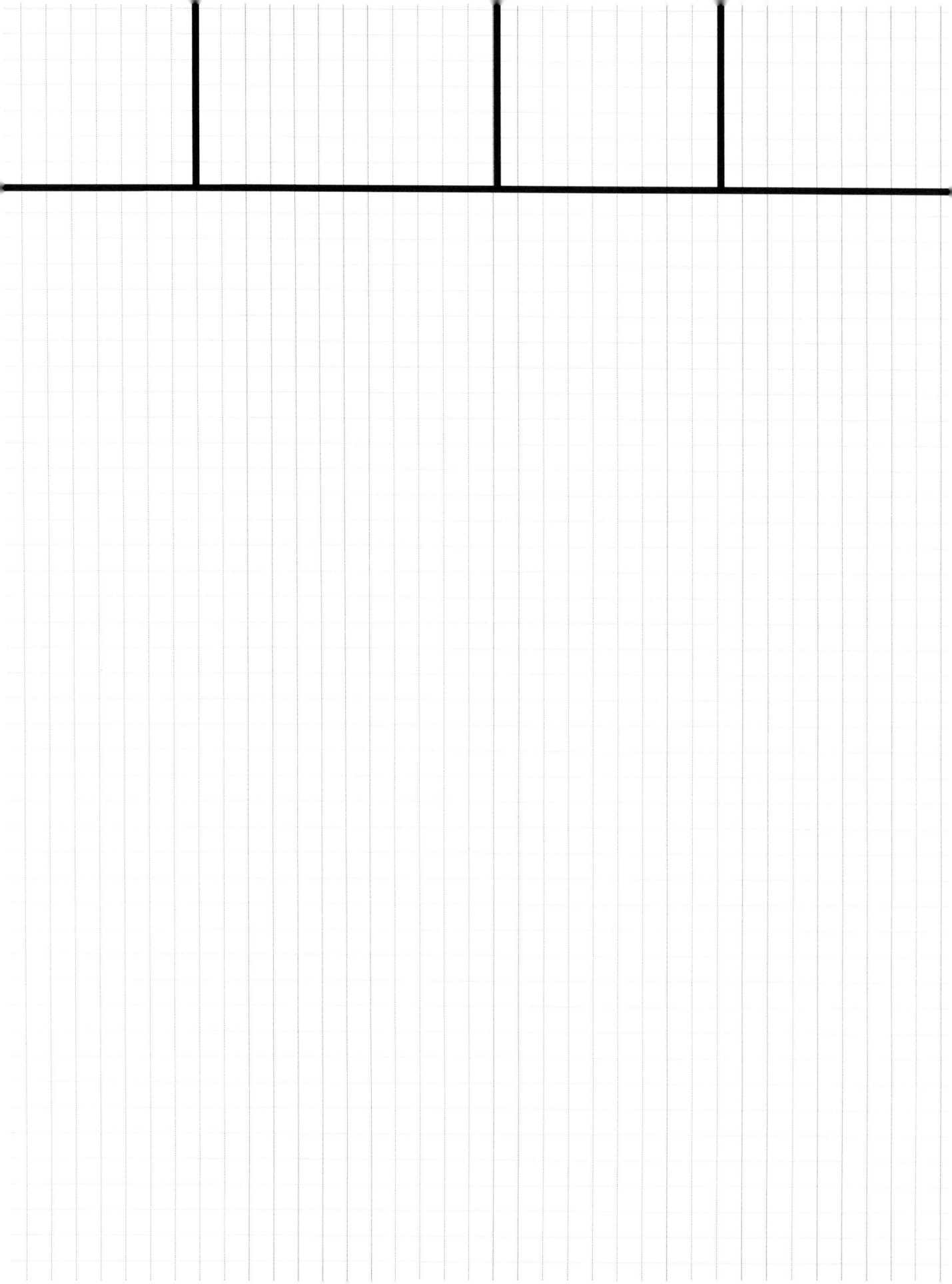

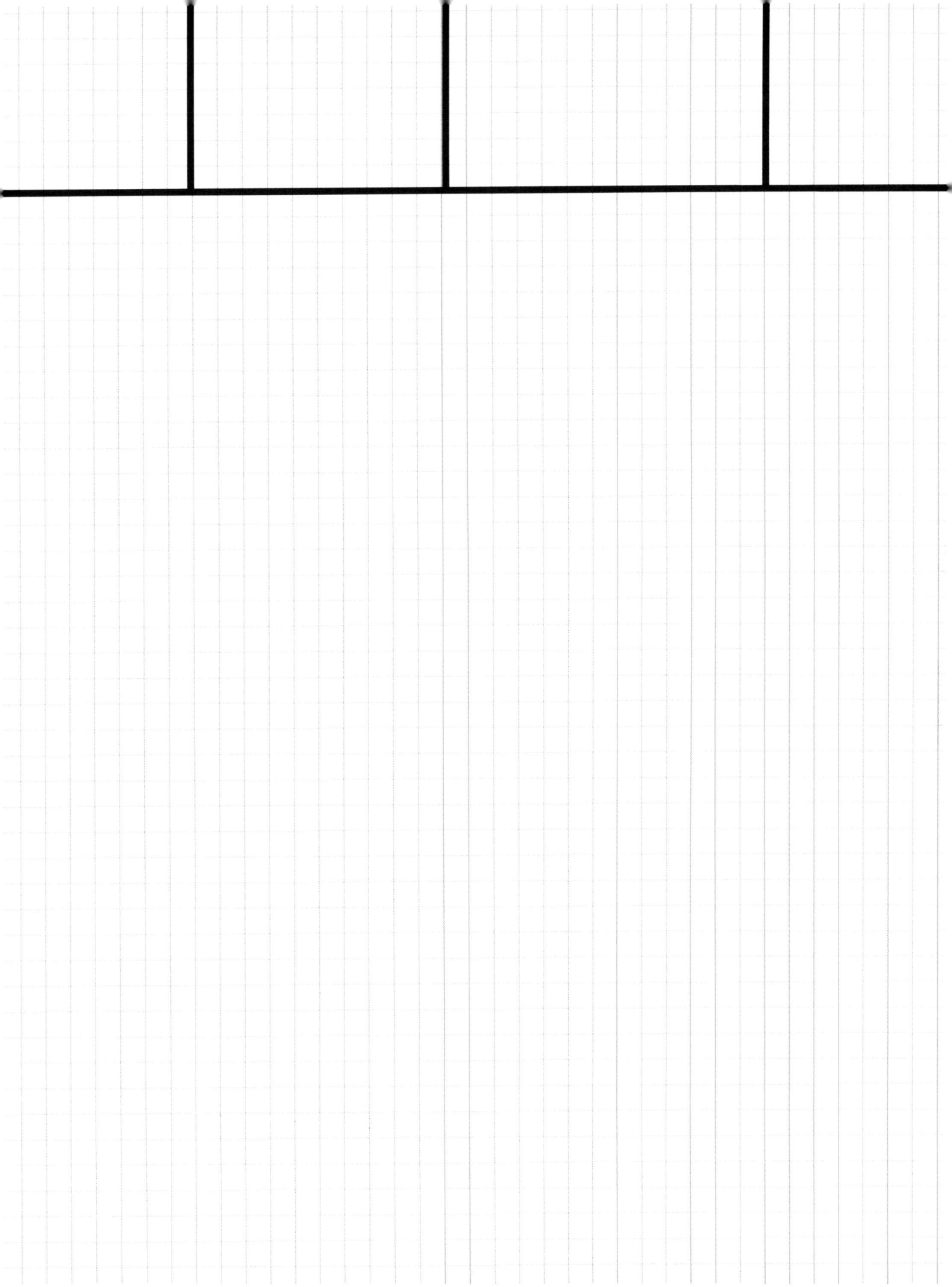

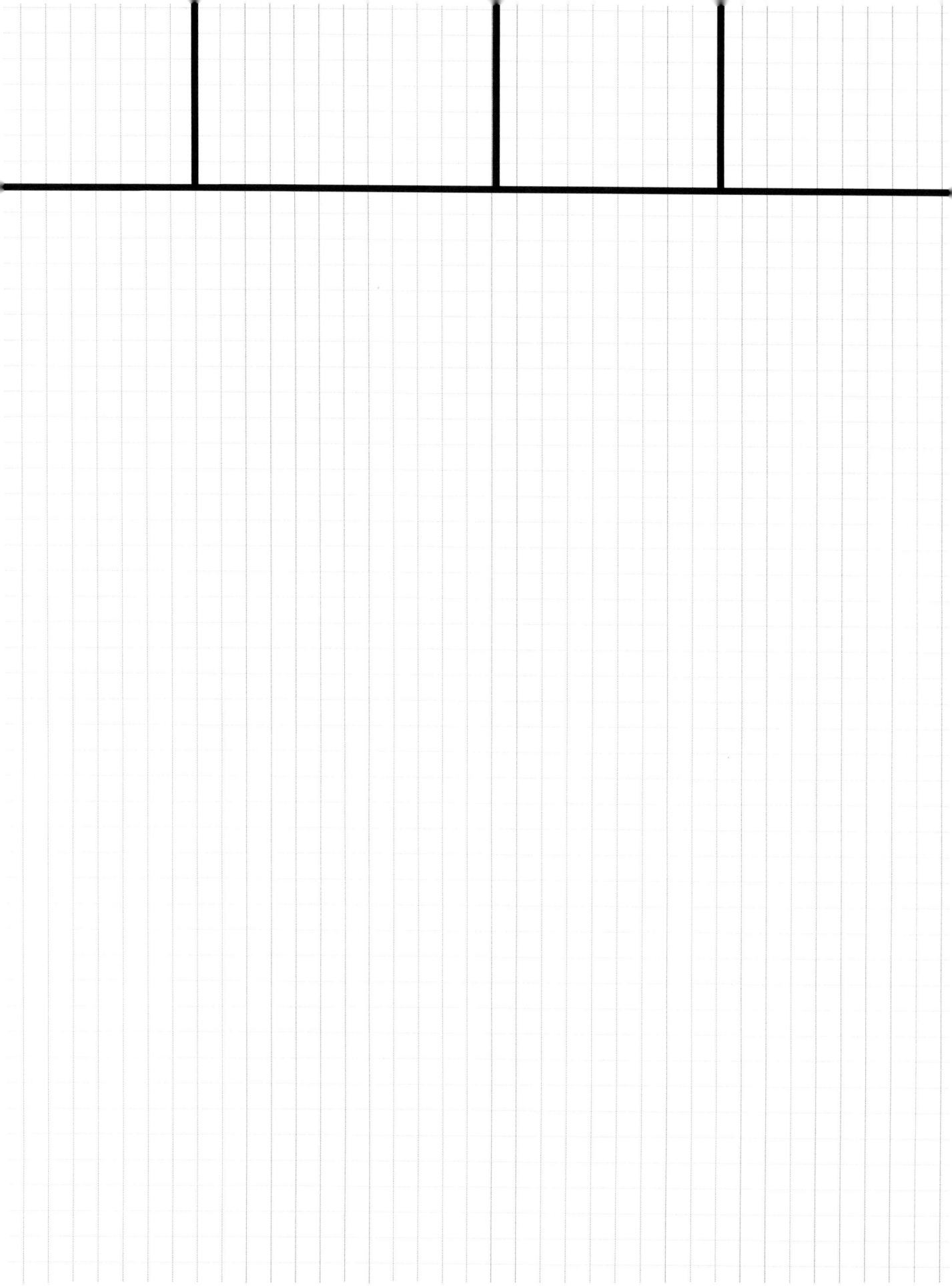

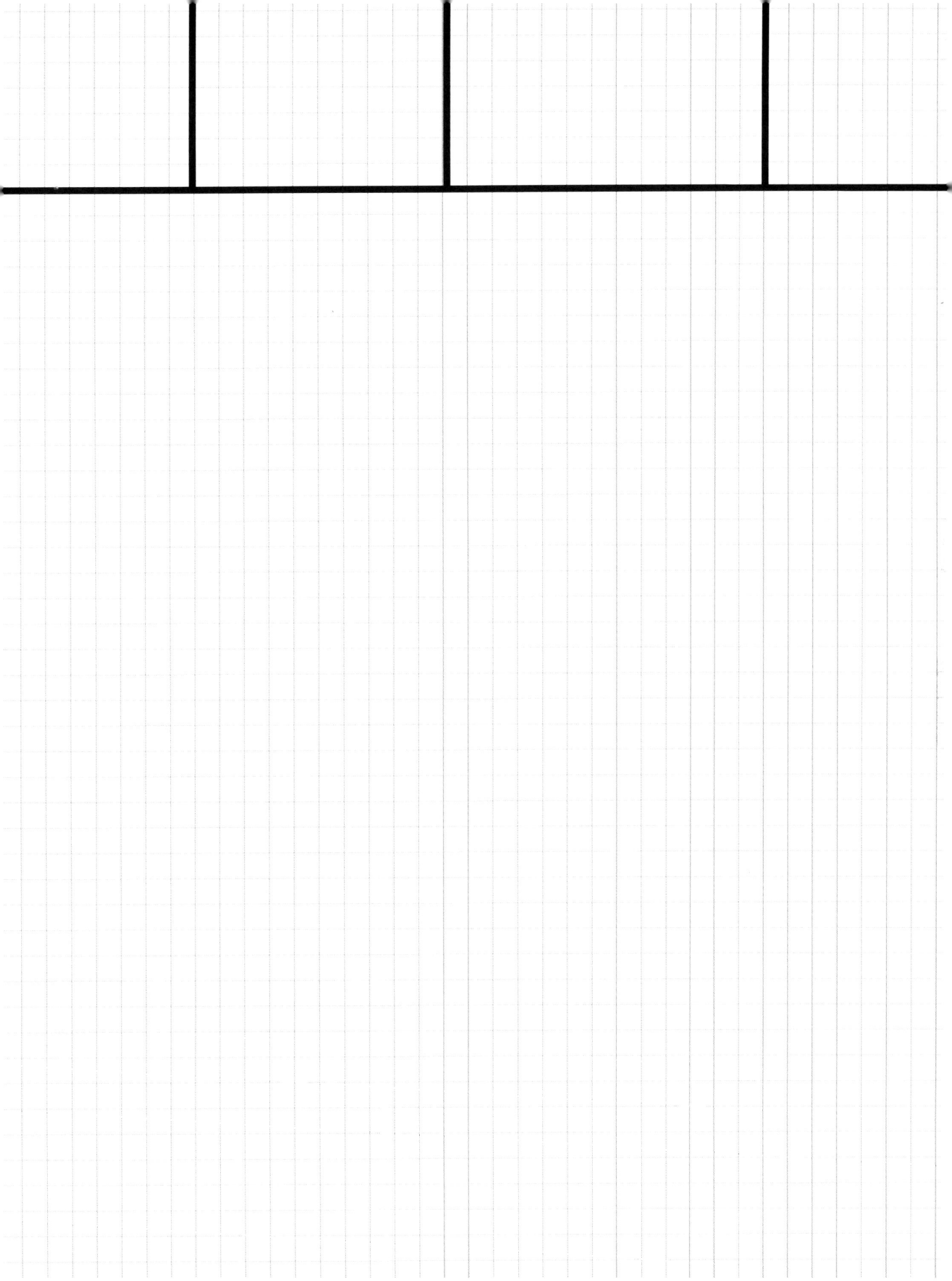

Made in the USA
Las Vegas, NV
17 December 2021